SATYR SQUARE

ALSO BY LEONARD BARKAN

Unearthing the Past:
Archaeology and Aesthetics in the Making of Renaissance Culture

Transuming Passion:
Ganymede and the Erotics of Humanism

The Gods Made Flesh:
Metamorphosis and the Pursuit of Paganism

Nature's Work of Art:
The Human Body as Image of the World

SATYR
SQUARE

•

A Year, a Life in Rome

•

Leonard Barkan

Northwestern University Press
Evanston, Illinois

Northwestern University Press
www.nupress.northwestern.edu

Printed in the United States of America

10 9 8 7 6 5 4 3 2 1

Library of Congress Cataloging-in-Publication Data

Barkan, Leonard.
    Satyr Square : a year, a life in Rome / Leonard Barkan.—
Northwestern University Press paperback ed.
        p. cm.
    Originally published: New York : Farrar, Strauss &
Giroux, 2006.
    ISBN-13: 978-0-8101-2494-3 (pbk. : alk. paper)
    ISBN-10: 0-8101-2494-7 (pbk.)
    1. Rome (Italy)—Description and travel. 2. Rome
(Italy)—Social life and customs. 3. Barkan, Leonard—
Travel—Italy—Rome. 4. Rome (Italy)—Biography. I. Title.
DG806.2.B36 2008
945.6320929092—dc22

                                                    2008013794

For Nick, who rewrote my life

CONTENTS

Whatever they say about roads leading to Rome, the traffic signs in the Piazza dei Satiri suggest that there are three ways out of it and no ways in. You could call it a sabbatical that had privileged me to be plunked down there, the fruit of many grant applications to go to Rome and write a book under the title Art from the Ground Up. *Or, in a different language, you could say I was a refugee, a displaced person who had slipped underneath the local radar. If Dante faced his existential crisis* nel mezzo cammin di nostra vita, *halfway through the biblical life span, I guess I was having mine about ten years late. Granted, my escape to Rome for a year—leaving behind the twin pressures of a scorched-earth academic culture that had lost its taste for pleasure and an unbroken horizon of middle-aged celibacy that was similarly joyless—didn't exactly constitute being abandoned in a savage forest "where the true way was lost." Still, I did find myself in a corner of Rome that was almost impossible for taxi drivers to penetrate.*

Though my book eventually changed its name owing to coercions from grammarians—"a preposition is not something to end a title with," intoned one academic lawgiver—it was exactly that offending "up" which really unblocked the impasse of Satyr Square. I had man-

aged to rent a quirky little misshapen apartment five stories above that ominously signposted ground, not only affording me a lordly vantage point on the immediate urban surroundings, endowed with an exceptionally full cargo of historical surplus, but also inspiring a notion that I could see all of Rome from my windows. This proved to be an empowering sort of fantasy, since the scholarly project that brought me there was nothing less than an attempt to add some new definitions to "Renaissance" by documenting its practice of exhuming ancient sculpture from deep in the Roman soil. And so, though I lived up, I worked down.

My subject, then, was Archaeology. But whose? Myself, I had never so much as touched a shovel to any historical turf. And when I bandied the term among my literary colleagues, all I got back was a 1970s-vintage Gallic vocabulary list ("reading—trace—decipherment—memory") whose terms were indeed haunting and suggestive but which I feared did not mean at all the same thing to me that they did to Foucault. And as for what ordinary people thought archaeology was—say, Heinrich Schliemann painstakingly layering his way through one Troy after another—that idea went out my fifth-floor window as soon as I made my first discovery about the Renaissance and its past. As it turns out, fifteenth-century Romans had no fully developed historical consciousness about the ground under their feet; for most of the period I was studying, every newly emergent arch or frieze, every Torso Belvedere or Dying Gaul, was just a brand-new one-off piece of strange and wonderful good luck.

Archaeology by Accident: that title, too, was short-lived, but the idea persisted. For the men and women whose culture I was trying to chronicle, the past was a whole lot of thrilling and beautiful fragments. And I needed to be the archaeologist who found those separate pieces—broken, detached, seemingly unrelated—and who honored the accident that brought them together. It wasn't long before I realized there was more than one archaeology going on here. Of all the apartments in all the neighborhoods of Rome, I had walked into a piazza named for a pair of unearthed statues, followers of the god Dionysus, ecstatic with drink and desire. That was my archaeology by accident, the first of many. And if Rome reposed on a storied past that formed the foundation of its present, if its geography was also its history, then I began to feel that I, too, was the jagged and gerrymandered sum of a past composed out of fragments. I, too, had a history that was a story.

But I wasn't just putting pieces of the past together. I had come to the Piazza dei Satiri with several years of occasional tourism in Rome but no deep familiarity—no underground consciousness—of the city; no friends or institutions were there to welcome me, nor was my Italian reliable. From the moment when I first reached the top of my little domestic tower, however, my life began to change. I was myself and not myself, alone and not alone. The statues I was gazing at, the wines I was pouring, the pages I was poring over, the streets I was traversing, the new vocabulary I was drilling into memory—all these things were changing the person who was reading the past, thus changing the past I was reading. If I had a story to tell, it was, like the archaeology of Rome, a heap, a mess, a jumble of now, then, and all time.

Also like archaeology, it needed a longer past to be told; it needed the space of recollection. I lived that late 1980s Roman year in its own present and past, but I could not really tell its story until it, too, had become sedimented, layered, tucked away in some deeper soil. History books, it is true, generally start then and move toward now. But the real shovel-wielding archaeologists, who ply their patient trade among the stratified traces of vanished civilizations, work from the top to the bottom; they tell history backward, from recent times down deeper into more ancient times. Backward history is the kind I find most congenial: it's retrospect, after all, that turns the past into history.

So to reach my year in Rome, I begin the dig a decade later. My Italian decade, as I think of it. The man who started writing his archaeological book in the Piazza dei Satiri celebrated its ten long years of composition with a sojourn on the Venetian Dorsoduro. The man who cautiously attempted carciofi alla romana found himself a little bit bolder, later, when confronted with fegato alla veneziana. The man whose Italian began by being parasitic upon the most outmoded and extravagant vocabulary of the opera house was, as time went on, ever more able to speak, and live, a passionate, confident vernacular in his own voice. But even that makes it all sound simpler than it really is. If the calendar in the story that follows is not always mappable, if the fragments of a life are not always recombinable, I can only urge readers to share my suspicion of orderly chronology and discrete particles of time. About Rome, the locals say "non basta una vita"; if that is so, then this must be a story not just about a year but about a life. And how does my Venice fit into my Rome? To quote an Italian friend of mine who was especially hungry for sweets: "La vita è incerta; mangia prima il dolce." *Life is uncertain; eat dessert first.*

Nor, to be honest, is chronology the only place to put a question mark here. Some maintain that it is possible to recount the past with perfect accuracy and that one is to be judged a liar by anybody who believes in a different version of the past; others contend that there is no foundation for believing in any consistent story about times gone by, that every story is a construct with its own self-defined truth claims. The first myth has paved the way to despotic certainties, the second to the tyrannies of rhetoric and solipsism, and to the heresy of believing that nothing really matters. I urge the reader, at least for the space of this book, to put aside both the seductive illusions of absolute veracity and the transient gratifications of believing that everything is true in its own way. In the pages that follow, it is the truth of memory that counts; and sometimes—to spare the feelings of persons who never asked to be put in a book, or for other, less noble reasons—even that truth has needed to be adjusted.

SATYR SQUARE

A CIRCLE OF SHADES

Venice, 7:30 p.m. While tourists trudge between San Marco and the Rialto, past strobe-lit international eateries manned by shills who extol displays of aging shellfish in four broken languages, a smaller group of individuals undertakes a different business in the remoter byways of the Serenissima. The workday is over, but it is not yet dinner hour: this is Venice's own snack time. Some locals, it is true, plant themselves at a single favorite establishment where they consume an unvarying sequence of food and drink. But the authentically hungry, searching for rarer satisfactions, pursue a jagged urban itinerary from bar to bar in a wanton incoherence of wines and noshes.

There's a dark-paneled melancholy corridor of a place on the far side of the Rialto Bridge where startlingly rare vintages of Tuscan reds are available by the glass; worthiest to accompany them are tiny, plump overstuffed little sandwiches called postage stamps, filled with prosciutto and Gorgonzola and something like pickles. Across the Grand Canal at another bar, as bright as the first is dark, as kitschy as the first is poetical, the wines are either banal or bizarre, and they can be redeemed only with some of the most utterly traditional local hors d'oeuvres: say, a glass of fruity pinkish Austrian-style Wildbacher beside the classic open-faced sandwich of buttered-up salt cod; or insipid flatland Soave washing down the local bony sardines covered in sweet-and-sour onions. Elsewhere again, past San Marco, you can find yourself among the trappings of the vulgarest tourism but blessed by the production of exquisite anchovies, held dripping over a slice of bread or over your mouth and performing a gastronomically imprudent counterpoint to some noble glass of Piedmontese wine, priced too cheaply to be resisted.

This pilgrimage the Venetians call *un giro di ombre*, a circle of shades. Why should a glass of wine be a shadow? No one is quite sure whether it refers to the respite from the afternoon sun as it crosses the cupola of St. Mark's or to the fact that the wineglass itself is darkened by drink. All the expressions surrounding this ritual are meant to be diminutive—*ombretta*, they say, for the drink (a *little* shade) and, for the food, *ciccheti*, something you've crumbled off of a larger slab. To do as the Venetians do, then, you move from place to place consuming bits and pieces in shadows while the day itself decomposes. Granted, it's not a full or balanced meal, but you've traveled quite a bit farther while nourishing yourself.

SHAKESPEARE AND NEW WORLDS

In many ways, Shakespeare and his culture were definitively isolated from the mainstream of European (and non-European) culture. But by the last years of the sixteenth century this isolation was coming to an end. In a paradoxical way, it may have been Europe's own adventure of new worlds—Asia, Africa, the Indies, the Americas—that helped promote a fuller awareness in insular England of all the crosscurrents of European politics, aesthetics, and culture. We will be studying three plays, each of which is notably concerned with the larger world: *The Merchant of Venice*, *Othello*, and *The Tempest*. Figures like the Jew Shylock and the Moor Othello testify to a vision beyond England and beyond Europe. But these outsiders also bring Shakespeare back to the familiar, or at least the more manageable unfamiliar. The fact that two of these plays are set in Venice and that the third replays a set of episodes in Italian politics only serves to remind us that Shakespeare's vision of new worlds is mediated by old worlds that are only slightly better known to his English contemporaries than are the lands of remote exploration beyond Europe.

Ten years of work had just gone off to the publisher, and I was ready for something new. Or, more precisely, something both old and new: from Rome to Venice, from immersion in the fragments of Renaissance archaeology back to my first love, Shakespeare. I e-mailed that course description to the Dipartimento di Studi Anglo-Americani e Ibero-Americani of the University of Venice, which had invited me to come as a visiting professor in the spring of 1998. Under its rather long-winded department title—Anglo-American and Hispano-American Studies—lurked academic schism. It seemed that recently the professors specializing in American literature had split off from those who taught English literature. The *americanisti* had managed to recruit the Hispanists who worked on Latin America, presumably causing them to split off in complementary fashion from the Iberians.

Academic politics as usual, and yet Venetian-style. In Venice, domestic politics becomes international politics, inside is outside, outside is inside, and there's no endogamy without exogamy. No surprise, I guess: Othello's marriage goes aground on the same shoals that beach the Turkish fleet; and Portia, on her way to marrying a fellow Venetian, dashes the hopes of a whole United Nations' worth of foreigners, gaily hurling racial and ethnic slurs in their direction.

At all events, the upshot for me was that, since my particular entrée came via the American side of the now-divided faculty, the only way I would be permitted to package Shakespeare was in red, white, and blue. No problem: New World exploration, colonialism, and the Other were in critical fashion. Yet in this movement to historicize—that is, to join the text with a revised history of its own time and a mirroring history from our time—we were in danger of putting it rather seriously at arm's length from ourselves. Under the right circumstances, that repressed was bound to return. For me, it would return again and again.

The afternoon before my first class, I was invited for *ombre e ciccheti* by some of my Americanist colleagues. A rather too well lighted bar, nothing like the quaint places I would discover in my own rounds. I scanned the meager selection and ordered a glass of Incrocio Manzoni, a dull wine but local and therefore true to my efforts at acculturation. My colleagues all ordered something called *uno spritz*, not a spritzer, but a cocktail whose name, they told me, signals that it was the preferred festive tipple of the long-gone Austrian soldiers who occupied Venice in the nineteenth century. No one in Vienna has ever heard of it. My *ciccheto* was Veneto lard, a slice of pure fat on bread; meanwhile, my youngest colleague munched from a bag of French fries.

They prepared me for the experience of the next day's teaching. "You'll be lecturing in English, of course," one colleague said. "They must never hear a word of your beautiful Italian, even under stress"; another, more senior, told me I must pretend I didn't even know Italian. This came as a shock, a denial of ten years in my life. Choking down my lard sandwich, I realized I'd been looking forward to the novelty of teaching Shakespeare's English in my Italian, of making the familiar into the unfamiliar.

In the privacy of the classroom, I blew my cover on the first day. I provided a little anthology of Shakespearean excerpts that alluded to the geography of the world, including a moment in *The Comedy of Errors* when Dromio of Syracuse describes the hugely fat woman who mistakenly claims him as her husband. In order to convey the immensity of her body, Dromio compares her to an entire globe, with each part of her corresponding to some foreign country. Antipholus asks, "In what part of her body stands Ireland?" to which Dromio responds, "Marry, sir, in her buttocks . . ." Up to that last word there had been nods of widespread comprehension in the class, even laughter at the punch lines. Suddenly, blank stares. I looked around to make sure no fellow professors were peering through the glass door, then stagewhispered *"Natiche."* Amid the hilarity, I reflected that any man who names his ass in Italian can't be trusted with secrets, even his own. Later, in front of drink and snack (a Bianco from the nearby Euganean Hills alongside some organ meat), I confessed to my colleagues, saying, I cannot live a lie. Later still, in more informal company—blessedly, this time the *ombra* is Chianti and the *ciccheto* is prosciutto—I rephrased this: I can *no longer* live a lie. Was anyone attentive enough to wonder what lie I used to live?

The Merchant of Venice, to begin at the beginning of my syllabus, has all the most delicious trappings of Shakespearean romantic comedy: true love whose course isn't running smooth; a girl who dresses up as a boy (three of them, actually); a real world versus a green world; multiple interlocking plots. I'd venture to say it's the most exquisitely poetical of all the plays—half the last act has no other purpose than the music of its words—but no one notices this aspect of the work because of its other, more peculiar distinction, which is that it's all about money. Ships go down in *Twelfth Night*, but we have no idea of the financial losses involved; marriages take place in *As You Like It*, but we don't hear any details of property transfer. In the *Merchant*, as the title tips us off, what links all the different actions is cash.

All three main characters are rich, and you can plot them according to some sort of primitive Samuelson. Portia is heiress to vast sums of old money, but its origins are mystified, and since her dead father's will prevents her from choosing her own mate, her wealth is blocked from free circulation in the modern world. Antonio, the merchant of the title, is one sort of economic alternative: a new-style mercantilist entrepreneur who is careful to diversify but still risks great sums on around-the-world import-export schemes; the other alternative is Shylock, whose riches are neither socked away in ancient privilege nor funding global productivity but, rather, operating in a closed circle of money-lending for interest.

No romance without finance. Portia's suitors have to identify correctly the relative value of gold, silver, and lead; and if they fail, they must go home and die unwed. The right answer is lead, not because it is the most (or least) valuable, but because it involves the most *risk*, which is, of course, the core value of merchantry. That in itself is a luscious mix of ancient fairy tale and modern economic analysis. What is more bizarre in the gaining of Portia is that you have to spend a lot of money just to mount the expedition across the water to compete for her. After all, what sets the plot in motion is that the suitor Bassanio needs even more money than he has already taken from Antonio in order to woo Portia. Antonio, temporarily illiquid, borrows from Shylock on the expectation of future returns; the ships go astray; Shylock is left with a contract permitting him to take a pound of Antonio's flesh.

Have I left anything out? Oh, yes. Antonio, sad at the beginning of the play and solitary at the end, loves Bassanio enough to sacrifice his own fortune and his life, with nothing to show for it. And Shylock is a moneygrubbing Jew who delights in the prospect of shedding Christian blood and is punished in the comedy's happy ending by impoverishment and forced conversion. God, I love this play.

Shortly before I go to Venice, I am sitting in a Greenwich Village noodle shop across from a much younger man, a musician and writer. Chris and I have known each other for years—he had been briefly my student—and we have been in the habit of lunches together when his wide orbits of rock-band touring and docu-fiction research intersect New York. One of these visits, about a year earlier, had introduced a variation in our routine: Chris came to dinner at my house. Whether I was anticipating, or plotting, or oblivious in advance of that evening, I can't now reconstruct. When I first knew Chris, he lived with a woman, then married another woman, then separated from her. Be all that as it may, I had made a first course that was highly savory (pasta with peppery pancetta and very ripe tomatoes, a little more oil in the sauce than would gladden the surgeon general's heart); the main course, short ribs, needed a lot of messy eating with the hands; and there was a pair of evocative and sappy wines, one from Friuli, the other from Tuscany. There may have been some Riesling and some Schubert along the way, but that would argue intent. I don't remember dessert, but I do remember that Chris didn't leave afterward. We had introduced a variation in our routine.

Still, weeks went by without communication, and months without seeing each other. Chris was, and is, epically penniless; if there were a Nobel Prize for living on nothing, he'd be hitch-hiking to Stockholm tomorrow. His trips to New York depended on some manipulations with airline tickets about which the less I knew the better. On what was to be the third or fourth post-variation visit, the travel scam collapsed, and I found myself for the first time conscious of missing him. On the phone I hazarded to say that I might spring for the trip.

That led to a much bigger variation, and to lunch in the noo-dle shop. I'd never known anyone before who could equal my passions for food and words. We had spent three days eating, talking, reading each other, and digesting what we had read and spoken, over feasts alternately extravagant and parsimonious. Somewhere between baba ghanoush and beluga, without our quite being aware of it, our desultory pattern was being shaken. A thousand miles, twenty years, and all the best modern defini-tions of sexual orientation separated us, but not a lot else. At Sammy's, two can eat fantastically well for $5.25 if one of them gets over his fear of looking like a panhandler. Over a single bowl of crispy chicken wonton soup, a dish that is warming and sloppy and unctuous, we find ourselves making a plan. I will pay for occasional flights to New York and for some of his expenses when he gets there; we shall read, talk, eat, and spend intimate time cohabiting on those occasions; no claims beyond those of loving friendship will be presumed or entertained. This arrange-ment will be referred to as "partial kept man status." I go off to Venice a new man.

To my Venetian students I make much of the fact that Portia's two failed suitors are Morocco and Aragon, the first designed by

Shakespeare as black, exotic, and sexy (a study for Othello?), the second as vastly imperious and self-confident. They never meet inside this play, but they stand as the two great antagonists in a centuries-old struggle between the European and the Other, only concluded in that fateful year 1492 with the expulsion of the Moors. In the interim, speaking of 1492, Spain has proved threateningly capable of subduing and profiting from quite a new Other, to be found well west of the Mediterranean. Shylock is yet another Other, Christianity's oldest, most intimate, most inextricable Other, not so easily sent off to another world in 1492 (or 1942), and raising the most unsettling possibility—namely, that the Other, *c'est nous*. To be saying these things to a classroom of junior Venetians ends up paradoxical. While I am selling the great wide world envisioned in 1600 by a northern islander who never traveled anywhere, I am also returning this great wide world to their own backyard. They gape at Shakespeare's mentions of the Rialto, or the Ghetto, or the Venetian trading empire as though they were picking out a few familiar faces in the painting of a vast crowd of the unidentified dead. I'm giving them a Shakespeare they can call their own.

Once the fatal loan has been proposed, Shylock asks to meet with Antonio, and he is duly invited to dinner. "Yes," says Shylock, "to smell pork, to eat of the habitation which your prophet the Nazarite conjured the devil into: I will buy with you, sell with you, talk with you, walk with you, but I will not eat with you."

Around the time I was sixteen, I started pretending I wasn't a Jew, and I didn't really quite finish with this impersonation, or with the lying subroutines that followed from it, until I was in my thirties. In this circle of buried memories are images of myself at age sixteen in lower Manhattan's St. Paul's Chapel, reassuring a Catholic woman who was terrified because she had unwittingly prayed in a Protestant church. (With some censoring I recounted this to my then aged mother, who asked, "Did she know she was getting this advice from a Jew?") Or, some years later, a vision in a dream on *erev* Good Friday in which I witnessed the crucifixion—I noticed that the sweat on Christ's upper legs made them resemble a roast basted with olive oil—and I was given secret reassurances concerning death. As comic relief to these melodramas, there was the weekly experience of New Haven's Christ Church, where stratospherically high Anglican rituals of holy water, Latin, incense, and confession were presided over by a nasal-voiced convert who looked like my uncle Irwin and was named Father Kibitz.

Was it the banality of being a Jewish boy in New York, of living inside what was in truth an exotic minority while construing it to be a tedious majority? Was it a revolt against our rye-bread ordinariness? Perhaps that was it. Or else I was feeling some terrible, ancient sense of exclusion from the feast. "I will buy with you, sell with you, talk with you, walk with you, but I will not eat with you." I was never going to utter that sentence, never going to refuse an invitation to dinner. Being gay almost looked simple by comparison.

When we first meet him, Antonio expresses an incurable sadness whose origins he cannot guess at. His acquaintances suggest that he is sad because he is worrying about the riskiness of his commercial ventures. No, it isn't that, he says. "Why then you are in love," proposes Solanio, to which Antonio replies, "Fie, fie."

For many of their contemporaries to the north, Renaissance Italians were proverbial for whole catalogues of vices, none more so than sex between men. *Ein Florenzer* in German was a bugger, and Venice was not far behind in the practice or in its fame. Historical research into early modern Italy has uncovered vast networks of persons accused of committing sodomy. What we learn from these researches is that the performance of same-sex desire was widespread but that it conformed in no way to the modern notion of a small minority of men who are permanently definable by what we call their sexual orientation. Virtually without exception among the hundreds or even thousands of cases, sodomy consisted of an older man enforcing his sexual will on a boy under eighteen. It was not always rape—though it was sometimes prosecuted under that term—but it was nearly always constrained, if not by force then by the status of the aggressor, and there was generally no sense that the recipient might be deriving pleasure from the act.

The consummate portrait of this disturbing practice is to be found in a magisterial piece of modern scholarship called *Forbidden Friendships*, which leaves no doubt that sodomy as defined and practiced in early modern Italy could have few defenders in any enlightened society, even if the judicial reaction, often consisting of torture, mutilation, and execution, is yet more abhorrent. It's a shockingly inappropriate title. The truth is that there were no friendships in this history of sodomy, no consensual love between equals, no erotic chemistry of mind, body, and soul. *Forbidden Friendships* must have been seeking an audience of modern readers who were looking for the historical roots of their own identities. Yet given the paucity of appropriate materials, this is a little like a history of the Jews that could rely only on documents authenticating their practice of drinking Christian children's blood.

Any account of male homosexuality past or present is wedged between the discourses of sodomy and those of love. Plato's ver-

sion, in which carnal relations between men and boys are anath-
ematized while spiritual relations are idealized, hardly speaks to
the full experience of desire. And what shall we say of Dante's
meeting with his cherished mentor Brunetto Latini among the
sodomites in hell? The disingenuous surprise that the wayfaring
Dante exhibits at this encounter (*"Siete voi qui, Ser Brunetto?"*)—
What's Dante surprised about? He put him there—signals a fatal
mix of homage to Brunetto as a classic pedagogue-pederast and
quite wayward reflections on what passed as love between the
poet and his teacher.

In short, the erotics of older men and younger men are something of a minefield, planted in explosive doses of violence and
exploitation, teaching and learning, frustration and desire. By
the eighteenth century it became possible to imagine and experience different unions. In Shakespeare, however, something of
sublimated Platonic pederasty and of criminal Italian sodomy remains. It is no wonder that in the case of Antonio and Bassanio,
this love might dare not speak its name, nor that we are uncertain what name to give it. If a historian can call a bunch of rapes
"forbidden friendships," it's hardly surprising that two fictional
Venetians in an obliquely expressed but financially grounded relationship might look strangely familiar to me, as though they
were sitting across from each other in a Chinese restaurant on
Sixth Avenue.

Early in my stay in Venice I accept an invitation to dinner, in
the Dorsoduro apartment of a middle-aged American who is living the life of the expatriate artist. The scene is difficult to take
in—Mike's own Hudson River School paintings of the Grand
Canal, work boots and proletarian manners, two volumes of the
New York *Social Register* on the well-stocked cookbook shelf. He

busies himself in the kitchen and sends his girlfriend, Maria, and me to the local *enoteca* for wine. That's probably a mistake, since I get deeply sidetracked at Il Cantinone in a discussion about the relative merits of Refosco and Valpolicella, and not sure what nourishment to anticipate when we return, I find myself succumbing to the temptation of a salt-cod crostino.

As we open the front door, an unexpected voice, musical and pontificating, fills the apartment. Lia, glamorous, athletic, expensively dressed, is Israeli but massively polyglot, the distinguished gentleman with her utterly silent. Her grandfather was a cabinet minister in Pilsudski's between-the-wars government in Poland; her father was on a train transport to Treblinka, but his mother managed to push his thin body through the floor so that he had a chance to escape; she is friends with the American ambassador to Poland, the Polish ambassador to America, other luminaries.

Maria, a Pole but certainly not a Jewish Pole, is impressed with Lia's pedigree and confirms that indeed there is a whole neighborhood back in Lodz named for Lia's family. Maria is also a rather sentimental student of post-Holocaust Lodz, and she brings out a picture book of ruined Jewish cemeteries all over Poland. Lia redoubles her rhapsodies of eloquence about the destruction of the Jews, while Maria, from the class that were alternatively servants or murderers of Lia's people, feeds her straight lines. Mike, who has gone off to arrange plates of badly matched hors d'oeuvres in the dining room, returns for a brief bout of proper hosting; when he names Lia's man, I realize that this taciturn gent is a great-grandnephew of a kaiser and probably in line to become Holy Roman Emperor.

After the departure of the royals, I reflect on the circle that had been enjoying this round of *ombre e ciccheti*: one from the people who organized the pogrom, one from the people who were on the death transports, one from the people who ruled all the ethnics of Europe from Vienna to the Russian border. And me, just sitting around eating Mike's pretty good pâté.

Curiously, the place in Poland spelled Łódź and pronounced "Woodge" has entered my Venetian conversation twice in a single week. A friend who lived in Rome when I did, and incidentally (or not so incidentally) the translator of my scholarly work into Italian, pays me a visit on his way back to Belgium, and we find ourselves sitting on a bench in the middle of the Giudecca telling language jokes. He has just finished producing a French version of Hegel's German; furthermore, he's an Italian in Brussels, which—given the city's indigenous dramas of two cultures on top of which all the mechanisms of pan-European community management have been layered—is itself something of a language joke.

My contribution to this Babel is my story of Roly and the Polish housekeeper, then quite fresh in my mind, since it revolved around my departure from New York for Venice. When I had first taken up residence as a professor in Manhattan, I acquired a smart, educated, and articulate cleaning lady from Poland whose English was impeccable. When she found a job more suited to her legal training, she passed me on quite seamlessly to a countrywoman of hers who was equally adept. But she, too, soon graduated from my employ, and this time I was passed on to her sister, who cleaned skillfully but did not speak one word of English.

To my surprise—what could be more disturbing to a man who lives by language?—this hardly proved a hindrance at all. Alice appeared to have been exquisitely instructed in every detail of my household habits, and communication between us took place smoothly with smiles and gestures.

Up to a point. Partly, I suffered from linguistic overreaching:

my pride would not let me remain speechless with this familiar weekly domestic visitor. I insisted on serving her a smorgasbord of phrases owed to recollections from Cold War movies and my grandmother. Alas, *ochen charashò* (after all, she had done a *very good* job on the closets) turned out to be Russian and not Polish, which proved culturally counterproductive. But it wasn't just language hubris that impelled me into bridging the gap. Sometimes there was a real need to communicate: I had found pillowcases in the tablecloth drawer; I worried about Windex being used on the piano; I needed to explain that mozzarella should never be refrigerated.

Enter a brilliant, jocund, funny-looking, affectionate graduate student named Roly. His days as a Ph.D. candidate were numbered because he was good at too many things: not only Shakespeare (his free associations in seminar about the portrait of Portia that signals Bassanio's conquest of her remain my final word on the subject), but also cartooning, children's books, and cinema. In fact, I learned when we started having regular coffee sessions after class that he had spent two years at the world-famous film school in the city of Lodz. So renowned, indeed, was this institution that its city was often rechristened Hollywoodge.

Among the fragments of post-seminar chitchat with my students, it wasn't easy to sequester Roly and introduce the idea of his playing the part of my cleaning lady's interpreter; and to be fair, though he consented gamely, he did disparage his knowledge of Polish with what I took to be false modesty. While I awaited his and her carefully triangulated visit later that week, I moved from room to room composing a roster of precise housekeeping details that would now at last be within my communicative command.

Unfortunately, there was nothing false about Roly's modesty. I stood there watching the two of them struggle with my list. He had forgotten to bring a dictionary, and faced with vocabulary like *lint, mildew,* and *waxy build-up,* rather than, say, *aperture, dolly,* and *two-shot,* he was helpless. Finally I retreated to the other end of the apartment lest my presence be inducing performance anxiety. A quarter of an hour later they both joined me in the kitchen, she with tears streaming down her face and he a picture of beatific happiness. It seemed Alice thought I had brought him there to fire her. In that situation, Roly did what he did best: not just reassure her but draw out, bit by bit, the entire dramatic story of her escape from Gdańsk. There might have been a super-eight documentary out of all this, but not much change in my housekeeping.

I would have dropped the project of communicating with Alice, but there soon arose a graver problem. How would I explain to her that I was on my way to Venice and for a time would have no need for her services at all—especially given the anxieties that had been so exquisitely wrung out of her on Roly's last visit? The only solution was more of the problem: Roly must return. This time he would have a dictionary; this time his brief would not extend to terms like *bleach* or *range hood* or *vacuum bag.* He was simply to announce the duration of my absence and express my fervent wish that she return to clean for me when my stay in Italy was over.

On the day I was leaving, Roly was instructed to join me at Alice's usual arrival time. She appeared at nine sharp, punctual as ever, though rather more smartly dressed than usual. And she made no move to put on her apron or to extract the cleaning materials from the broom closet. Rather, she handed me a note, which read in block letters "I GO BACK POLAND NOW WILL COME YOU TOMORROW IVANA IN STEAD." With which she smiled and started for the apartment door.

Where was Roly to explain that this arrangement was quite

unnecessary? Of course Alice had arrived promptly: she was a person accustomed to hard daily work. But Roly was a bohemian, an intellectual, a cineaste. He probably didn't even get out of bed much before noon. Now, with Alice halfway out the door, I was stuck with a phantom Ivana who couldn't be telephoned, since I was several domino housekeepers away from knowing any phone numbers, and what language would I use if I could contact them?

Italy, I thought. That must be comprehensible, even in Polish. I stood between Alice and the doorway, pointed to myself, pointed away, and formed every pronunciation I could imagine of *ITALY, ITALIA, ITALIANSKI.* She smiled with the same fervor and vagueness that had met all my efforts at communication. Then she seized my hand warmly—perhaps our first-ever physical contact—and was on her way. Italy meant a lot to me but nothing to her.

About an hour later, Roly appeared, bleary and grinning. He was holding a Polish-English dictionary and several drafts of a statement to explain my travel plans. What could I say? He was doing me a favor; he was a student of mine; he was funny and charming; he was making a movie about clowns; he was the soul and spirit of discussion in my graduate course. All I could think of was to grab the dictionary and look up the Polish for Italy. *"Włochy,"* it said. *Włochy?* No wonder I had failed to communicate with her. Why would Italy be called Włochy? Then I realized: Wallachia, Gaul, Wales, Galicia, Galatia. From the British Isles to Asia Minor, this strange formation was a kind of universal word for some group of foreigners or other. *The Dying Gaul* is no Frenchman; he's a Persian. "Are they *turchi* or *vallachi?*" asks Despina in *Così fan tutte* after the young men have donned impenetrably alien disguises. And I could hear my grandmother say contemptuously of the Jews she didn't like, *"Galizianer."* Forget

Paolo's gossip about multilingual Brussels. The real melting pot is
Włochy.

The phone rings late at night in my living room. I scramble out
of bed and sit by a bank of windows that overlook the Giudecca
Canal. For almost the entire length of my (expensive, collect)
conversation with Chris, a Swedish cruise liner is making its
slow progress across the luxurious field of vision that my borrowed apartment affords. Chris is uncharacteristically gloomy.
Life in St. Louis is becoming difficult. Though it is his hometown, and though he is welcome to crash at hippie pads stretching from Ladue to Granite City, he really has no place to live. He
has been seeing a sweet Mexican girl, but he feels unable to
make the greater commitment that she wishes. The local jour-
nalism beat is drying up. Worst of all, there's no wood floor big
enough for him to do his yoga. I restrain myself from offering to
solve his problems, though when I finally get back to sleep, I
dream about my considerable expanse of parquet on Washington
Square.

In next morning's class I am on the third act of the *Merchant*
when I burst into tears. Just when Bassanio has chosen the lead
casket and triumphantly won Portia, a messenger comes from
Venice (no late-night phone calls in Shakespeare) with bad
news. Bassanio reads Antonio's letter aloud to Portia:

> Sweet Bassanio, my ships have all miscarried, my creditors
> grow cruel, my estate is very low, my bond to the Jew is
> forfeit, and (since in paying it, it is impossible I should
> live), all debts are clear'd between you and I, if I might
> but see you at my death: notwithstanding, use your
> pleasure,—if your love do not persuade you to come, let
> not my letter.

Then I went on to elucidate another passage, in which Bassanio explains the whole financial picture to his new betrothed:

> . . . When I told you
> My state was nothing, I should then have told you
> That I was worse than nothing; for indeed
> I have engag'd myself to a dear friend,
> Engag'd my friend to his mere enemy
> To feed my means.

It was on the word *engag'd* that I heard my throat choke. Portia and Bassanio have just become *engaged*. Bassanio chooses this moment to refer to his friendship with Antonio as, also, an *engagement*, on top of which he names Antonio's fatal contract with Shylock as yet another *engagement*. My verbatim lecture notes on the subject:

> 3 engagements = all the "bonds" of the play
> Betrothal only legitimate "engagement"
> Antonio/Bassanio engagement gives way
> Shylock/Antonio engagement potentially fatal
> However you look at it, Antonio *disengaged*
> B and P victorious over crippling enmity between Jew and Merchant

Looking over those notes now, I can only ask who exactly was being crippled by the enmity between Antonio and Shylock.

In St. Mark's Square you may see both all manner of fashions of attire, and heare all the languages of Christendome, besides those that are spoken by the barbarous Ethnickes; the frequencie of people being so great twise a

day, betwixt sixe of the clocke in the morning and eleven,
and againe betwixt five in the afternoon and eight, that . . .
a man may very properly call it . . . a market place of the
world, not of the citie.

Unlike Shakespeare, Ben Jonson's friend Thomas Coryate actually visited Venice, publishing a lengthy account, which he
called *Crudities*, "hastily gobled up in five Moneths travells," as
the 1611 title page puts it. Everything fascinates Coryate: the
giro di ombre in the Piazza San Marco; public torture; women performing onstage, a thing unheard-of in England; vast and exotically stocked food markets, affording his first-ever sight of a
watermelon, as astonishing to him as the fact that in Venice
great noblemen do their own grocery shopping.

But his fullest version of any human encounter takes place in
the Ghetto. That dinner invitation which Shylock at first refuses
would have been quite impossible in real-life Venice, where the
Jews, in a complicated politics of economic exploitation, interde-
pendency, and containment, had been confined to a single island,
which admitted neither entry nor exit at night. Coryate goes
there in the daytime, with a relatively open mind. He notes the
beauty of the women and the riches of their dress, exceeding that
of English countesses; he hates the endless babbling in the synagogue; he is impressed by the zeal with which they keep the Sab-
bath, but he is offended that they don't show enough respect in
the house of God to remove their hats; he notes the wealth they
have gained through usury; he regrets not being able to witness a
circumcision. He reflects on the fact that in Italy all the property
of Jews is confiscated when they convert to Christianity, which,
he points out, slows down the conversion rates as compared to
those in Germany and Poland. He engages a rabbi in spirited theological argument concerning the status of Christ as Messiah

(Coryate's rabbi proves to be something of a Unitarian). Suddenly the rabbi has reinforcements: forty or fifty Jews surround Coryate menacingly, and he is saved only by the opportune appearance of the English ambassador, who rescues him in a boat.

Shylock despises Antonio "for he lends out money gratis." But does he? If Antonio offers zero-interest loans, Bassanio appears to be his only client. Is lending out money gratis a euphemism for keeping a boy? Antonio despises Shylock for the usual millennia's worth of reasons. He has spit on Shylock's face in the Rialto—the same Rialto that I cross every day to shop for fish and cheese and vegetables in the same market that fascinated Coryate—and he promises to do it again. The Jew and the queer, anti-Semitism and homophobia, sodomy and usury. Inside the play they are opposites. Do I double the problem or cancel it out? For Dante—and who deserves more pride of place in a circle of shades?—this is no opposition. He calls usury and sodomy similar forms of "despising nature and her bounty." But he can't even bring himself to name the two sins involved; he just declares them to be "under the sign of Sodom and Cahors." Cahors rather than Gomorrah because that French city was notorious in the later Middle Ages for usury. I know it only from the bitter taste that its tannic black wine leaves in my mouth. According to the official line, which reflects all that fascination with taxonomy which has fueled both scholasticism and bigotry from Aristotle to Aquinas and beyond, sodomy and usury belong in the same folder because they are barren. And you can file Jews there as well because they practice usury and because, wanting salvation, their lives are also barren.

———

It was easier for Coryate to cross the strait from Christian to Jewish Venice than it was for me. Over the years of my many visits
to the city, I could never bring myself to take the ritual guided
tour of the two beautiful and solemn little spaces, to be the kind
of Jew who ignores the Doge's Palace in order to make aliyah
among Shylock's people. My opportunity came with the visit of
two American friends—a male couple, as it happens—of unim-
peachably Christian credentials, one a Missouri boy philosophy
professor, the other a WASP to the point of being nearly albino.
When I was finally surrounded by suburban Americans with expensive clothes and moist but uncomprehending eyes, I spent
the hour of the tour in an agony of self-cancellation, clinging to
my two Christian friends as though their proximity would bleach
and straighten my hair.

There were, to be sure, surprises. The grandest of the syna-
gogues contained rows of gorgeously carved private pews, most of
them with ancient brass nameplates. They bore names of the
dead among which one could read the European diaspora in its
most aristocratic form: Tullio Gomes de Silva; Emmanuele Levi
y Lopez. But a little farther along, on the same ornately fluted
molding, names of the living were pasted on with Scotch tape:
Saul Schapiro; Arthur Lustgarden; Menachem Goldberg. The
guide noticed immediately that my eye had strayed to these inscriptions. She anxiously interrupted her monologue to explain
that of late a Lubavitcher group had taken up residence in the
community. Her face was a study in pained impartiality.

After we finished the tour, I saw that the one large commercial space in the Ghetto Vecchio was occupied by a kind of su-
permarket of Schneerson paraphernalia, complete with a colossal
photograph of the messianic candidate himself. Some things, I
thought, never change. There's always someone trying to convert the Jews. I turned away from the Moshiach merchants to a

much smaller commercial space, where a little grocery shop advertised *pane azzimo*. They handed me a dimpled rectangle that looked something like a very stale crumpet. It was as though anchorites had conveyed the specifications of matzos to Martians. I chewed on it while crossing the bridge that would lead me back to Christian Venice, just about where Coryate had escaped the rabbinical posse.

With no paleface to accompany me, I steer clear of the Ghetto thereafter. Still, it is hard to keep my own past from Shylock's gaze. More than ever before, I notice how he looks into the hearts of the Christian Venetians and turns their own contradictions against them. You called me a dog; is it possible that a dog has the money you need? You want the quality of mercy; how about those slaves you keep—what mercy are you showing them? You think you have a monopoly on the immortal soul—let me threaten to take a pound of your flesh and we'll see how cocky you are about salvation. If Shylock can see so well into the goyim, imagine what he's doing with me.

Whole passages of the play to which I'd never before attended are starting to point in my direction. The same two acquaintances who wondered if Antonio was in love and who brought us the bad news about his bankruptcy also recount the parting of the two friends. Antonio, they report, told Bassanio not to worry about the Jew's bond when he is with Portia: "Let it not enter into your mind of love." And then, "his eye being big with tears, / Turning his face, he put his hand behind him, / And with affection wondrous sensible, / He wrung Bassanio's hand." "Affection wondrous sensible": this is not so much an affection that shows common sense—hardly—but an affection that is wonderfully perceptible to the onlookers. Holding Bassanio's hand, Antonio's love almost dares to speak its name, though Shakespeare tucks the whole scene offstage, where it is not so *sensible* to us. The final word from this pair of narrators on Antonio and Bassanio: "I think he only loves the world for him." The knife starts cutting a little too close.

There is the whole issue of where to locate the pound of flesh. "In what part of your body pleaseth me," says Shylock suggestively when he names the terms. Later, as Antonio's life and love are threatened, the part localizes itself at or near the heart, which might be thought of as weighing about a pound. But who knows where Antonio's heart is, exactly, and what pieces of his flesh the play has already lopped off? One of the standard— inevitable and enduring—punishments for sodomy is castration; that, too, might add up to about a pound.

I keep thinking about the pounds of flesh—kilos, actually— that I was always buying from my friend Maurizio the butcher. Feasting on pounds of flesh is what tourists who stream by the garishly lit restaurants near San Marco are hoping to do, too, and they think they're going native by confining themselves to a menu of fish, even though the lagoon is mostly either polluted or overharvested. But my own culinary discoveries of a season in Venice have been the glorious cured and smoked meats of the inland north—speck, *lardo*, and a kind of rolled bacon wrapped around goose breast. From Maurizio I have learned the difference between prosciutto that is *biologico* and prosciutto that is *super-biologico*. Naturally, both groups of pigs have nothing but organic upbringings. It's just that the *superbiologici* are given homeopathic medicine when they are ill. I found myself disturbed by my food's diseases of the flesh, and not only because of Shylock's reference to the Nazarene prophet who exorcised demons by driving them into the souls of pigs.

When the contract is first made, Shylock assures Bassanio

that he will never require the gruesome payment, because there isn't enough profit in human meat, unlike mutton, beef, and goat. But the prospect of an edible pound of flesh is never quite dispelled. As sodomites are associated with castration, Jews are associated with cannibalism. For a thousand years or more, the provocation to pogroms is that Jews are killing Christians and drinking their blood. Shylock is given the grace and favor of his bond because Venice, with its dependency on commerce and its communities of foreigners, is a rigorously contractual society. But the loophole that undoes Shylock, a card brilliantly played by Portia cross-dressed as a learned judge, is that he may not shed a drop of Christian blood. That blood, the play suggests retrospectively, is the all too familiar goal of Shylock's kind.

Then there are his own problems with eating: "I will buy with you, sell with you, talk with you, walk with you, but I will not eat with you." Forget the problem of *treyf*: the reason why Shylock doesn't want to go to dinner with the Christians is that he wants to eat *them* for dinner. In fact, he eventually accepts the invitation. "But yet I'll go in hate," he declares, "to feed upon / The prodigal Christian." Ultimately, the prodigal Christians will feed on him. Venice, it should be noted, was famous for exotic feasts. Some of those look like the one Veronese painted for Venice in 1573 with his drive-in-movie-size *Last Supper*—when the Inquisition objected to all the realistic particulars, the artist insisted on leaving the food, drink, and service as it was and simply renamed it *Feast in the House of Levi*—and some look like my circle of shades. But they all require pounds of flesh.

Chris eventually transferred his yoga to my floor, and it all happened the day I got back from Venice. He was already on one of his New York swings, so I was able, burdened and jet-lagged, to catch sight of his bare feet off the end of the bed as I came in the door. The next hour was one of the most eventful of my life. We made love; he told me he had met a new woman who lived in Brooklyn; I asked if he was putting an end to our relationship, and he said he didn't want to; he asked if I wanted to put an end to it under the circumstances; I said he should move to New York and make his voyages across the East River rather than across the continent.

By then it was 7:30 p.m.—past one in the morning where I came from—and we were both starving. We sealed our curious engagement by a trip to my favorite French bistro. There must have been something radiant about the two of us: as we walked uptown, people stared in our direction. I had just crossed the sea, and Chris was about to cross the earth. We didn't eat a proper continuous dinner but ordered every starter on the menu and gobbled at them from the center of the table. A bite of onion tart, an oyster, a crunchy mouthful of frisée and bacon. I bought him his first taste of fresh foie gras, with the provocation that I wasn't going to tell him how it was made. He insisted, and I said it was something the French learned to do. Only the French? No, I said, it was now produced in America. Ever the pedant, I recalled later that the Israelis had also overcome any scruples about extracting this bloated organ from the goose. Yet another pound of flesh.

Antonio writes to Bassanio, Don't worry that I'm going to die. All debts are clear between you and me if you just come see me before the end. Then, in the courtroom, not knowing Portia is present, Antonio says, Commend me to your wife, say how I loved you, and when you tell this story, "bid her be judge whether Bassanio had not once a love." Once a love: Does that mean once before or only once—in other words, only when Antonio was the lover? Of course Portia *is* a judge, but she never tells us how she judges her competition. What she does do, when the danger is past, is to torture her husband (playfully?), claiming that she doubts his fidelity to her. One more time, Antonio puts himself on the line: "I dare be bound again, / My soul upon the forfeit, that your lord / Will never more break faith advisedly." Last time he pledged only his body, this time his soul. His reward is to be a solitary wedding guest. The Merchant of Venice becomes the Ancient Mariner. He even gets back his foundered ships, but now that Bassanio has married the big bucks, what's Antonio got to spend his money on? Portia is paying for the feast.

The woman in Brooklyn, feisty, mercurial, barely tolerant of the unorthodox arrangement, was not a keeper. After a few months there was a woman in Queens who held Chris in ways that neither her predecessor nor I—nor he himself—imagined. I began to realize that Chris was hers and not mine. Our bond was dissolved. To me it seemed, for a long time, like a tragedy— something beautiful and impossible that died young—but with another turning of the seasons it felt more like a comedy, as Chris and I reached a happy ending by making ourselves equal partners in a binding, indefinable friendship, signaled by a ritual of dinner on Wednesday nights. I stopped inventing sexy menus for him. We'd usually go to a bargain Belgian restaurant and order one big bowl of mussels, going at them from opposite sides of the table, each with his own little fork.

The day that ended in New York with Chris and me sliding out of bed and into every appetizer on the bistro menu had begun almost as momentously in Venice, where my last step on the shores of the Adriatic had very nearly been a misstep. Resolute against any acts that were too touristical and too expensive, I had never taken a water taxi before—a gondola ride would be even more taboo on the same grounds—but the increment in my possessions over the course of a semester in Venice made it necessary to use transport that could launch me directly from the steps in front of my house to the airport. I had never had any trouble alighting on the customary water-bus. The deck of the vaporetto lines up with the bobbing dock so as to produce a broad threshold sufficient for two or three passengers abreast to cross in comfort. The sleek taxicraft, on the other hand, put down at the edge of the oceanic Giudecca Canal, had no such reassurances.

The boatman secured his craft, reached across in a single smooth motion to transfer my three bulging bags into the vessel, and waited for me to join them. The currents grew choppy, and he held out a strong, doubtless practiced, arm. But the ten or twelve inches that separated me on terra firma from him on the water taxi might as well have been the Caspian Sea. The fear and embarrassment of my clumsy posture soon gave way to something worse: I managed to plant my left foot on the slick flooring of the boat, but there seemed no power on heaven or earth that could induce me to heave the rest of myself across. For a long, turbulent moment, I remained in two mutually exclusive places at the same time.

I won't say that my life passed before my eyes during the transit, but I did have time, as the taximan and I subsequently tore through the lagoon, to do some past and future reflection. Surveying my life and possessions from the speedboat, I thought about excess baggage. If my suitcases had arrived in Venice trim and now returned to America bulging, part of the difference was due to the complete works of Shakespeare in competing Italian versions that had been showered upon me during my visiting professorship. Not just *Il mercante di Venezia*, but *Molto rumore per nulla*; *Pene d'amor perdute*; *Tutto è bene quel che finisce bene*. Much Ado; Love's Labor; All's Well: when you translated the titles back from Italian, they started to seem like predictions of the future or judgments on the past.

Or maybe fragments from fortune-cookie messages at the conclusion of a ten-year meal. This sojourn in Venice celebrated the end of a decade spent far from my first love, Shakespeare, a decade I had spent living and writing Roman archaeology. As soon as I had written my book on that subject, I had returned to Shakespeare, with the import-export scheme of my own that brought the *Merchant* back to his fictional hometown. Had I been indulging in some perverse attempt to cohabit with old and new loves at once? Adultery or miscegenation? *Traduttore traditore*.

No. I might have been stuck momentarily executing that nautical split, but I had discovered something about thresholds during the months on that Giudecca shore. And Shakespeare, who traveled nowhere but arrived everywhere, had been my guidebook—not only to Venice but also to myself. I had spent thirty years reading Shakespeare; now, in Venice, I had let Shakespeare read me.

A decade earlier, I had made an even bigger leap. And, I realized now, in the first long year I spent in Rome at the start of that adventure, it wasn't just Shakespeare, but whole libraries, picture galleries, opera houses, and wine cellars that could read me. When I first arrived in those thrillingly, ominously enclosed spaces of the Piazza dei Satiri that were to be my abode for my year in Rome, I was even more in need of guidebooks than I was to be in Venice. But I was armed with only an opera, a couple of other Romance languages at varying levels of fluency, and an eye with some practice in recognizing classical statues as they peered out from under the surfaces of Renaissance paintings. I had imagined a scholarly project for which I was almost totally unprepared, come to a city where I knew no one, rented an apartment sight unseen, and hazarded my lifelong need for conversation in a place where I lacked both means and persons for communication. I had cast the fortunes of an already wavering, solitary life upon a place that, a little bit like Shakespeare, I knew from dreams—and mostly other people's dreams.

Reading and being read, going from Rome to Venice and back, discovering that I could go home again but also that I could leave home again: my Italian decade, like the *giro di ombre* itself, opened out into circles. I began, mute and inexperienced, sitting at a table with the dead in Rome, trying to dig up their shades, disentangling the many layers of their space and time. Making my way in the city of Shylock and Antonio, picking up the pieces here and there, visiting myself while living among foreigners, revising and refining my circle of tastes, I sat at a table with the dead in Venice. But if the living have joined in the feast—and after all, Shakespeare lives, Chris lives, libraries and galleries and delicatessens and even gardens of ancient sculpture fragments are filled with life—then I owe some unpayable debt to the places where my own archaeology was first brought to light.

ONE YEAR OF SOLITUDE

There were a hundred and three steps up to my top-floor apartment in the Piazza dei Satiri. They rose in a long stone spiral said to have functioned as a military watchtower for several centuries before the building it now served was constructed as an afterthought to it. At this moment, within days of my arrival, I had not yet counted the steps, of course. That act of classification would only come months later, born of a cross between exhilaration and muscle strain as I hefted home the complete works of Pliny the Elder, or else of my determination to master the strains of life in Rome, perhaps inspired by a notable success, or failure, in the archives.

The steps were innumerable and the memory of hauling upward a taxiful of excess baggage still fresh. I had mastered nothing about the route homeward except that the man who drove me from the airport, after gamely consenting to help with the suitcases once he was tipped in lire sporting many zeros, had taught me a new vocabulary word. As we wheezed our way upward, he gave me to understand that we were passing one, two, three, four, and arriving finally at my—fifth—*pianerottolo*, or landing.

Eager to increase my word power, I had just tried this expression out on a friendly shopkeeper—I was choosing between the purchase of a TV and the rental of a piano, the one project ultimately postponed, the other abandoned—but where I expected to impress with my conquest of domestic Italian, I was faced rather with philological comeuppance. Yes, he said, you could describe the space in front of my door that way, but mostly the word was used to talk about neighborly proximity, to establish your bond with the people next door by saying that they lived on the same *pianerottolo*. Like so many words, it seemed to describe a thing but really described a relation. My building, an accidental composite, now rather dilapidated, of separate constructions from the first, the eleventh, and the seventeenth centuries, had only one apartment per floor. Without a close neighbor, I could have no *pianerottolo*.

Perhaps it was the conversation with the piano man that inspired the tiny act of madness I was about to commit on this upward climb. Then, too, it was dark (the staircase was never well lit), and I was as yet so far from having a Roman routine that I had not even learned to count landings, let alone steps.

At all events, on this particular late afternoon I found myself well above street level in front of a door inside my building, poised to enter. Why I did not simply extract the keys from my pocket I am not sure. It can't have been that I forgot about them: their boxy, exotic shapes produced a vexing bulge in my clothing that I never learned to smooth. Let us just say, and not for the last time, that I was slightly disoriented.

What I did was, I knocked on my own door.

A voice responded, *"Chi è?"* (Who's there?), and I said, *"Son' io"* (It's me). A completely unremarkable exchange. Except that there was no one in my apartment; there could be no one in my apartment; in my whole adult life I had lived with no one. Furthermore, it was especially impossible for there to be anyone in this apartment, since I knew not a living soul when I came to Rome, nor had I since my arrival met anyone to whom, judiciously or injudiciously, I might have offered a set of those cumbersome keys. I had exchanged a life without a partnership for a life without even an acquaintanceship.

The mystery, I suppose, is not much of a mystery: I was intruding on the siesta of the elderly lady who lived at the fourth, rather than the fifth, *pianerottolo*. No surprise that she would react to a stranger by asking "Who's there?"; but whom did I think I was talking to when I replied, "It's me"? And what was I to say when she very reasonably responded, "Me who?"

I covered my tracks by blurting out some hastily concocted form of "Please excuse me, I've made a mistake, I'm at the wrong door." *Ho sbagliato porta, ho sbagliato porta*, I repeated to myself upstairs after consulting dictionaries and phrase books, though I never again needed to say it. And from then on, I learned that to get home in the Piazza dei Satiri, I had to climb until there were no more neighbors and no more stairs to climb.

Yet the whole episode is not so strange when you realize that I came to Rome precisely to hear voices. In fact, I had been taking part in displaced conversations for a long time. When I taught *Hamlet*, students eager to tackle existential paradox had to endure my endless riffs on the play's first two lines, in which a lonely soldier guarding the dark battlements of Elsinore cries out, "Who's there?" only to be answered by another soldier, newly arrived for his watch, who responds, in effect, No, *you're* the one who's supposed to answer *me*. Who's there, indeed.

But I wasn't in Rome to hear the voices of Danish soldiers, or Shakespeare, or even Dante, much as they would keep resounding in my head, even here. Poets' voices, I had come to feel, were too easy to hear, which, oddly enough, meant that their voices

were being drowned out by too many professors—my colleagues—speaking on their behalf. I came to Rome to hear
voices hoarse from much longer silence, the voices of material
objects, statues of marble and bronze that had lived the public
and private life of ancient Rome, then been buried under a thousand years of decomposing civilization only to reappear in the
Renaissance, anonymous and mutilated, speechless and demanding to be heard.

Take those satyrs who had given my piazza its name. All the
neighborhood regulars, like the elderly proprietor of the ballerina-
friendly restaurant who held court outdoors in bathrobe and
slippers, or the young go-getter whose paint shop permanently
displayed a handwritten sign reading TODAY: GLUE, could tell
you that twin statues of satyrs had been dug up right here five
hundred years ago. I happened to know these guys. Leering,
paunchy, goat-legged, and, as statues go, well hung, they were
now tucked inconspicuously among more eloquent antiquities in
front of the Capitoline Museum. Yet if you listened carefully,
they might tell quite a story. Once, they had supported a door-
frame in Pompey's Theater; a millennium later, detached and
armless, they became prized collectibles. Pristine in 44 B.C.,
they witnessed the assassination of Julius Caesar; eroded in 1513,
they were carried like totems to celebrate the inauguration of fat,
art-loving Pope Leo X. I was proud to live at the sign of such a
sexy pair, even if they were both carrying filigreed marble fruit
baskets tucked between their horns.

Alas, it was my job to listen to them even more carefully.
Once I did that, I discovered that my little satyr community
wasn't entirely authentic. No document records where these
statues were found in the 1400s, and it's only in recent times that
they have become associated with my home square. Worse than
that, this bit of turf was given names that sound like *satrio* and

atri (which bespeak no satyrs) as early as the Middle Ages, long before such statues could possibly have been dug up. And when you come down to it, they're not really satyrs, they're fauns. Most likely, the story about the hunky eponyms is a nifty mythic back-formation invented around 1800, and the truth is, I live in the Piazza of the Theater, or the Piazza of the Atrium, or maybe even the Piazza of Satire. Only much later did I notice that it's the cross street of my building, Via dei Chiavari, that is endowed with authentic sexy potential. Literally, it's the street of key makers, but regular late-night guffaws from drunken young Romans suggest that *chiavare*, putting the key in the lock, has other idiomatic meanings. You have to listen to the voices of the living as well as the dead.

That takes a lot of practice, especially in an unfamiliar environment, and at this moment I was still being deafened by the reverberating sound of the voice in my own head. Within a very few days of arriving, I had perceived that my sabbatical in Rome meant one year of solitude. Like all such thunderblows, this realization came not from experiencing the dreaded condition itself, but from the efforts to stave it off.

Before leaving the States, I had—masochistically, as it turns out—cultivated circles of acquaintance among those who had spent research time in Rome. They all had their own nostalgias for bands of institutional camaraderie, and there were some diabolically effective storytellers among my informants. Even now I can recall the vicarious sensations of spending New Year's Eve atop the American Academy or of engaging in coffee-room gossip sessions among the manuscripts at the Vatican Library as though they were taking place before my eyes. They never would take place before my eyes, as the storytellers themselves regretfully made clear. The awkward, unkempt Evanston antiquary whose whole life was a downhill slide compared with his year at

the American Academy, the raven-haired Marxist beauty who
had organized an ongoing international salon during break times
among the medieval codices—these and others were haunting
me as I did my lone shopping in the streets near my new house.

The day before, there had been a chance encounter with an
art historian I knew only slightly, via a mutual friend with whom
my relations were so pained as to be undiscussable. We sat in a
café, I babbled like a madman for half an hour—released from
utter silence—and then, looking for churches to which we might
pay a learned visit, we combed the nearby streets. But we were in
the midst of midday closure, and all we ended up doing was inventing a quattrocento artist named Divieto di Sosta (i.e., No
Parking), a peripatetic muralist who never learned how to work
in fresco. As we parted, she recalled that she had been invited to
dinner with a professor at the University of Rome—he was connected to me via the same troublesome mutual friend—and she
offered to insinuate me along. It all seemed easy enough, but
when I left my apartment in the Piazza dei Satiri for my errands,
I discovered a note from her admitting that she had not summoned up the courage to ask the professor if she could bring me
with her.

Now, on my rounds with a packet from the pharmacy in one
hand (Band-Aids, eyewash) and from the stationery store in the
other (airmail envelopes, note cards), I found myself circling
Piazza Cairoli before completing the return trip home. It is as
ugly a space as Old Rome affords. A pompous, blank-faced family palace from the seventeenth century, with impeccable archi-
tectural credentials but disfigured by the shops from which I
fetched my goods; a grand, uncharming, rarely visited church of
similar time period whose interior contents include *The Derision
of Christ* and *San Carlo Carrying the Sacred Nail to the Plague-
Stricken*; a one-pump gas station in the midst of a tiny slot of

parkland, including half a dozen trees planted in dirt otherwise covered with refuse and parked motorcycles—those are the high points.

I stopped under the green neon cross that signals drugstore and reflected on the expectation of fifty more weeks in the neighborhood. This kind of adversity—sadness in prospect—I knew very well how to handle. From childhood onward I had made myself the poet, dramatist, prosecuting attorney of my own unhappinesses. For selected audiences I had staged my every potential sorrow into cycles of saga underpinned by airtight syllogisms against all well-meaning objections that things might, after all, not turn out so bad, that I might have a fulfilling career, or that friendships might ripen into loves. And I had been infallible in choosing my partners for this game, those who could keep the volley going indefinitely between the proffered illogic of open possibilities and the well-oiled engine of certain despair. Mother, lover, best friends, or just acquaintances with whom I felt the secret handshake of common addiction to this strategy: whomever I had played with, I had always experienced a charge of negative energy at the end of the session. I would walk away or hang up the phone having demonstrated that no accident of pleasure or success could invade the closed system of sorrow.

Once in a while, the scheme didn't work. Standing naked at a New Haven draft board in 1970, or, ten years later, holding my beloved German shepherd Sasha in the midst of an epileptic seizure—these prospects were too real, too absolute. In these cases, I wished only to be reassured. And since I could not take the risk that my friends' comforts would be unconvincing, I asked for nothing from anyone. I kept silent, as though, absurdly, I were some kind of stoic. That's how you know I'm in real terror: when I don't complain about anything.

It's easy to see all this now only because I figured it out that day in Rome. What kept me in Piazza Cairoli was a paralysis. If I climbed the stairs at home, I could pick up the telephone. True, I would be staring at the meter that registered 200 lire every 1.8 seconds, with its clicks, or *scatti*, playing disco beat to every transatlantic conversation. Still, regarding the fears of a whole year without friends or acquaintances, without flirtations or banter, without embraces or conversations, I could readily unload and then await all those cheery counterclaims for which I had answers well prepared. But I just couldn't do it. I remembered Sasha and the draft physical; I even remembered how it felt to anticipate swimming practice every Monday afternoon in junior high school after I had walked heedlessly into the deep end my first time at the pool. I was too scared to talk to anyone.

Upstairs, at the fifth *pianerottolo*, all was quiet. There remained some disarray from the previous evening, when a cloudburst had been followed by long, heavy rain. Just as I had finished unpacking the last of my clothes and stowing them in the dim space under the staircase that led to the tiny loft bedroom, the lights had gone out. Moments later I started hearing the dripping—no, gushing—of water. I stumbled into cupboards, felt my way for containers, then homed in on leaks.

As I now returned, my eclectic efforts at damage control were still in evidence. A mug and a bucket sat under the pair of wooden African fertility gods that framed the interior doorpost. Several layers of dry-cleaner plastic had rescued the shiny new stereo rig that had so delighted me when I first entered the apartment, though the adjacent record rack, whose emptiness had disappointed me, was quite awash. A toolbox, rusted open, was centered beneath the Romanesque brick ceiling arch that topped the doorway between the two main rooms. And at the foot of the whole wall that was covered with Roy Lichtenstein prints ("BRATATATATATA!" emerging from primitive aircraft and sci-fi cannons) I had wadded up rags from the bathroom armoire. Or at least they had seemed in the dark to be rags; now I noticed fringes of lace and threads of embroidery soppily entangled in them.

Scarcely had I visited all the trouble spots in my little dripping empire when, for the first time ever, the doorbell rang. For this contingency I had been carefully coached by the elderly couple, parents of the regular inhabitant, who would throughout my time in Rome act as my—variously—affectionate, enigmatic, inaccessible, and malevolent landlords. During a brief orientation session at her house in a much grander neighborhood, Signora had said very little about the heating system, the shower, or the washing machine, but she had done virtual performance art on how to let friends into the building. The unstated corollary was, of course, how to keep the wrong people out—a point she got across in some difficult-to-follow asides concerning a previous subtenant whose alternative lifestyle she had nothing whatever against, only she wished he hadn't opened the door to all the little boys in the neighborhood.

The building was far too primitive to possess an intercom, Signora had explained apologetically; indeed, one was considered lucky to have a button on the ground floor that could ring a bell on the fifth. It took several run-throughs of verbal explanation and mime before I was sure I understood the drill that would get visitors past the locked front door without my having to go to the street myself. She began with a great flourish by extracting a special key from her pocket—she was wearing something that could have been a lace bathrobe or a wraparound suitable for wearing at state occasions—and then pointed to the little weight attached to the key. It appeared to have the shape and bulk of a fishing sinker, except that it was enclosed in a formfitting crocheted sheath. She held this object out from her body, took a few

mincing steps in place, then did a pushing motion with both
arms and leaned forward. Only at this point did she speak slowly
enough for me to understand her perfectly. You have to look
with great attention, I understood her to say. Then, with a liftoff
gesture such as I had learned from my childhood piano teacher—
come to think of it, she rather resembled Signora, both in appearance and in range of moods—she let the key drop to the
floor. She then turned to her right, took a few more steps, and
held her arms akimbo in what I took to be the international sign
for Awaiting the Guest.

Now that the doorbell was ringing for the first time, I felt
ready. I seized the weighted key, walked to the front window,
opened it wide, and looked down. Only then did I realize just
how inadequate the rehearsal had been. I stared down all five
stories in a myopic haze. I never had good eyesight; worse, I have
never known how to coordinate my eyes and my hands. My parents took me at age five to something called the Gifted Children's Clinic, where I was given tests that proved I could read at
ninth-grade level, but not draw a chair if my life depended on it.
And throughout my school years I spent eternal minutes at
home plate thinking, The bat in my hands is so thin, the thing
he's heaving is the size of an orange, there is so much air all
around us in the universe, what are the chances that this stick is
going to connect with that ball?

When I looked down now, key in hand, any number of people were milling about in the piazza, and it was just that hour
when it begins to get dark but the streetlights have not gone on.
How would I recognize the bell ringer? Furthermore, the piazza
was full of parked cars, and right under my window was a perpetual fountain with a large drain full of urban debris. What were
my chances of delivering the key where a guest would find it—as
opposed to, say, having to fish it out of the sewer or under a

parked car or from inside a newly cracked windshield? As I gazed out the window, no one seemed identifiable (how *could* they be?), but in the spirit that had led me to swing at baseballs I couldn't see and, more recently, to knock on my own door, I hurled the key to the ground and guiltily drew back inside. I waited for a greeting, a scream, a bang, a splash. Nothing.

Just as I allowed myself to lean back out the window and search for anyone who was scrambling after the key, I did hear sounds. But it was the locked door of my own apartment opening. There in the entryway stood my landlords, laden with care packages and smiles and, of course, brandishing their own passkeys, which had made the whole throwing ritual superfluous. Highly pleased with themselves, they were contributing some little *amiglioramenti*—improvements—to launch me on my life in their son's house. Extra towels, which I didn't need, and a floor lamp, which I did need. There was also some promise of a comfortable chair, which I needed desperately. About the dripping water and various soppy linens, they appeared to be indifferent, which was a great relief.

But my anxiety soon shifted to retrieval of the weighted key. I didn't quite have the words to explain this problem, nor had they remained at street level long enough to be aware of what I had done. I don't know what they thought when I bounded down the stairs while they were busying themselves with installing their various gifts. As for the key, it had landed in perfectly clear open space, under a streetlamp, and precisely in front of the door. Beginner's luck.

Carrying my little prize in some triumph, around the fourth *pianerottolo* I began to hear the couple in animated conversation. Signora, who outtalked and outweighed her husband considerably, was asking some sort of question, to which he was responding, "I don't know, I'm not sure, I'm still looking." When I got inside, she was pointing to the sofa-daybed that would remain my principal place of comfort in the apartment (like many other promises, the easy chair was never delivered) and demanding insistently, "*Fodera?*" Or perhaps it was *federa*, or maybe *fodero*. Possibly even *figaro*. She moved around to other sites—a little trunk containing religious ornaments, a pile of folding chairs leaning against the rickety dining table, an open pipe that came out of the wall in the midst of the bookshelves occasionally emitting gray ash—with the insistent question, "*Fodera?*" Signore pointed to other objects—cushions, cupboards, piles of linen—and he seemed to answer, "*Fodera!*" But she remained unsatisfied.

Finally she sent her frail husband up the nearly vertical steps to the scantily furnished attic crawl space, my bedroom. After a few moments he returned empty-handed but in glory: "*Sì, c'è!*" he announced definitively, and Signora was duly reassured that the necessary object had been tracked down. Later I climbed the stairway and scoured the area, but all I could find were dust balls, a few wire hangers, and my pajama top, none of them likely candidates for *fodera*. Only now do I consult a definitive dictionary. *Casing? Scabbard? Tribute of rations imposed on a conquered enemy district?* I thanked both my landlords and sent them off to their dinner at home.

It was just as well that they were unfazed by all the leaks in the apartment. I could do nothing for the soggy beamed ceilings with their remnants of peeling paint, or for the terra-cotta floor. Nor had I any means of stemming the tide that had cascaded down the lavish built-in bookcases, anomalies in this genial and shabby space, whose tightly packed contents exhibited a long history of seepage.

Nonetheless, I owed them. Those books, wet and dry, were in the process of saving my life. Excessive as my first day's baggage had been, it was lighter than it was supposed to be. Four large cartons, filled with all the indispensable volumes I expected to need day and night by my side as I began my research, had been impounded by customs, whose officials were carefully studying the minute list of their contents that I had misguidedly been urged to prepare while still Stateside. And they were threatening to charge me 23 percent of some imagined monetary value attributed to the contents.

This is how it happened. I had followed instructions and listed every title I packed. At the top of page one—it was a big book, and I guess I put it in the bottom of the first box—was:

Drawings of Michelangelo

It seems that the customs inspector looked at this and decided that my boxes included not *Drawings of Michelangelo*, but drawings of Michelangelo. And, I picture him thinking, just imagine all the other dutiables signaled in the remaining five pages of the document. For instance:

Splendours of the Gonzaga
The Sexuality of Christ
Truth and Method
Brown Fisherman's Sweater

Actually, the Brown Fisherman's Sweater *was* a brown fisherman's sweater, which I had folded into a half-empty carton so that the books wouldn't roll around. But as for all these other possessions, I sympathized with the customs inspector. Who could put a price on Renaissance art collections, or modern hermeneutics, or God's genitals?

Perhaps it was the deprivation of my own reading matter that made me so assiduous a browser among the apartment's heavily laden, now soggy bookshelves. The city of Rome lay all before me, not to mention the archives, the statue collections, the prospect of a triumphant conclusion to research. The enterprise of launching myself in one of those social circles of international scholars about which I could anticipate future nostalgia—this, too, lay before me. Yet for the whole time that my own books were impounded, I made no such moves. Instead, I kept voraciously reading the happenstance library of my rented home.

Either it was daytime and I was coiled in lotus position on the saggy sofa bed—oriented with the east-facing window over my left shoulder as the light progressed from blue-white morning sunshine to golden afternoon reflection off the cranberry walls across the piazza—or it was late night and I was struggling for a comfortable position on the thin mattress that spread across the low-ceilinged sleeping loft while I maximized one lamp and a bit of streetlight passing through the circular window that looked into the cupola of Sant'Andrea della Valle.

I have a photograph of me standing just inside the apartment (a visually minded person who has entered my life more recently looks at the picture and says, "Beautiful doorway, lonely man, neat bookshelves"), and from it I can reconstruct large stretches of the library I had at my disposal. From across this gap of time it looks like an archaeology of fashion for one stylish post-1968 historical moment. A few classics, like Jack London and the late Fitzgerald; stray readings in French theory and Italian Marxism; international-scene contemporaries like Kundera, Grass, and Kosinski; the loftier literature of the drug culture, with titles like On Hashish and The Peyote Dance. I am reading these off the picture because they have otherwise passed completely from my memory. Faced with these bookshelves, I did not give myself a liberal education. I became obsessed.

I guess it started innocently enough. It was bedtime on the

first or second day, and I searched for the volume that promised to be my hottest companion in the little sleeping loft. For all its show of being countercultural, the apartment's library was curiously prim and high-minded—rather like Italian culture in general, as I later learned. Still, there was an entire shelf devoted to an author I had never read but somehow knew to be rough and provocative.

I was attempting my first novel . . . I set a goal of ten pages a night but I never knew until the next day how many pages I had written. I'd get up in the morning, vomit, then walk to the front room and look on the couch to see how many pages were there. I always exceeded my ten. Sometimes there were 17, 18, 23, 25 pages.

When I came I felt it was in the face of everything decent, white sperm dripping down over the heads and souls of my dead parents.

"You're a whore."

"Yeah? Well, if there's anything worse than a whore it's a bore."

"If there's anything worse than a bore it's a boring whore."

Why always more women? What was I trying to do? New affairs were exciting but they were also hard work. The first kiss, the first fuck had some drama. People were interesting at first. Then later, slowly but surely, all the flaws and madness would manifest themselves . . . I was too old and I was ugly. Maybe that's why it felt so good to stick it into young girls.

"I want to fuck you," she said. "It's your face."

"What about my face?"

"It's magnificent. I want to destroy your face with my cunt."

"It might be the other way around."

"Don't bet on it."

"You're right. Cunts are indestructible."

No oral sex. My stomach was too upset. I mounted the famous doctor's ex-wife. The cultured world traveler. She had the Brontë sisters in her bookcase. We both liked Carson McCullers. *The Heart Is a Lonely Hunter*. I gave her 3 or 4 particularly mean rips and she gasped. Now she knew a writer firsthand . . .

I was fucking a culture-bitch. I felt myself nearing a climax. I pushed a tongue in her mouth, kissed her, and climaxed. I rolled off feeling foolish . . . She would have been a better fuck in Greece, maybe. America was a shitty place to fuck.

Why was it that every time you saw a woman like that you were always with another woman?

I don't recall which was the first Charles Bukowski novel I took to bed with me; it doesn't really matter, because they all turned out to be one logorrheic profusion. Within a week of late nights, I had devoured them all, sometimes even descending from the loft to fetch another volume should I happen to finish one book after midnight and still need more. A bond of dependency attached the fastidious, correct, unwillingly abstemious man stretched out on his narrow sleeping pallet to the scrofulous, profane abuser who gets laid on every page. If you had asked me at the time, I would have said that wish fulfillment entered into it. Not just the desire to overturn a lifetime of seeming sexually invisible, but a longing to encounter every new object in the world—women, men, artifacts—with the capacity for yet another hard-on.

But that's only part of it. Some years later I was invited to a seminar at the University of Rome, where I gave a paper on narrative theory—I had translated it myself—in which I made much of recurrence, reiteration, and echoing in Ovid's *Metamorphoses*. I had worked hard on the Italian, but I'd had to guess at the precise rendering of Freud's "repetition compulsion"—itself, of course, an English translation of *Wiederholungszwang*. I had settled on *costrizione di repetizione*. My uncertainty was doubtless audible when I first read the phrase, and I paused long enough for a student to interrupt with the correct Italian version.

Unfortunately, she was a bit shy, and I didn't quite hear it. Consequently, the next time I wanted to say repetition compulsion, I was even less certain of the Italian. By this time several people blurted out the proper translation, which made it still more difficult for me to understand. The phrase comes up rather often—coincidence? I think not—in the paper. As a larger number of students came to my aid on each repetition, the intoned expression got ever more indistinct until the group started to find its rhythm. By the fifteenth or sixteenth iteration, I was finally able to conduct a unison chorus of COAZIONE A RIPETERE.

What's so special about Bukowski is that he writes as he fucks. *Coazione a ripetere.* There's no plot and no satisfaction. He climaxes, but his books don't. Their story lines consist of the moves that get women into bed, after which there is nothing to do but start it again. A life lived so that experience is short-circuited by orgasm whose only result is the repetitious text: 17, 18, 23, 25 pages, vomit, coming in the face of everything decent. Always more women; indestructible cunts; sticking it into young girls; boring whores; 3 or 4 mean rips.

And if he writes as he fucks, that's the same way he got me to read him. I turned the pages just as he turned from one woman to another. In fact, you could probably substitute *book* for *woman*, and the whole of his oeuvre would be a story about me. Not only Bukowski's books, but all my modules of scholarship. A book with a plot belongs to a life with a goal. But I lay scanning episode after episode, always wanting more and never satisfied with more, because I was turned on by an emptiness that lay on the other side of extravagant experiences I'd never have.

What shall I say, then, of my other page-turning obsession during these first days? It seems impossible to guess at the state of mind of someone who cannot tear himself away from sentences like, "The study of autobiography is caught in this double motion, the necessity to escape from the tropology of the subject and the equally inevitable reinscription of this necessity within a specular model of cognition."

And yet it is so. I was by night prowling the dark side with Charles Bukowski and by day prowling the even darker side with Paul de Man.

It's poetic justice that up to this time I had never read de Man, only played with his name. *Demain?* Every [de] Man? He de man? De-man-ic? I was influenced by hearing a German colleague refer to a yet more eminent poststructuralist as *Der die das*, also by a spontaneously composed Olde English ballad of deconstruction with the chorus "Derrida, down derry, Derrida." Words seemed to crumble and recombine at the very sight of these guys: that's all I knew for sure. At the moment when I was pulling *Blindness and Insight* off the shelves of my Rome apartment, I was about as virgin to contemporary literary theory as I was to Charles Bukowski's sex life. And I had reason to believe that some scary analogy operated between the two.

It wasn't just the sensation that lurid pleasures were on offer just outside my reach. For more than a decade, my life in the academy had felt just like watching my landlords run around the apartment indicating various objects and shouting *"Fodera!"* What exactly were they pointing at? Was this a new name for old things? Did the things change when you called them by this name? Was *fodera* not a noun at all, but some sort of optative verb or relational adjective? If I pointed to something and shouted *Fodera!* would I get away with it? I guess I started reading de Man at this moment because Italy was just an extension of my life at the university—a place where everyone was speaking a foreign language that I only intermittently understood. In fact, they all seemed to be having a great time together. They may have been screwing like Bukowski or, alternatively, building passionate lasting relationships: I didn't have the experience to judge or the invitation to find out. I knew there were still pockets of people who spoke my language, but by comparison to these passionate foreigners, my kind seemed crochety, pasty-faced, and unsexy.

I, too, had a theory, or maybe a substitute for a theory. A brilliant in-your-face professor had handed me face-to-face history. She made me read a book by the German philologist Ernst Robert Curtius which declares that modern literature begins when Dante meets Virgil in the opening canto of *The Divine Comedy*. Once Dante put it into my head that Virgil is not a book but a person, that his conversation is open-ended, that you can talk back to him, that you can even reinvent him, I began to choose some of my closest friends from the past. Ominously, de Man says that if you make "the absent, deceased, or voiceless" speak, some kind of fatal symmetry kicks in and you find yourself struck dumb in return. So, while exotic theorists sat in cool cafés chattering away in quaint but difficult foreign tongues, my social life consisted of talking to the dead in their own language.

For the record, what de Man was trying to do in that wadded-up sentence about tropology and reinscription was to blow the whistle on autobiography. Writing about oneself promises the supreme authority of language over subject matter; and since no writing possesses authority outside language itself, autobiography is a particularly insidious act of deception. I already knew the general drill: "the priority of lexis over logos"; "stability of meaning . . . does not exist"; there's no "nonverbal 'outside' to which language refers"—in short, it was not I who should be reading de Man but my adversary at the customs office, who had such blind faith in that list of book titles.

What I didn't know before this reading, however, is that when language loses all its power to deliver reality, other breakdowns follow. Literature that tries to summon up a deep and distant truth is "itself a cause and a symptom of the separation it bewails." History, too, is threatened, since there is no substantial way to make the absent present or the invisible visible. Biggest surprise, though, is the collapse of desire: "The error is to believe that the possession of a particular person could be sufficient to fill a void that does not exist on an interpersonal but on an ontological level."

I suppose I kept turning these pages, rotating on the sofa as light moved from the east to the south window, because I was mesmerized by reading about reading, asking myself whether my reading was following the theories of reading I was reading. All that labor to disentangle impossible sentences. There was an irresistible paradox in winning the brainteaser game of correct decipherment when the sentences under view were telling me that there was no such thing as stable meaning. To me, reading had always meant granting authority, reality, and presence to the text. Now I began to realize that meeting the writer face-to-face was the inverse of theory, and I couldn't turn my eyes away from the gory wreck that de Man had made of writerly language. Bukowski by night was teaching me how to read de Man by day. His endless angry pages of sexual exploits were, in fact, giddy with the power of language: "It was a joy. Words weren't dull, words were things that could make your mind hum. If you read them and let yourself feel the magic, you could live without pain, with hope, no matter what happened to you." And the pages worshipped at the altar of poetry as truth. In one story the narrator meets up with his bitter friend Randall, who explains why he is currently living with an older woman:

"She's a good lay," he said, "and she gives me some of the best sex west of St. Louis."
     This was the same guy who had written four or five great love poems to a woman called Annie. You wondered how it worked.

His own doubts are answered when he reads Randall's new poems: "They were all powerful. He typed with a very heavy hand and the words seemed chiseled in the paper. The force of his writing always astounded me."
     You can see the whole problem in that heavily incised typewriter paper. De Man would look at it and see all the power of language denied any reference in the real world. But Bukowski has no doubts. The chiseled typewriter strokes of Randall's love poems aren't a failure to signify; on the contrary, they substantively deliver the only thing that matters: desire. Did Bukowski

know the joke on *pen* and *penis* that goes all the way back to the Middle Ages? He didn't have to; on every page his writing depends on his fucking. Quite different from the literary critic who puts misguided desire at the pinnacle of all failures of signification, saying, in effect, if desire is inauthentic, we can't know anything about writing. De Man: "The erotic mode is not contrary to the pattern of authentic consciousness, it is merely inadequate, it does not go far enough." Bukowski: "I gave her 3 or 4 particularly mean rips and she gasped. Now she knew a writer firsthand." As Virgil knew Dante?

Still, de Man had a thing or two to tell me about Bukowski. In one of Bukowski's stories, there is a psychiatrist (he admits to having been a Nazi, which has its own equivalences to deconstruction) who, instead of confronting the narrator's tormented sexuality, turns to pure language: "He broke down the word for me. I forget if it was woman or female or what it was, but he broke it down into Latin and he broke it down from there to show what the root was." After the session, the narrator reflects that everyone is suffering all the time: "It seemed to me that this was quite a discovery. I looked at the newsboy and I thought, hmmmm, hmmmm, and I looked at the next person to pass and I thought hmmmm, hmmmm, hmmmmmm." That may be Bukowski's catchiest tune, and it told me more about his life than he knew. The repeatable, extendable *hmmmm* is his real autobiography.

As for de Man, despite his insistent denials of meaning, his essays started to look like the authoritative autobiography whose existence he denied. He didn't know that he was recounting the absolute soul of his own nihilism in all that impossibility of reference, of history, and of desire. What both writers didn't know turned out to be their greatest truth. Blindness and insight.

Moments of genuine humanity thus are moments at which all anteriority vanishes, annihilated by the power of an absolute forgetting.

And the war, everybody was talking about the war in Europe. I wasn't interested in world history, only my own. What crap.

Is it any wonder that both these men played Nazi in 1940, de Man publishing hate literature in Belgium, Bukowski going to America First rallies in Los Angeles? Nearly half a century later I was finding myself alone in a Roman garret, attempting to write some history while all around me were negating history, and I was wrestling with my own desires while the others were denying or denaturing desire.

Solutions are always less interesting than problems. The key I so anxiously threw out the window proved easy to find on the pavement; and the problem about my books, which had been growing more mysterious by the day, was settled, if not explained, once I phoned the American consulate and had the good fortune to be connected to the diplomatic corps' in-house intellectual, who said he could not countenance the separation of any scholar from his research materials. Within an hour the unopened book boxes were piled up in my living room, delivered from an unlabeled truck by nonuniformed moving men who seemed to know nothing about either customs office or consulate. I didn't even get my chance to execute the key maneuver: they appeared right at my living-room door without so much as ringing the downstairs bell.

Once I had shelved my own books—judiciously in out-of-the-way places untouched by the recent deluge—it was as though I had transited from sojourner to resident. It wasn't that I started reading them; it was just that I felt easier in their company. Bukowski and de Man receded and were not replaced by other hyperconnected readings. I was freed to leave home and explore Rome.

As I bounded to the bottom of the staircase, I realized that I had forgotten to bring a map. Whether by accident or design, I had embarked on a novelty. Years earlier, when I was an annual two-week vacationer in the city, booking a single room at one quaint historic hotel after another, I used a map to get around. I tolerated the curbside embarrassment of unfurling the origami accordion, a constant mockery to my pretensions at street smarts, so that I could learn to equate the two-dimensional ground plan with the four-dimensional reality.

Now, leaving the map behind and refusing the arduous climb to retrieve it, I was undertaking a personal dare. It was a test of my memory from the earlier visits, combined with a willingness to get lost—or rather a shape of my time, in which I had no fixed target and could afford serendipity. And like it or not, I suppose I was still under the influence of de Man and Bukowski. They had been such implacable guides and left me so little freedom of motion, yet both of them seemed to be telling me that ultimately, there was no place to go. So it seems appropriate that I should close their last chapters, never touch either author again, walk down the hundred and three steps without a sheet of paper in my hand, and elect a simple, utilitarian crosstown destination.

Actually, I did have sheets of paper in my hand, and my destination was a desperate necessity. I had resisted sending up a distress flare by telephone in those first days, but now, with books and reading in their respective places, I spent a whole morning writing some letters home. My smattering of local urban legend had already instructed me in the unreliability of the Italian postal service and the advantages of entrusting my correspondence to a higher power. So this first walk would take me to St. Peter's Basilica and the Vatican post office. I'd heard it said that this mailbag went straight through to Zurich, where it landed in the irreproachable hands of the Swiss; that was the roundabout route I chose toward a world where I knew people.

My own pedestrian route, straight or crooked, had to be improvised, beginning with the first steps outside the spiral staircase of my tower. From that original taxi ride into the Piazza dei Satiri, all access and egress had taken place along the Via dei Chiavari, which performed a straight shot in both directions, each toward its respective busy thoroughfare. This time I decided to turn away from it, on a route that had no visible outlet. It was well into midday mealtime. The streets were not quiet—raucous television programs emanated from open windows while apartments full of people enjoyed the daily second hour of family lunching—but they were nearly empty. I felt as though I were taking a meditative private excursion to the accompaniment of a cacophonous sound track.

Perhaps it was the staginess of that picture, and of standing in a graciously open space formed by buildings rendered almost two-dimensional in the afternoon sun, that enabled me for the first time to notice the full contours of where I lived. My bold new route out of the piazza seemed blocked only because the facades of the structures at the far end were curved. They were curved, I realized from my recollections of urban archaeology, because they followed the outline of Pompey's Theater, built in the first century A.D. Of course, no one who had constructed the later buildings along the arc—including a showy seventeenth-century multistory noble palazzo with a tire-repair shop taking up half its street level, a trim little bourgeois house four windows wide, and a tiny, dilapidated churchlike edifice with no visible sign of religion about it—had ever seen the Theater of Pompey. They were simply piling foundation upon foundation, stretching back to some Dark Ages Ostrogothic hut whose makers had squandered their own good fortune of looking backward toward a prior half millennium of splendor.

If I didn't understand fully at the time that I was walking in a space where the past was both visible and invisible, that was because I was receiving a quite different taste of the uncanny. I was headed for the Vatican post office; I wasn't interested in studying the ancient arc but in escaping it. As I pursued its course past what I could see from my front door, the landscape became progressively more motley—a hotel, a narrow sideways structure housing a tiny watchmaker's shop, a grimy trattoria—but it perfectly maintained the curve. I began to despair that there was any exit in this direction, but at the same time I realized that I was looking at more than a few remnants of what was once a theater in the round. I was standing at the farthest extension of a perfect semicircle whose focal point, dead center and the object of my gaze, was my own building.

As I turned to face the curve, once more in search of the exit, I remembered *Julius Caesar*. The Ides of March murder took place at the opposite end of the ancient theater complex. On a line between the outer building wall where I was now standing and the site of the assassination, my house would (once again) have signaled the midpoint. Now, on an afternoon dramatically drenched in sunlight, I commanded the arc of what had been a thirty-thousand-seat auditorium. At my back was the site of the ancient stage, which had recently become my home. That made me a Roman actor soliloquizing to no one.

I might have needed to run the full 180 degrees back to the Via dei Chiavari and take up my habitual (though misdirected) exit from home had I not glimpsed a little sign on the crumbling church that sat at the apex of the semicircle. I would never learn what Academy of the Superfluous meant, but at this moment I pondered its significance long enough to see that next to it there was indeed a passageway out of the arc toward the city beyond. Nothing you could drive a car through, just a sequence of steps and gates leading to a narrow tunnel, full of rot and graffiti, that issued in a small open square dominated by a shapely Renaissance palazzo from whose vantage point all traces of Pompey and the semicircle were unreadable.

Not ten minutes out of the house, and I had discovered a secret shortcut that pivoted me like a time machine, I thought proudly, not yet aware that this corridor had its own mysterious and inexorable schedule of lockdown. I had also passed from alarmingly enclosed spaces to an embarrassment of open possibilities. Piazza upon piazza surged to the left and right of me. Freed from tight surroundings and concerned that the Vatican post office was as famous for its whimsical schedule of closure as for its efficiency, I opted for the nearest, widest expanse, and soon I was hustling through the familiar sweep of the Campo de' Fiori. I counted eight streets leading out from the Campo that qualified, according to my intuitions, as possibly heading toward St. Peter's. To assay the situation, I centered myself where the Inquisition burned Giordano Bruno and where the nineteenth century put up a statue to remember him.

In the morning, the Campo is a vibrant clash of market colors and smells; by night, almost equally populous, it dresses in the chic tones of drinks and dinner. For a few hours in the afternoon, however, it is almost deserted. Doubtless my memory plays tricks on me, but I can recall no other occasion when I was alone with Bruno, when I might without distraction make a circle around him and see, from straight on, a robed Dominican friar and from all other angles a giant furled umbrella. I stared at the inscription, then as now enigmatic:

A BRUNO

IL SECOLO DA LVI DIVINATO

QVI

OVE IL ROGO ARSE

I knew that Bruno was a mystic Copernican heretic with ideas about an infinite universe that were unacceptable in 1600. So even in haste, I got the drift: Bruno foresaw the future; on this spot he was burned alive. But what exactly was the relation between those two statements? He lived outside his own epoch, but he died where I was standing. He shakes the hand of my century, but I can't save him. Time is indeterminate; space is fixed.

This was precisely the wrong message for someone who must find his way to the Vatican post office before it closes for the day. Bruno's gruesome fate thus propelled me a bit faster on my impromptu itinerary. Like the proverbial sinner, I chose the broadest way, and I found myself once again pivoted into another world. The Campo de' Fiori's style is piecemeal, functional, vernacular, solicitous. Now I was facing a grandiose and forbidding urban space, dominated by the vast facade of the Palazzo Farnese. Adored as a kaleidoscope of Renaissance styles, all it showed me at this moment was miles of wall and inches of doorway. Worse, on this afternoon it was in its most teasing mode. I already knew that the French, who have been masters of this place on a one-lira-per-century deal negotiated in 1871, never let you in to see the gorgeous mythological frescoes. But at this moment the plate glass covering on the loggia in front of them was so squeaky-clean that I could make out footmen serving a banquet, and if I squinted, even a bit of Hercules' flexed leg seemed to pick up the rosy reflected light of afternoon.

Taking in the broader picture, I found the whole square monumental, foreign, uninviting. Nothing of human scale. I peered across the piazza's cobbled expanse for ways out, but they were obscured by the double centerpiece of gigantic quatrefoil fountains surmounted by ancient granite bathtubs fit for Gargantua, if he'd had any taste for hygiene.

Still, I managed to find a corner with two modest streets, either of which might take me where I was going. The option directly in front of me terminated after one short block at the facade of a picturesque bijou church whose portal was adorned with skulls and bones. I made for the alternate pathway. It led to a street of sumptuous storiated portals, lofty French windows, and alluring glimpses of inner courtyards, every one of them locked, shuttered, or barred. Which is probably why, just as I reached the point where I had to decide on the next phase of my route, I was stopped in my tracks by a tall, apparently nondescript residential structure. It was in a shape carved out by two narrow streets that joined in a blunt angle at a piazza: four stories of tiny windows amid wide stretches of unarticulated wall, as though the place were so ancient that its builders feared it would fall down if they left too many openings for light. As elsewhere, every one of the windows was shuttered.

Except at the top. Five floors up—just the height, I judged, of my own apartment—was a span of magnificent semicircular windows, each occupying a full side of the building's truncated triangle. No shades or shutters except for a bronze curtain rod hung, strangely, on the outside, with a many-colored velour drapery that was flowing sharply upward in the breeze. Perhaps it was the identification with my own humble residence that enabled me to imagine I was seeing the city from inside that three-sided parapet. I had my first decisive glimpse of the city's ground plan. I knew at once that the room had precisely the shape of the Tiber bulge and that it sat in parallel to the land around it as though it were a hub around which the whole city flowed. As soon as I pictured that vantage point, I could see my way perfectly to the Vatican.

The streets began to be peopled; shops opened; cars impeded my route. Still, once I accepted the great straight way of Via Giulia, Renaissance Rome's monumental Main Street, I was delivered to a Tiber bridge that brought me into the visible immediacy of St. Peter's. And how many different approaches to the great monument I was able to traverse in haste! The river view itself, with all its treelined curves; the dingy foregrounding hospital, complete with elderly madmen wandering behind the open latticework fence, which occupies what ought to be the choicest piece of waterside real estate; the hard-edged triumphal boulevard that the Fascists constructed to celebrate their agreement with the pope. Then, finally, irresistibly, the sight of the basilica itself. Even half a mile away, it dwarfed and trivialized the onlooker, except for the strange anatomy of the colonnade, which extends first straight from the facade and then curves around envelopingly like a lover or a harvesting machine. As I followed the heavily determined route of approach, the scale seemed to alter at every pace, with those extending arms, unimagined by any of the original architects, ever more sure that they were equal to the task of accommodating me to the vast structure from which they hinged outward.

There seems no resisting: the cityscape turns you into an automated pilgrim. And whether the role pleases you or not, you are surrounded by those who have come from all over the world just to feel helpless in its grip. I felt each step confounding power, religion, and beauty. I knew what sort of climax lay inside the building—golden throne, monumental altitude, art of kitsch and sublimity. Not for today, though. Today I ducked under the colonnade, observed its more pedestrian offers of rescue. On the left, the toilets; on the right, the post office. I chose the second

option, and at the nearest window I held out three airmail envelopes and paid one thousand lire apiece. I was now officially in
touch with Westport CT, Newton MA, and Libertyville IL.

Of course, I hadn't come to Rome just to write letters home.
The Vatican walk, which was a lifeline in early September, soon
became a subplot, a recreation. One morning I might be in touch
with St. Louis MO via a Vatican route that took me past the
prison of the Queen of Heaven, its massive fortifications belying
both its name and the gracious surroundings of Tiber and Trastevere. Or else a letter would get posted to Halifax NS after a walk
through that multiform cityspace where the frail, desanctified
church of San Simeone Profeta stands opposite an indecorously
grand fountain carried there by Mussolinian urban renewal. Or I
would send up a flare to Palo Alto CA, having circled the broad-
beamed facade of San Giovanni dei Fiorentini, whose banal ex-
terior immortalizes its founders for flunking Michelangelo's
designs on the grounds that he was too old to build a church. Between the fixed points of Satyr Square and the Vatican post office, a solitary man could, day by day, describe many crooked
lines.

But the real daily grind that autumn was my journey to the library where I undertook most of my research—or at least the
kind that could be done from books. I had come to Rome with a
grant proposal, a nice little fellowship, and only the sketchiest
idea of what sort of book I could write. It was Shakespeare—as
he was in the past, as he would be in the future—who led me onward. On this occasion, it was Sonnet 55:

> Not marble, nor the gilded monuments
> Of princes, shall outlive this powerful rhyme.

I had long since absorbed the astonishing boastfulness of the
claim. I had admired, without being able to emulate, the speak-

er's amorous gambit: Love me and I'll make you live forever. But recently, having experienced my own fatigue with the immortality of verse, I had started to ask, Is this true? Do poems really last longer than statues? Books, after all, are a hell of a lot more fragile than blocks of stone. Rocks, scissors, paper: I needed to figure out just how that game played itself out in the Renaissance. I wanted to know what happened to all these marble monuments, how they got made and broken, buried and saved, discovered and copied, why it was that they seemed both dead and alive. I wanted to take a census of ancient stones, to meet them face-to-face, to trace their family histories.

Which meant assiduous attendance at the Bibliotheca Hertziana, the German-run art-history library that, more than anywhere else, spanned Rome of the ancients and Rome of the earliest moderns. With that great pile of Teutonic learning as my destination, I felt that I could hardly indulge in such casual circulations as those I sought en route to the Vatican post office. This time I would consult maps—worse, bus maps. I would become a commuter, toting my briefcase to work on public transport. But Rome has a way of derailing purposeful travel, and it took barely a week for this sober scheme to come undone. The 62 bus, which I could pick up near home, left me quite a distance from the library; the 58, good for the library, was a long walk from home; and the little electric 115, which offered a viable compromise at both ends of the journey, ran so infrequently as to be popularly christened the Biennale—i.e., every two years. And so, while earlier I had forgotten the map, now I proudly renounced it.

Like the Vatican mail run, this journey, too, involved fixed points—my fifth-floor walk-up in the lowlands of Rome to a doorway in the form of a mannerist monster mouth that, situated at the top of the Spanish Steps, was probably at exactly the same altitude as my point of departure. At first I imagined that an invariable daily itinerary would connect these dots, that I would find the most efficient route. I began by following the crowd—"Wide is the gate and broad is the way"—which swept in at one end of Piazza Navona, amid beggars and mimes and portraitists in charcoal, and swept out toward the Corso, jagged avenue of a modern Rome that purveys haberdashery to tourists, faded nineteenth-century boulevard of sagging balconies, its irregular throughline a memory of triumphant antiquity whose celebratory arches were demolished so that the city might have a Main Street in which to see and be seen.

Too little nourishment for the soul on this route. By October, I had carved out the Beauty Walk. On an outside wall on the Palazzo Massimi, just a few dozen steps from my front door, a panorama of frescoed stories could be extracted from the invisibility of grisaille and urban decay, if one took the trouble. From there, three swiftly executed right angles aimed in the general direction of my workplace would place me at the Pantheon, though all I allowed myself to see was a triangle, a rectangle, a semicircle, and some abbreviated lapidary text. No such quick escape was possible from the enveloping curves and angles of Piazza Sant'Ignazio, shaped by a monumentally delicate baroque maze of buildings that seems to trap the pedestrian inside a vast urban armoire. This probably accounts for my prodigal lunge toward the north, placing me at the church of Sant'Agostino, whose spotlessly curvaceous Renaissance front, joined to side buttresses with the perfect industrial geometrics of futurism, offered the antidote of blankness after all the articulations of the previous landmarks.

Perhaps it was a few chill winds of autumn, maybe even the imminence of Halloween—who knows?—but tiring of pretty urban pictures, I managed to sculpt a different itinerary. Call it the

Mystery Tour. By swinging away from the Navona crowds and the more rarefied pleasures of the little piazzas, I found myself in an orbit around a gleaming white marble spiral loftily silhouetted against the sky, animated with a sequence of tiny figures (angels? scallops?) that seemed to be leaning over a balustrade edging toward heaven. Such a celestial helix had to be the top of something, and yet, by whatever direction I approached it, there was nothing at street level but lumpen blockish structures fronted by government security guards.

A few steps in the right direction would bring me to a more earthbound enigma—Bernini's pachyderm saddled with an obelisk that sits in front of Santa Maria sopra Minerva. Struck by the jaunty way the little beast rolled his eyes and swung his trunk, I learned to make an entire route of obelisks, each speaking in a different tone, as though sculptors of hieroglyphics had their own distinctive handwritings. In front of the Minerva, the carving is spare and laconic. A few steps around the corner, opposite the Pantheon, the obelisk sports cool and confident calligraphics. At my next stop, in front of the parliament buildings, Pharaoh Psammetikos is memorialized in fragments and whispers. And the trip culminates in the busy, nature-abhors-a-vacuum garrulousness of the Trinità dei Monti obelisk practically opposite my library door.

Not that I was always so eager to arrive at this threshold. Perhaps it was the human reception, or lack of it, at the library—my difficulty in understanding the etiquette of the various reading rooms, why it was that when you opened the door to some of them, you were met with a unison forbidding gaze from all the occupants, whereas other seemingly identical rooms could be entered without a flicker of public attention—that began to raise questions about the journey versus the arrival.

Or perhaps it was what I was learning at the library. Ancient marbles did have their own route to immortality, which drove straight through the middle of the Renaissance. For some uncanny historical reason, by the middle of the fifteenth century people started rediscovering beautiful objects that had reposed in the ground for a thousand years. A farmer digging on the Esquiline— the wrong side of the city for my walks to the Hertziana—happens upon the *Laocoön* and calls Michelangelo, who comes running to look at it. A mason building a nunnery's wine cellar accidentally unearths a bunch of Dying Amazons and Falling Gauls. A humanist walking down the street notices a boy wearing a medallion around his neck, and he recognizes it as a chalcedony miniature by the hand of a great ancient master. I, too, was a humanist walking down the street; if I had to be alone in a crowd, why was I rushing through the Roman groundscape so that I could devote more time to reading books about the Roman groundscape?

The morning after I transcribed the story about the boy with the beautiful medallion, instead of noting with distracted pleasure the outdoor frescoes of the Palazzo Massimi, I stopped. I stared at the dozens of classical figures in magnificent layerings of garment—a warrior holding a baby, a queen conducting a tribunal, cavalry and infantry in combat, an assassin about to plunge his scimitar into a figure sleeping under a rippling canopy, while elsewhere on a different bed a man lay inert in sleep or death. I had no sense of the artist's name or the subjects or the occasion, or even whether I was looking at a painting of life or (given the monochrome and the massively static body forms) a painting of sculpture. No matter: I felt I was witnessing one of those imaginary pictures that poets describe but no artist could ever execute, the way Homer oversees the entire universe on Achilles' shield or Keats the whole life of antiquity on his Grecian urn. What I mostly thought was, Here is a picture gallery that does not bar its doors to me, a reading room where I feel at home.

As the morning trips repeated themselves, I began even to broach interiors. One day, not only did I find myself at street

level of the scalloped spiral that had seemed to float indepen-
dently in the sky, but I discovered it with all its encircling doors
wide open. Later I learned that the opening times for Sant'Ivo
alla Sapienza were legendarily infrequent, but now I walked
unchecked through courtyard and portal as though entering my
private chapel. Or was it my tomb? Inside this jewel box in the
shape of a bullet nothing disturbed the tripartite symmetries of
star and circle and square; nothing intruded on the white marble
upsweep of right angles and curvatures leading me toward dead
center, where I could place myself alone at ground zero of the
swirling lantern I had first seen from afar.

Not every day did I enjoy the blessing, or curse, of such aus-
tere and solitary contemplation. Sant'Agostino's facade was my
restful space of simplicity, but just inside I got to know the riotous spectacle of the *Madonna of Childbirth*. Lush and brown,
corpulent and sinuous, she is arresting enough as Renaissance
art, but the real show is the gold, jewels, and candles that devo-
tees have encrusted around her, guided by the papal caption on
the pedestal to the effect that adoration of this statue brings a
guaranteed two hundred days of indulgences. Not being covered
by this type of insurance, I was left to seek human connection.
But the bodies turn one way and the faces another, and when I
placed myself in the way of mother's and child's eyeless gazes,
what most reached out to me was the Madonna's prosthetic
golden foot—the original marble having been eroded by the
kisses of the faithful.

Saint Matthew, down the block at San Luigi dei Francesi, was
altogether more promising. Balding and bearded, his graceless
frame stooping over a heavy book while he uncertainly wields a
pen—this guy I knew. But I also recognized the fear and yearning
as he looks upward toward the muscular spirit who hovers at an
unbreachable gap of distance. Could Matthew read whatever in-

spiration it was that the heavenly muse was counting out on those slender angelic fingers?

From those queries I took refuge in the Pantheon, which afforded all kinds of company. Among the living, the tourists. Among the dead, all the majestically buried kings of modern Italy; indeed, the blessed Raphael himself, lying inside a crypt upon which Cardinal Bembo, buried nearby under a humble slab, had written that Mother Nature herself feared to die when Raphael died. But none of this could equal the companionship of geometry—the perfect circle open to the sky at the top of the dome. And of cosmology—the brilliant rays of the sun describing their round of the year upon all the coffered squares of the dome. Standing at the base of that ancient solar circle, I was by myself, once again, at a spot the ancients constructed for the center of the universe.

The same zeal that had propelled me so distractedly through the books in the apartment I now applied with greater focus to reading literary Rome at home, half in preparation, half in substitution for these morning jaunts. Yet where Bukowski and de Man had proved so absorbing, these texts, for all their promise of relevance and edification, only served to distance me. James's Isabel Archer, almost in the grasp of her future husband, spends the happiest days of her life walking where I was walking. "The sense of the terrible human past was heavy to her, but that of something altogether contemporary would suddenly give it wings that it could wave in the blue . . . She went about in a repressed ecstasy of contemplation." But I neither plummeted with the past nor soared with the present; repression and ecstasy were equally foreign to me on these streets.

And Hawthorne's *Marble Faun*, with all its lurid sentimentalities about the art and sex of ancient sculpture, seemed to pander even more shamelessly than *The Portrait of a Lady*. Two or

three mornings a week, in fact, found me in front of the Tower
of the Ape, whose shrine of the Virgin with ever-burning lamp
Hawthorne made into the site and symbol for his saintly heroine.
It was all rather disappointing in the present day. The only light
I could see was in the shiny window of the street-level barber-
shop, and as for our thrilling first experience of the scene in the
novel, when Miriam beholds a flock of white doves "skimming,
fluttering, and wheeling about the topmost height of the tower,"
I had to suppose that pollution had killed them off.

Just when the weather began to dictate more time in the library and less in the cityscape, I found myself, perversely, crossing the continental divide between the books and the streets.
Why read about the *Bed of Polyclitus*, that sinuous and sexy relief
of a man and a woman contorted in positions whose elegant *con-
trapposto* had all but given birth to Mannerism, when I could enter the courtyard of Palazzo Mattei and, by twisting my own body
almost as much as theirs, squint at the remote second-story spot
where the very thing itself was immured, a part of the building's
fabric? Why pursue the endless paper trail of speculation about
the great bronze equestrian figure—was he Constantine? Com-
modus? Marcus Aurelius?—when he was so vividly on display,
offering his gentle right hand straight out to any viewer strenuous enough to climb the Capitoline staircase?

Then, one day, the texts and the living city started to converge. Chasing down footnoted material concerning colossal
statues on the Quirinal, I came upon a letter that Petrarch wrote
about his own walks through Rome in 1341. I confess I was
struck by something a bit frivolous and unscholarly in the English version of the headnote: "To Giovanni Colonna of the Order of Preachers, that one must love not sects but the Truth," a
message that became intriguing only when I happened to read it
aloud. Of course, Petrarch could hardly have foreseen English

phonetics. Still, he was engaging in his own little in-joke. Petrarch's taste for walkabouts makes him into a Peripatetic—in other words, an Aristotelean. The trouble is, in philosophy's virtual metropolis, he's too peripatetic to be a Peripatetic. Sometimes he wants to hang out downtown on the Stoa among the Stoics; other times he hits the suburbs to join the academics at Plato's academy. Petrarch has a surfeit of invitations, but there is no such joy of sects for me.

No matter: it might still be possible to tag along with Petrarch and his friend. As they walked around town, he boasts, "At every turn there was present something which would excite our tongue and mind."

Here was the palace of Evander, there the shrine of Carmentis, here the cave of Cacus, there the famous she-wolf and the fig tree of Rumina with the more apt surname of Romulus, there the overpass of Remus, here the circus games and the rape of the Sabines . . .

Here the head of Servius glowed; here sitting in her carriage cruel Tullia crossed and made the street infamous because of her crime. Here is the Sacred Way, these are the Esquiline Hill, the Viminal, the Quirinal . . .

Here Perses was compelled, hence Hannibal was repelled; thence Jugurtha was impelled . . .

Here Caesar triumphed, here he perished . . .

Here it snowed on the fifth of August; from here a stream of oil flowed into the Tiber; from here, according to tradition, the old Augustus, following the Sibyl's advice, saw the Christ child . . .

Here Christ appeared to his fleeing Vicar; here Peter was crucified; here Paul beheaded; here Lawrence burned. But why do I run on?

Here—where? Here was I, alas, traipsing through unreadable, or at least uncompanionable, spaces toward a well-stocked library, while Petrarch, making geographically impossible leaps from Janiculum to Campus Martius, from Castel Sant'Angelo to the Capitol, could enter into a millennium of Roman lives without benefit even of a Hertziana. I longed for his circle of friends, but I had trouble believing in his locomotion. In fact, he was not really traveling across the map at all. His trajectories are fueled by the thrust from turning pages of Livy, the torque from reordering Christianity's early folk legends, the liftoff gained by translating ancient history into a series of interlocking verbs. It's not a tour bus; it's a time machine.

Reading elsewhere, I encountered a different and rather unexpected fellow traveler, who toured the city in another kind of vehicle:

> Let us, by a flight of imagination, suppose that Rome is not a human habitation but a psychical entity with a similarly long and copious past—an entity, that is to say, in which nothing that has once come into existence will have passed away and all the earlier phases of development continue to exist alongside the latest one. This would mean that in Rome the palaces of the Caesars and the Septizonium of Septimius Severus would still be rising to their old height on the Palatine and that the castle of S. Angelo would still be carrying on its battlements the beautiful statues which graced it until the siege by the Goths . . . In the place occupied by the Palazzo Caffarelli would once more stand—without the Palazzo having to be removed—the Temple of Jupiter Capitolinus; and this not only in its latest shape, as the Romans of the Empire saw it, but also in its earliest one, when it still showed

Etruscan forms and was ornamented with terracotta
antefixes.

Walking the streets of the city, it was easier to spin Freud's fantasy than Petrarch's, easier to read history up and down than
across. Of course, Freud had a special stake in preferring the archaeological to the chronological. He was, after all, creating a
science of the mind, in which the time-bound sequences of historical change were meant to decompose under all the strata of
repetition that are begun and determined in childhood. *Coazione
a ripetere* all over again.

Juggling all this companionship in memory, with the determination to see histories and not just sites, my daily walks gathered
new kinds of shape and momentum. Spaces changed and started
to take on transparency. As I passed from Sant'Agnese in the
Piazza Navona to Palazzo Chigi at the base of the Hertziana's
hill, I found myself reciting, "Here Pope Alexander VII, having
turned his back on all the family riches, slept each night with a coffin . . . Here the body of Pope Innocent X, every revenue of his
sacred office having been squeezed dry by his wicked sister-in-
law, lay abandoned and awaiting a pauper's burial." Alternatively,
at the midpoint of the same itinerary, I could stop long enough
to see the piazza where eleven massive second-century pillars
supporting a vast triangular pediment had become the ex post
facto skeleton for the squared-off blocks of modern Rome's
stock exchange, and I could expostulate, "This would mean
that Agrippa's temple dedicated to the deified emperor Hadrian
stands where scurrying functionaries look out banal casement
windows framed by crumbling Corinthian columns as they calcu-
late the Dow and the Hang Seng."

Perhaps I could gather materials for a vast three-dimensional
map that would do justice to all the strange layerings and jagged

chronologies that emerged from my many walks. The filigree of skulls and bones that I had seen adorning the dark little church that I avoided on the way to the Vatican turned out to be the center of a network that collected the bodies of murder victims and used their spare parts in decoration. Conversely, the riverside hospital I usually passed shortly afterward, where I saw nothing but genial madmen, turned out to house a sort of lazy Susan for infants that permitted unwanted babies to be placed discreetly on an outdoor conveyance which would rotate them into monastic sanctuary on the inside of the building while the fallen women who were their mothers could escape notice.

Death to birth to death again. The frescoes I repeatedly perused outside the Palazzo Massimi proved to be the external casing of spaces closed to the public, where early in the sixteenth century, five vengeful sons of the family conspired to murder their new stepmother and all died miserable deaths, some at each other's hands; and where, later in the same century, San Filippo Neri miraculously resurrected the fourteen-year-old heir apparent of the family, only to discover that the boy opted to stay dead.

Minutes later on the daily library route, at Santa Maria sopra Minerva—Freud loved it because even its name came in layers—I discovered that I was not merely browsing in a candy sampler of buried heroes and villains; I was entering a land of renunciations. Kneeling in the Inquisition-happy adjacent convent, Galileo had uttered his famous recantation and, simultaneously, his legendary disavowal, "and yet it *does* move," while a century and a half later the slippery social climber Cagliostro—alchemist, Rosicrucian, fence and fall guy in the affair of Marie Antoinette's fatal necklace—commuted his death sentence to life in prison at Castel Sant'Angelo by performing a different public disclaimer. And even Barocci's shadowy altarpiece of

Christ instituting the sacraments—which had intrigued me because so much space was given to the kneeling communicants and so little to the apostles—it, too, contained a history of abnegation. The painter, it seems, had originally inserted Satan whispering in Judas's ear, but the pope expressed disapproval of such intimacy between God and the devil and insisted on its erasure.

So many scraps of knowledge, so many continuities and simultaneities, so many bewildering proposals for order! I could hear the Trevi Fountain gush in the same language for Hawthorne as for Hollywood, or I could see the delicately ornate precincts of the Piazza Sant'Ignazio juxtaposed with a somber chapel where, it was said, Jesuits whipped themselves for fifteen minutes every night in the dark. Walk after walk, and without the requisite community of faith in Christianity or the unconscious, I struggled to integrate horizontal and vertical histories. What sort of guides, after all, had I chosen for myself?

Petrarch begins his letter, *"Deambulabamus Rome soli"*—we walked *alone* in Rome—a difficult grammatical construction for a reader whose solitary walks were exclusively in the first person singular. His friend Colonna, who accompanied him on these walks, has asked for the text of Petrarch's monologue, since it was inspired by their walk through the city. But it cannot be recaptured:

Give me back that place, that idle mood, that day, that attention of yours, that particular vein of my talent and I could do what I did then. But all things are changed: the place is not present, the day has passed, the idle mood is gone, and instead of your face I look upon silent words.

Petrarch, now alone in the singular, draws back step by step from fulfilling Colonna's request: I'll try to write it here—better yet,

I'll send you to some other authors—no, I'll repeat the words I used back then—what am I saying? the subject is too large and this letter is already too long—how about I put it off until tomorrow?—never mind, it's not material for a letter, even tomorrow—okay, here's what I'll do: I'll write a book. But that book never got written, unwelcome news for this latter-day reader, a writer with no face to look upon.

And Freud designs his map only to demonstrate that no geographical place can house such living depth. What he really cares about is not Rome, but the "sensation of 'eternity,' a feeling as of something limitless, unbounded, as it were, 'oceanic.' " He wants to explore those individuals who feel "an indissoluble bond, of being one with the external world." The subject leads him on to the passion for aesthetic beauty and the transports of being in love. But Freud has no use for all these extravagant sensations of belonging. Grown-ups who fall desperately in love, or feel at one with creation, or lose themselves in front of great works of art are regressing to that infantile condition before they learn to distinguish between the mother's breast and their own body. On the streets of the city, it turns out, I was just another nursling who needed to be weaned.

If I tried to banish these authorities, I was left with a pair of bad angels—familiars, the Elizabethans called them—on my shoulders as I spent mornings going from effigy to effigy among tombs and inscriptions. Bukowski whispers to me about a turbulent liaison with a woman who molds him in clay.

> We split up at least once a week . . . but always managed to make up, somehow. She had finished sculpting my head and had given it to me. When we'd split I'd put the head in my car next to me on the front seat, drive it over to her place and leave it outside her door on the porch. Then I'd

go to a phone booth, ring her up and say, "Your god-damned head is outside the door!" That head went back and forth.

So did mine. De Man would probably look at that head and see another compulsive love affair, only for him it was the delusion of all aesthetics and representation—"a movement of conscious-ness toward something that it has lost, toward something that it wants to possess in order to be complete." As for pursuing the de-composing artistic remains of the past, all these inscriptions are "not only the prefiguration of one's own mortality but our actual entry into the frozen world of the dead." The whole thing—epi-taphs and autobiographies both—is "the fiction of the voice-from-beyond-the-grave."

Another Bukowski hero buys a mannequin for $17.50. He names her Stella, slaps her around, takes her to bed, and falls in love with her; when his real-life girlfriend finds out, she rips the dummy apart:

> He stood in the hallway and could see the head under the chair. He began to sob. It was terrible . . . He just stood in the hallway, sobbing and waiting. Both of Stella's eyes were open and cool and beautiful. They stared at him.

Love objects, art objects: they start to look like so many dis-embodied heads and decapitated torsos. Like the Rilke sonnet about a fragmentary statue of Apollo that is supposed to cinch de Man's case for metaphor's bad faith. Despite having no head or eyes, the torso glows, it gazes, it smiles, it blinds, it shimmers, it radiates. It sees. De Man's verdict is that this power is delu-sional, nothing but verbal construct. "What appears to be the inwardness of things, the hollow inside of the box, is not a substantial analogy between the self and world of things but a formal and structural analogy between these things and the figural resources of words."

Making my way past the incinerated Bruno in marble or gazing at the childbirth Madonna whose foot has been eroded by too many kisses, I could willingly embrace these nihilisms and read Rilke's confusing first twelve lines—full of detached body parts and contrary-to-fact subjunctives—as the empty wish fulfillment that de Man wants it to be. But then I was face-to-face with the last two lines, where suddenly everything gets very clear.

>   . . . for there is no place on this stone
> that does not see you. You must change your life.

De Man doesn't hear that voice; Bukowski can't look into those eyes; Petrarch is alone with some inexorable theology and Freud with a selfhood as big as history. All four of my would-be friends are frozen in an impregnable solitude. So what voices would I hear if I let Rome's fragmented body look at me?

I set out a little late one warm November morning and so opted for the straightest lines that Rome can muster, on a library route that bisected perfectly: the first half due north from my front door, the second half precisely northeast, with the pivoting angle of 135 degrees in the midst of dark, arcaded structures and a sooty fountain too ordinary to signal such an important crossroads. I might even have made the unprecedented decision to go straight to work had I not just learned something new about one of my favorite sights along the way.

It started with a shameless piece of self-identification in Caravaggio's Saint Matthew in three parts at San Luigi dei Francesi. In the left-side painting, the saint is summoned by the pointing chiaroscuro hands of Christ and Peter and by a thrilling shaft of illumination whose origins are irrelevant to the brightly framed open window. But this fellow, with all his radiant surprise of being caught in the spotlight, is too young and eager-faced, and too gaudily accompanied by gamester companions. In the right-side painting, of his martyrdom, Matthew is foreshortened into near invisibility and further obscured by a dance of more eye-catchingly fleshy torturers.

Matthew in the middle was my man, uncrowded in a strangely vertical composition. He winds his cloaked body around a stool by a table, and he rests one hand on a big book while the other delicately wields a pen in midair. But he pays no attention to all of that. His apprehensive gaze is drawn upward to the angel who inspires him. I had already understood that he was a scholar, a Socrates, a distracted middle-aged writer, bald and bearded. I had seen that he was staring anxiously at a youthful angel who was swathed in a whirlpool of garments and yet half naked. I had noted the mysterious look that is passing between them and the curious precision and purposefulness of the boy's finger gestures. Most of all, I had registered the perfect separation between the two figures. Garments, wings, bodies, halo: all swirl recklessly in space, and yet a strait of blackness forces man and boy to keep their distance.

What I had just learned was that this was Caravaggio's second try, substituted when the priests turned down his earlier effort. Stuck in my head that day was a contemporary comment on their reasoning: "He has neither the decorum nor the look of a saint, sitting there with his legs crossed and with his feet grossly exposed to the public." Stuck in my hand was a crumpled photo of the original—refused by the church, snapped up by a more lib-

eral patron, exhibited in seventeenth-century Rome, acquired by
the Kaiser, and then incinerated with most of Berlin in 1945.

This first, lost Matthew is indeed a man of flesh rather than
spirit, burly and cross-legged, his grimy feet kicking forward just
where the priest would be saying Mass at the altar. His twist of
limbs seems to betray the lordly elegance of the ducal chair in
which he hunches. He looks down at the book in his hands like
someone who has never seen a book before. His left hand man-
handles the pages as no reader would, and his right hand
clenches up as though he has never held a pen. This angel does
not fly or swirl or convey cryptic messages. He envelops Matthew
in waves of glimmering garments and an expanse of pure white
wing that even provides what passes for a halo around the saint's
thickly molded head. And no safety zone separates these two.
The angel's body curves around Matthew, their legs both parallel
and intersecting. Together their forearms frame a personal space
whose vanishing point is the boy's breast. At the bright center of
the whole composition—the object of Matthew's stupefied gaze
and the boy's firm but sidelong glance—is the book, and the radiant, angelic fingers resting on the fat, curled hand of the man
as though they were playing him like a harpsichord.

Now, as I stood before the official Matthew, grasping the little
black-and-white reject in my hand, I began to feel strangely inhabited by the space between the two. Was the first Matthew
simply left behind by history—here Saint Matthew was a brick-
layer . . . here Saint Matthew is a philosopher—contradicted,
superseded by his successor, as canceled by Caravaggio's later
canvas as he was by twentieth-century firepower? No, it was
more like archaeology. In the same space where the anxious classical scholar prepares to write his book while looking across the
unbridgeable gap toward a well-built youth, forever sits the
brawny laborer, fingered and encircled by a guardian spirit with
blond spit curls.

Maybe Rome really is the map of the unconscious. Man of betrayals and conversions, Matthew, né Levi, the Hebrew turned Roman tax collector turned follower of Christ—"Who me?" his face proclaims in the brightness of the left-side picture—is prompted by the angel, who counts on his fingers to compose the gospel that numbers the Judaic lineage of Jesus; maybe he dreams of a less layered, less contradictory existence where he is a muscular illiterate who is not instructed but played by the angelic hand. Some say the picture was rejected because it was blasphemy to suggest that Matthew was a mere mouthpiece of the angel; some say it was because the two were in an unseemly posture. But to the later Matthew, mute and set apart—"Who me?"—it comes to the same thing, the dream of being grasped and mastered, held in an embrace that inspires, spontaneous and involuntary, the writing of miraculous text. "Instead of your face I look upon silent words," I heard one voice say, and another: "Nothing that has once come into existence will have passed away and all the earlier phases of development continue to exist alongside the latest one." On my copy of the first Matthew I could just make out what we are not allowed to see in the final picture, the gospel itself, represented by a few majuscule Hebrew characters on a still almost empty page: "The book of the generations of Jesus the Messiah, the son of David, the son of Abraham . . ."

I was enjoying the scrupulousness of those historical strata, the ecumenism of honoring the Jew behind the Christian, until I realized that it was all wrong. The New Testament is not a Hebrew book at all: to arrive at that showy calligraphy, the Greek of the gospel had to be translated into the Latin of the Vulgate, whereupon someone invented a Hebrew that existed in nobody's Bible. As I looked at the two Saint Matthews—the one wearing a toga, the other clutching fabricated Hebrew—times and places seemed to stagger, and I found myself shunted toward another piece of my current reading, out of another church, affording another occasion of seeing and being seen.

"Who is this son of Abraham who found life, grace, and bliss in Rome?" I heard a highly educated, cosmopolitan foreigner ask this question in his painstaking autobiography. Alphonse Ratisbonne is lonely from the time he leaves Strasbourg, hoping always to make friends on the way, but New Year's 1842 in Naples brings him no greetings, no one to hold in his arms. An emancipated, secular Jew, he arrives by a mix of error and destiny in Rome, where his values—or valuelessness—come under siege. He devours ruins ancient and modern with "monotonous admiration" and piles them in his imagination and in his journal. Surrounded by ancient vestiges, he thinks about the obsolescence of his own religion: "We must make haste to escape from this old temple, whose remnants are collapsing on all sides, if we are not to be shrouded in its wreckage." He writes from the perspective of having escaped both pagan and Jewish rubble. "All I can say is that the veil fell from my eyes; not just one veil but all the multitude of veils that had enveloped me disappeared swiftly one after another, like snow and mud and ice under a scorching sun." Now he finds grace at Rome's bosom; now he prays to Mary, Mother of the Word.

For me, this Ratisbonne story had started with a piece of surprising punctuation. Flipping guidebook pages one evening, I read, in a description of Sant'Andrea delle Fratte, "The third chapel on the left is remarkable for a modern miracle (?) annually commemorated here." What really struck me was that "(?)." Was I to be skeptical that a miracle took place or skeptical that it was a miracle? The uncertainty launched a paper trail that acquainted me with Ratisbonne, whose experience, it turns out, could also be plotted on a map of Rome.

At the Church of the Aracoeli, he is "moved, penetrated,

transported" by music, architecture, and history. In the Piazza
Nicosia—exactly where I was planning to make my 135-degree
right turn—he visits the home of a French Protestant turned
Catholic who coaxes him into wearing a medal of the Madonna.
(He has his own geographical coincidences. At the same address
earlier that day, he had bought a ticket for Naples that he will
never use: "I travelled a long way to arrive at the point where I
began—the itinerary of more than one human existence!") He
begins to feel religious stirrings and one night dreams of a
strangely shaped black cross empty of Christ. The next morning,
at the Spanish Steps, his convert friend catches sight of him at a
café and invites him on a ride through the city but then remembers that he has to make a brief stop at Sant'Andrea delle Fratte.
Rather than wait in the carriage, Ratisbonne goes with him into
the church.

From the Matthews in San Luigi dei Francesi, I could take a
more direct route to the same destination. If I made my way past
the Pantheon and the stock exchange, past an obelisk, a parliament, and a street named for the Propagation of the Faith—still
on a beeline for the Hertziana—I would come to the spot where
the veils dropped and where the question mark might be cleared.
As I moved through the streets, I recalled Ratisbonne's deliciously protracted windup to the moment of his conversion:

You woke up a Jew and you will go to bed a Christian . . .
   Alphonse, in fifteen minutes you will worship Jesus
Christ, your God and Savior, and you will prostrate yourself in a poor church, and you will beat your breast kneeling at the feet of a priest.

I had admired the arresting biform upper stories of Sant'Andrea delle Fratte on various laps toward the library, the one part

a broad-beamed brick mausoleum in the sky, the other a psychedelic filigree of heads, monsters, balustrades, and torches topped
by a quartet of reptile segments supporting a crown of spikes. But
now, seeing the interior for the first time, I had to agree with
Ratisbonne that the place was "small, poor, and deserted."

When I arrived at the church, I knew nothing; when I departed, I saw clearly.

I have the impression of large central expanses and tiny side
chapels—a fat cross with shallow scallops. From a distance I see
the pair of Bernini angels, surplus from an overcharged Tiber
bridge project, that earn guidebook mention but point nowhere.
As I work my way along the walls from right to left, the place
seems a garden of death monuments. Vast allegorical personages
in white marble cast a faint gleam on moldering inset portraits of
the actual decedents. Moving toward the high altar and past it, I
start noticing different necro-genres, lean geometric graveyard
slabs or bulbous catafalques all covered in text. Above them I
glimpse two winged skulls (the remains of angels?). In the dim-
ness, I let the texts, above all the names of the dead, guide
me through the pictures. There's a hook-nosed mathematician
named Pessuti. A profile relief, Roman senator–style, sits atop a
tablet with a great deal of Latin, including the name Angelica
Kauffman, but whether she designed the monument or is buried
in it I cannot tell. A pale, sculpted face stares almost eyelessly
out of a deep niche: Can his name really be Schadow?

I was coming out of a tomb, out of an abyss of darkness,
and I was alive, perfectly alive.

Finally, the third chapel on the left, and the right piece of
text in headline bold atop the arch: "Here appeared the Ma-

donna of the Miracle." Even in this artistically unprepossessing environment, Ratisbonne's chapel is disappointing stuff. The surroundings, in geometric pastel marble inlay, appear expensive, suburban, funereal. The Madonna herself emerges from the clouds, dressed in high yardage of crinkly draping, the obligatory stars around her head, her arms stretched limply out and down in a gesture that might signify the embrace of sinners or the conclusion to a torch song. She wears a Queen of Heaven crown several sizes too big for her head. Was this what Ratisbonne saw?

The whole church disappeared, I saw nothing, or rather—
O my God—I saw one single thing.

I was like someone born blind who suddenly sees the light of day; he sees, but he cannot define the light that illuminates him and in whose bosom he contemplates the objects of his admiration.

I saw something like a veil in front of me. The church seemed to me all dark, except for one chapel in which all the light of the church seemed to be concentrated. I raised my eyes toward the chapel radiant with such light.

I sought several times to raise my eyes toward the Holy Virgin, but reverence and splendor made me lower them again.

Did he see or not see? Blindness or insight? Certainly he didn't see what I was seeing. The tacky decorative program in front of my eyes falls stylistically somewhere post-deco and pre-modern; it screams 1950s.

How delicious to feel what Ratisbonne felt:

I was prostrate, bathed in my tears, my heart outside myself.

> I did not know who I was, I did not know if I was
> Alphonse or someone else, I experienced so total a
> change that I believed I was another self. I tried to find
> myself again, and I could not. The most ardent joy
> erupted in the depth of my soul, I could not speak.

In an empty space, Ratisbonne saw the Virgin Mary and left behind him a piece of fluffy kitsch that sits outside history and inside eternity. Everywhere I went in Rome, I was chasing down the artifacted records of what had happened in another time or at another place. Here Trajan built the Pantheon; here they buried Raphael; here Caravaggio painted Saint Matthew, who, long ago and elsewhere, had been summoned by God to write his book. But what angel or book could I expect from Saint Matthew so long as I remained so stubbornly myself, by myself, in the chapel where they existed merely as paint on canvas? And even here, where it wasn't the garish glow of the bejeweled Virgin that mattered, but the idea of real presence, what did I expect from this question-mark miracle at three removes, in the companionship of such a disturbing double, the man whose portrait bust I noticed to my left—dashing, swarthy, Semitic, his eyes ardent and his beard in a sexy tangle? What would it take to be summoned—"It's me!"—and to be inspired, to lose myself and find myself?

Below the bust was an inscription:

ON THE 20TH OF JANUARY 1842, ALPHONSE RATIS-
BONNE OF STRASBOURG CAME HERE A HARDENED
JEW. THIS VIRGIN APPEARED TO HIM JUST AS YOU
SEE HER HERE. HE FELL DOWN A JEW AND HE
ROSE UP A CHRISTIAN. FOREIGNER, TAKE HOME
WITH YOU THE PRECIOUS MEMORY . . .

I stopped reading in mid-sentence, still on my feet and uncertain what memory to take home. Just as I see her here? God forbid: I was in Rome for Laocoöns and Michelangelos; I could never find my new life from some daub one step removed from painting on velvet. And what about the old life: Is it destined to be added to the rest of the rubble?

You will renounce the world, its pomp and its pleasures, your fortune and your hopes and your future. If necessary, you will renounce your fiancée, the affection of your family, the respect of your friends, your attachment to the Jews.

Easy for him to say. Through a brief isthmus of loneliness Ratisbonne passes from one full life in Strasbourg to a commonwealth of Romans working on his conversion. From there he joins the embrace of the priesthood in order to make more Jewish converts. No wonder that as he lies dying in Jerusalem—another city of ruins, another place of pilgrimages and visions—he declares, "All my desires have been satisfied."

There is no place on this stone that does not see you.

I had to get out of these dark, overdetermined surroundings as fast as possible. A brief and arduous upward zigzag, leaving the now incongruously playful Borrominian towers behind me, led me face-to-face with the Hertziana's Monster Mask. We looked each other in the eyes—not for the first or the last time—and I realized I had no head for the confined spaces of the library. I turned around to gaze at the very opposite of confinement, the western panorama of Rome dominated by the great dome of St. Peter's. God knows, by this time I could find my way to the Vatican, even to penetrate beyond the post office and the toilets. I had now retraced Ratisbonne's path to the Spanish Steps; from there, it would be almost a straight shot past the Augustus mound and the vast Hall of Justice that the Romans call the Ugly Palace. Then I remembered the family joke about a miracle. Many years earlier, a pair of cousins were vacationing in Rome with their strapping and obstreperous firstborn son, age four. To keep him out of mischief on their touristical rounds, they wedged him into a baby stroller. In front of St. Peter's, he broke loose. The myriad faithful, ever loitering thereabouts, took one look at the oversize child in a pram and concluded that he was a cripple; now, as he ran amok through the colonnade, they crossed themselves and shouted, "*Miracolo, miracolo!*" No such enactment today: I couldn't bear the thought of yet another Jewish miracle.

If not the Vatican, then, I could make my way down to the Piazza dei Satiri. From this wide-angle dream of an urban perch, all I had to do was swivel in place and I could pan my way home. Or so I thought. But once I had identified the earth-toned mound that tops the Pantheon and the dizzy white spiral of Sant'Ivo, the whole panorama seemed a blur of belfries and cupolas, a flat cyclorama, as though it had already become a tourist's snapshot and not a living place. That massive double-columned dome at ten o'clock: Was it the one where the pope slept in a coffin or the one where Satan used to make cozy with Judas or the one where Ratisbonne had his first Christian goose bumps? Among the palatial monuments to family grandeur, I knew there was one where it was the French and another where it was the Italians who wouldn't let me in, but I couldn't identify either. And where was Hawthorne's birdcage, where was Petrarch's overpass of Remus, where was Freud's palazzo piled on Jupiter's temple?

Then I realized it: the Tiber was missing, its every meander untraceable in the wild geometry of cityscape before me. The Tiber was both the signpost and the enigma of the city for me. At different times on different walks I kept willing the river to flow dependably north and south, like the Hudson, or east and west, like the Thames. In fact, the Tiber cuts a very jagged slice, describing not a straight line but a hooked nose, a grinning mouth, and a big, determined FDR-style jutting chin. I lived across from the Vatican and inside that open jaw, on a great bulge in the river, a fat interruption in its verticality on the map, which made all my personal shortest distances between two points into vast curvatures, as when Euclid's geometry is plotted in the roundness of real space. If the river was gone, Rome had no shape for me. And if Rome had no shape, then, as I searched for that ancient enveloping semicircle in the midst of which I lived, I asked myself how I could continue to entertain the fantasy that it was home. No help from the Academy of the Superfluous this time.

The love of my God has so taken the place of all other love . . .

Other love indeed. In the search for intelligence on life in Rome that I had undertaken months before I actually arrived here, I had covered more subjects than the American Academy and the Vatican Library. A square- and stubbly-jawed theologian—a Rome veteran and critical link in my apartment-hunting chain—had sat me down in a smoky Chicago bar to lecture me on the vitals. In the semidarkness I had scribbled names and numbers on a hank of perforated computer paper: how to cash checks, print business cards, access private collections. Then he laid his meaty hand down on my notes, pushed them slightly away, and took a pause. "Rome isn't much of a place for having fun," he said. "But if you want to see some action, head for the streets around the railroad station." Since he was a man distinguished for his deep aura of sexual undecidability, I found this piece of information even more cryptic than he intended—in addition to which, "seeing some action" always makes me think of World War I soldiers in trenches. I was left with a picture of life around the Stazione Termini both lurid and nebulous.

A potent combination. Now, scanning the western horizon from Rome's high point, I recalled the conspiratorial tone and the broad arm across my notepaper. Without a map, I had no very precise idea where to find the railroad station, but I knew that it was opposite St. Peter's, invisible from my current roost, and to be reached only via the passageways of a very different Rome from what I had been traversing in all my cherished itineraries. A quick descent through some last picturesque urban spaces; a sudden flash of white fountain glimpsed from a tight passageway; a church with a comical sequence of curves and columns; a self-enclosed piazza of extraordinarily gracious symmetry that debouched into an utterly incongruous prospect of country gardens traversed by crumbling stone footbridges that would not have been out of place in Watteau.

Then suddenly I came face-to-face with four lanes of trucks and buses laboring up a steep hill and a right angle, long stretches of identical storefronts in all directions divided up between souvenir stands and *bureaux de change*, and a big sign advertising Rome's wax museum. I had found my path. From there, it was just a question of how many bland commercial spaces on sites of faded glory I could traverse, how much traffic I could dodge, and what my instincts were for reckoning the approach of my goal via the progressive decay of the surroundings.

I gave myself little time to ponder the railroad station itself, though it loomed as the biggest surprise—a gleaming geometric structure, somewhere between plastic and marble, in no style known to me from either Italy or railroad stations. The streets seemed desperately nondescript, the pedestrians even more so. I summoned my courage to stare at a burly, ruddy-faced house-painter—he was carrying buckets and a ladder; what was I think-ing?—and then noticed a frumpy little family trailing single file behind him. A clump of age-indeterminate women, Poles per-haps, their suitcases bound with tape and rope, their faces both frightened and inquisitive, seemed, on the other hand, to be giv-ing me the eye. A mother and three Gypsy children, forcing sheets of cardboard in front of passersby as some kind of begging-pickpocketing strategy (or so I had been led to suppose), unac-countably paid me no attention whatever.

Perhaps I was too close to the station entrance; perhaps these pedestrians were actually there because of the trains. I began to trace the unendingly long sidewall of the building, where there were occasional arcades that might offer refuge. In the very first niche—I couldn't help noticing the similarity to Ratisbonne's side chapel—a thin, hirsute young man, scarred across his chin, leaned against a garbage bin reading the newspaper. So that was it: I had discovered a series of shopwindows where goods were on display. No need to seize the initial opportunity, and anyway, by the time I had formulated this thought, I was already walking to-ward the next alcove. The next alcove was empty; in the one af-ter that, a pair of women were smoking and laughing; then two old men selling lottery tickets, then a nun with a collection plate. I started moving faster, uncertain whether to turn back to my beginner's luck in the first recess. I saw a tweedily dressed middle-aged man with a briefcase, who smelled of perfume, then a broad-shouldered young tough. But these two weren't exactly framed by their niches; they seemed busy with other enterprises.

Were these really display cases, then? Two tall women—maybe not women—then a leering blond with acne and makeup on his face, made me feel I was back on track.

You must change your life.

This was no track I wanted to be on. The hours of the midday siesta were drawing to a close, and I started to see more pedestrians. I could no longer tell—if I'd ever been able to tell—who was there for action and who was just there. Glimpsing one person after another, I started to give them names: sultan, parachutist, Hegelian; asthmatic, countertenor, endomorph; Quaker, linguist, hand model. I started to feel stupid and vulnerable. Piles of closely penciled note cards, an entrance ticket to the Hertziana with the grinning little photograph and my address in the Piazza dei Satiri, a couple of letters from friends back home that I had nabbed in my vestibule but not yet read: it was ridiculous to risk losing my possessions or being found with only those possessions. The hollow inside of the box. I had seen enough action. I wanted out of the trenches, but now I had progressed into territories where all the bus numbers were unfamiliar.

I turned a couple of corners and lost sight of the railroad station altogether. Then I was on empty streets with no identifiable landmarks. A man was leaning against a lamppost. He was not young, had a beard, wore glasses; I caught a look of intelligence and irony in his eyes as he slowly turned toward me. I was flooded with unexpected sensations. Then, God, I thought, what's someone like that doing here?

I veered into a narrow passageway that led to a crowded commercial street, and somehow I was again facing those station arcades, now far more populated. But the sad, miscellaneous loiterers looked nothing like advertisements for themselves, at least not for any product I could stomach.

I turned away, only to be struck by a mirage. Standing out from a row of junk shops and filthy cafés across the street, there appeared a magnificent two-story emporium with great stretches of plate glass decorated in curving art nouveau walnut. *DISCHI*, the tasteful sign read. That was it! Notes from my fleetingly sala-cious historian friend had included an encomium to Rome's best, and least heralded, music store, but though I had copied down "2 flrs, best classical, imports, disc. prices, nr. RR station," I had not recorded the precise location. My apartment sported a stereo and nothing to play on it. From time to time I happened onto a classical radio station, but it gave out so little verbal information that I felt as though I had a symphonic robot in the house. Music of my own choosing, the little repertoire of works I had cultivated through countless replayings—that, too, was compan-ionship I had been missing. I looked from one side of my vista to the other and contemplated: lumberjack, caregiver, monsignor; Bach, Beethoven, Brahms. At last I had found action at the rail-road station.

The shop provided lordly shelter, and I admired the rows of shiny boxes that enclosed the music. So much world lay before me that I knew I might lose myself in yet another impossibility of choices, another paralysis of unforeseeable delights. Why strike into the unknown when I saw my oldest musical friend in a newly decked-out package? As a college freshman, I had owned one record album. Repeated, many times repeated listenings en-abled me to mouth its words from beginning to end even though I didn't really know the language; I could also perform all the parts in a clumsy, singable English translation. If I couldn't score at the railroad station, at least I could score *Don Giovanni*. In front of me was a reissue of the very recording that I had worn bald in my youth. I could hear the opening monologue of the witty sidekick who waits in the street for his master to hammer home another sexual conquest:

Night and day it's toil and sweat
For a master hard to please,
Out in weather cold and wet,
Often down on hands and knees.

Just as soon as the 64 bus could take me home—barring pick-pockets, for which it was notorious—I would climb the stairs and try to repeat, with Ratisbonne: All my desires have been satisfied.

2

INVITING THE STATUE

TO DINNER

The first time I bought *Don Giovanni* I didn't yet own a record player. I was seventeen, away at college, and subject as never before to the endangering influences of my equally adolescent peers. I was paired with a boy who took apart motorcycles in our room (how could this happen at Swarthmore?), I was forced to square-dance and meditate during orientation week, and I was left with too much time for solitary brooding during the mile-long walk from the classrooms to my ramshackle dorm, whose seclusion made it the proud haunt of student radicals but a nuisance to me.

In fact, nothing was quite right. What to wear: equally uncomfortable in blue jeans and suits, I can remember one morning picking out of my still unpacked trunk an ensemble of shirt and pants in identical pale green. Coeducation, which I had never experienced, bewildered me. I didn't drive or smoke or play bridge. There was no lock on the bathroom door. Strangers scared me, especially when so many of them went mountain climbing or enjoyed political punditry, spoke non-Indo-European languages or dabbled in leatherwork.

But then there was classical music. At the piano I could play some of the more bombastic Beethoven sonata movements and the easier *Pictures at an Exhibition*, but I had never been much of a listener. And then I met my next-door neighbor, a fellow freshman, when we were both threatened with reprisals after the unlatchable bathroom we shared leaked spectacularly on the possessions of a surly senior who lived downstairs. Having faced his terrible wrath together, we bonded, and suddenly I was the sidekick of a teenage savant who knew more about classical music than I knew about anything. Our paths drifted apart in later college years and even more in later life, but I find myself even now remembering strange details about him: his mother's maiden name; a certain click of his tongue just before he began to laugh; how once in a game of Botticelli he asked me if I had scored my requiem for fourteen violas (he was asking about Fauré, but I was Flaubert).

Most of all, I remember his patient lectures on the great composers, which—only later did I realize the oddity of it—were almost never accompanied by actually listening to the music. He himself had already heard, played, and probably memorized the scores. What he passed on to me was a riveting romance in words. Not just the lives of the composers or the stories their music told, but the geometries of thematic development, the surprise of modulation, the tease of withholding the tonic, the satisfaction of ending where one had begun.

So I found myself one day at Sam Goody, needing more than anything in the world to own a recording of *Don Giovanni* because I knew that somewhere in the opera there was a shocking, vertiginous key change from E flat to D; that three trombonists wait around a whole evening to make a brief hallucinatory appearance late in the second act; that Mozart is supposed to have spent a night of melancholy extramarital flirtation on the eve of conducting the premiere in Prague; and that this is one Don

Juan who never gets laid. There was more to my anticipatory pleasure, of course—hell and Kierkegaard, sex and violence, rococo and romanticism, Sturm und Drang. In each of these, no doubt, I rejoiced as I grasped my bargain discs (only one version managed to do the opera in three records rather than four, which saved me 25 percent). All that lay between me and my pleasure was finding a hi-fi.

In Rome, it was the other way around. I had the shiny, late-model stereo (far more up-to-date than any other appliance in the apartment), but only now, finally, package in hand, was I able to provide the music. Or almost able. Faithful to some quite new rituals of solitude, I was determined to lay out my dinner in all its necessary stages: that way, by sequences of cooking and eating, I could pass an evening in the best company my senses could afford.

The D-minor chords that open *Don Giovanni* return me to my freshman self, clutching that first boxed set and without funds for even the meagerest audio system—still less, now that I had bought three records. Penniless but, as it turned out, not without resources. What little spending money I had was earned by working in the college language lab. Ten hours a week, often stretching late into evenings when no one showed up, I sat within a grim warren of booths awaiting beginners in French and German. My job was partly to operate the equipment—low-tech even for this remote period of history—and partly to help students develop pronunciation skills. In fact, each night, while irritating my German pupils by insisting on the varying places in throat and sinus where *ich* and *ach* were produced or shocking my French pupils by revealing how few sounds are required to enunciate all the letters of *qu'est-ce que c'est que ça*, I was sitting in a room with twenty-four record players.

The term is a bit grandiose. These were eight-inch rotating

platters designed for flexible pieces of mucus-colored acetate, suitable for repetition of foreign speech acts but hardly to immortal Mozart. No matter: one evening, with no customers in sight and a little furtively, I unwrapped the cellophane, opened the box, and placed the first disc atop the puny turntable. Pulling the arm far outside its intended orbit, I dropped the similarly maladapted needle on the record, clipped the hard plastic earphones around my head, and, with some astonishment, began to hear the overture.

Scary material, the opening of *Don Giovanni*, thirty bars like nothing that had ever been written before. It is amazing, among other things, that Mozart was willing to hand over terror music from the opera's high point when the audience were barely settling into their seats. Yet it works because during the couple of hours of buffo and sentimentality we enjoy before returning to the hair-raising dramatic climax, these first sounds hang in our subconscious like the threat of Judgment Day: long chords whose notes are played for different durations by the different instruments, trills and dissonances between adjacent tones, jerky dotted rhythms subliminally placed in the underscoring, syncopations that blur the bar line, finally a rising tide of up-and-down scale passages in a sequence of familiar yet unidentifiable keys. Great stuff, and even better when played on the language lab's wobbly turntable. Subject to the haphazard rpm's of unsteady speed, trills and dissonances were indistinguishable from one another, all chords were rolling, all rhythms dotted, all meter blurred, all tonalities unsettling. Hell stared me in the face from bar one; I am not sure the music has ever thrilled me as much since then.

Just as well, perhaps, given my mood that night in Rome. I organized my antipasto. Slices of braised fennel, browned almost to mahogany in olive oil, remained from the previous evening: slightly overdressed in vinegar, they sat well in an envelope of sweet-and-salty air-dried beef, and the dark monotone common to the inside and outside of the package was balanced off by a dusting of parsley around the wrap. With this mix of lush and tangy, I settled with some relief into the prettier phases of the overture, whose later moments of high drama—a sudden lurch from *piano* to *forte*, a deviant tour round the circle of fifths—are protectively encased in the gracious little fanfare tune that first rescues us from the terrors of the beginning.

The more I listened, the more I discovered that for all the imminence of damnation, *Don Giovanni* was very good at providing just the comfort I needed. No matter what the suffering heroics as the Don careens through failed conquests, Mozart cannot help himself from crosscutting them with beauty in one direction and irony in the other. Even Donna Anna, who has been threatened with violation in her own bedroom, goes a little bit over the top when she counts how many emotions are undulating around her heart. Intricate modulations attend the discovery of her father's corpse; and who wouldn't be cheered by the simple diminished sevenths that accompany the doggerel rhyme of consolation offered by her tenor lover, who teeters on the brink of parody? As for Donna Elvira, previously seduced and abandoned: Is there no tongue in cheek at all when "I will rip out his heart" is sung to ecstatic vocal pyrotechnics on a perfectly sweet major triad?

Not only that. The death of Donna Anna's father at the end of Don Giovanni's sword point takes place in a male trio harmonized with proto–*Moonlight* Sonata triplets that land somewhere past kitsch into bliss. As I listened for Leporello's bass line in this death scene, I realized that it was he who was protecting me from the abyss in all the heights of drama—the underclass as undervoice. He was the one who made it impossible to believe in the suffering of the divas, with his incessant commentaries all but robbing them of solos. No surprise that he was the one I sang along with as I returned to the kitchen. If I worked fast enough, I could actually produce my pasta course as the Commendatore breathed his last. I had been doing a weekly sampling of store-bought gnocchi around the city (Thursday in Rome is sacred to gnocchi), and all they needed was a quick boil and then a sauce that consists of tricked-up molten Gorgonzola. If mac and cheese was kitsch, this was bliss. Between bites, I could manage, as I had for decades, "*Sta a ve-der che il ma-lan-dri-no mi fa-rà pre-ci-pi-tar*"—Wait and see how this scoundrel is going to get *me* into trouble.

I couldn't always have executed that bass line. Back in the days of the language lab, I had no Italian at all. But night after night I followed the libretto in faithful lip sync. While I monitored others around me repeating *Voilà le facteur! Bonjour, M. Guillaume, est-ce que vous avez du courier pour nous ce matin?* or stumbling through lists of German prepositions that take the dative case—*aus, außer, bei, mit, nach, seit, von, zu*—I was mouthing Italian expressions that turned out to mean things like "What crime, what excess! Within my breast I feel my heart palpitate with fear." More than my students, I was like a child beginning to acquire language—surrounded by inscrutable adult goings-on and starting to mimic whole paragraphs of sounds without really knowing what they meant. No surprise that I was listening to *Don Giovanni* in my Rome apartment: it was pretty much the lexicon of all the Italian I knew.

Which almost made me feel that I belonged inside this opera. Everyone is forever stumbling in darkness. Giovanni wears a mask at the opening and declares to Anna, "Who I am you'll never know." After the duel, Leporello isn't sure who died. Donna Anna can't find her father, and when Don Ottavio tries to console her, she mistakes him for the murderer. Elvira can't find Don Giovanni. Later, it's the darkness of the courtyard followed by the darkness of the graveyard. In fact, it was these expressions of confusion and ambiguity that formed my own beginning Italian:

> *Chi è morto? voi o il vecchio?*
> Who is dead? You or the old man?

> *Io manco. Io moro.*
> I faint. I die.

> *Sposa. Amica.*
> Bride. Friend.

> *Il padre mio, dov'è?*
> My father, where is he?

> *Hai sposo e padre in me.*
> You have husband and father in me.

Such lucid paradigms, such oceans of ambiguity. Now that I was beginning my Italian residency, this was to be my native vocabulary.

Sensitive to these confusions and clarities, I stopped in the midst of preparing my main course—I wanted to experiment with guinea fowl, new to me and, I thought, in need of some flavor coaxing—on a snippet of recitative that I had paid no attention to before. When Elvira tries to insist on her betrothal rights, Giovanni eludes her by declaring that he had his reasons—*ragioni forti*—for abandoning her; and when she is unsatisfied, he fobs her off on Leporello as he slips into the darkness. Leporello's "reasons" run, roughly, "Madame, truly, in this world, provided that, as it may be, so to speak, a square is not a circle." To a twentieth-century man, it seems like a joke on the Age of Reason. In this drama of passions, fulfilled and unfulfilled, where the hero chooses hell over order, why shouldn't reason become nonsense and geometry become tautology? I halved the bird so that the dark meat, moistened with stock, wine, and apples, could be carried over into tomorrow night's dinner, where it would fill one of the little *zucche* that were starting to appear in the market. As I considered my private food chain—from the fennel of yesterday to the pumpkins of tomorrow—I looked out from my window once more into the Piazza dei Satiri, and I had to agree: a square is not a circle.

When I finally coaxed myself out of contemplation and into action, my first encounter had to be with the *Spinario*. This naked little bronze guy, sculpted two thousand years ago and famous ever since, sits on a rock, left leg crossed over right knee, and hunches over intently while working with both hands to extract a thorn from his upturned foot. That's all there is: nothing mighty or monumental, nor even particularly beautiful; just a three-foot-high kid doing a little self-surgery. Why, of all the ancient sculpture that has survived millennia of destruction, has this piece grabbed hold of so many imaginations? And why was I evading the official monuments of classicism, like the *Apollo Belvedere*, with all his histrionic right angles? Winckelmann's stentorian formula of "noble simplicity and quiet grandeur" sounded like chalk on my personal blackboard.

Poring over the *Spinario* archive at a Hertziana library table, all I developed was more questions. Statues represent gods or heroes; mere mortals deserved sculpting only when in torment or ecstasy. There is no god of thorn-pulling; inflammation of the sole is not a tragedy. I knew that for centuries people had tried to flatten these dilemmas by inventing names and narratives for this kid. He was the beautiful Absolom from the book of Samuel; he was the month of March; he was a young Roman who ran for miles with aching foot to carry a message to the senate; he was an allegory of penitence. No: my instinct told me he was just a boy with a thorn. But what was the purpose of a boy with a thorn, and why were we all so taken with him? The answer could come only from seeing him face-to-face in the Capitoline collection.

Courtesy of an English acquaintance, I was invited to a reception one Sunday morning; it was just right for killing an hour before the museum opened. Wherever I moved through the grand top-floor apartment, among many hallways and strangers, dodging offers of mediocre bubbly and oversweetened pastries, I kept noticing the same young man, though he always seemed to be facing away. After various sightings I started to get a composite of him: rather small but with extraordinarily large hands; a closely cut round head of red-blond hair and a beard to match; dressed with an incongruous elegance—black jacket and trousers, not quite matching, one tweedy and one shiny, a starched white shirt, and a florid bow tie. Could there have been a pince-nez? Everything slightly out of place or out of time.

I was about to leave, not disgracefully early, with a bare sense that I had done my duty, spoken to quite a few people, exercised my Italian, run the gamut of party topics. In the act of bidding farewell to the hostess, however, I found myself mentioning that I had heard she had paintings in the apartment, and I asked if I could see them. Suddenly, at the mention of pictures, the young man materialized as my guide. Taking me by the hand, he led me to the study (a lush, badly drawn Caravaggesque Madonna, so shiny that it looked as if it had been painted yesterday) and then the master bedroom (something after, long after, Tiepolo). He

was so proprietary that I thought perhaps he owned the apartment; he certainly owned *something*. At the foot of the canopy
bed, he turned to our hostess with a gracious and old-fashioned
gesture and said he could not go on talking to me without a
proper introduction. When she complied, he executed a bow;
suddenly his whole costume looked Victorian, Pre-Raphaelite.

Gabriele and I were together, alone. "Marina tells me that
you are a very intelligent man—that's all I know," he said. But
he seemed to know about my research, and he went on with
what might have been a poem or a song concerning his own
work, something Byzantine, but whether he was an artist or an
art historian I couldn't make out. We stood in the space of a
large window, which somehow gave us a commanding position.
Other party guests came in to look out the window—the view
was of the piazza where Agrippa's temple had been homogenized
into Rome's stock exchange—or else to be with Gabriele. One
fellow got paid so little attention (I later heard that he was *molto
depresso* and everyone ought to be nice to him) that he left the
room almost unnoticed. A young lady appeared, and Gabriele
introduced me to her, saying, "This man is a genius," promoting
me from mere intelligence. A professorial gentleman came to the
window and said Gabriele looked familiar and wondered how
they knew each other. Polite but uninterested, Gabriele offered
some of his curriculum vitae, including the name of a school.
The other fellow had attended that very school, he declared triumphantly, and pressed for more details as to what year Gabriele
graduated. "No," said Gabriele, "I only went there to use the
swimming pool," and he named a fancier-sounding alma mater.

We were alone again. He said he worked in Milan; I said I
was planning to visit Milan. Addresses and phone numbers were
exchanged. Was that a way of concluding our romance? He was
pulled away by someone who said it was time to go, that after all,

they would all see each other later, at dinner. But no one went anywhere, and for the rest of the time at the apartment, I gently pursued Gabriele, with little resistance on his part. Around this time he began to speak German, which he said he was studying from one to three in the afternoons (and Russian from three to five). In German, I was *Herr Professor* and addressed as *Sie*, though in Italian we were calling each other *tu*.

I was ready to try anything so that I would be issued an invitation to this dinner. Cooking, I said, was my second-favorite activity in the world. I gave him that opening, but in case he didn't step into it, I added, "But I'm afraid of bending over the hot stove." I was unsure whether I should create a mental image of myself naked, but Gabriele found this dazzlingly funny. Or was he laughing at my mistakes in Italian? (*Second-favorite* was very hard to render.) Now, as we were the last guests in the immense foyer, he leaned across the exit door and, eyes twinkling into mine, began the long windup to some great pronouncement. "I don't want you to think I'm just saying this, and I hope I am not being too bold, but . . ."—I thought he was going to tell me he was falling in love with me; it wasn't impossible—"how does it happen that Jews are more intelligent than other people?" Then he added—more likely, corrected himself—"Or more amusing." He whirled around and was suddenly halfway down the stairs. From the next landing, I heard him shout up to me, "*Ci vediamo presto, a cena!*" See you soon, at dinner.

In later years, the accessibility of the *Spinario* turned into a long-running tragicomedy in my life. I had only to show my face in the Capitoline and either that single gallery was closed, the museum was under massive reconstruction, or the entire complex was brilliantly reopened in a gorgeous new installation but this one statue was temporarily shipped off to Paris and replaced by a little framed picture. But this time I had beginner's luck.

There he was, strangely off-center in the gallery, atop a squat marble column. Photographs had not prepared me for how he was miniature and yet life-size at the same time, how his strangely elegant coiffure stayed upright even though he was bent over, how the flecked patina of the bronze looked at once like the flesh of a child and the husk of something infinitely aged.

But truth to tell, all of that came only after a while. What struck me first—indeed, I was thrilled and disturbed and almost burst out laughing—was the discovery that the *Spinario* is exhibited on a turntable. At either side of the bronze platform on which this child's two-thousand-year-old foot is resting, museum visitors have at their disposal two little brass erections enabling them to spin the whole construction around at will, as though it were a ship's wheel or a game of chance.

Alone, once again, with a rotating art object, I took control of the tillers. Instantly, of course, I realized what no picture can reveal: the *Spinario* is 360 degrees of beauty. From the front, he is a piece of complex right-angled topology, with the cross of his legs balanced by the oblique angles of his arms above. A quarter turn in one direction, he is a human arc, face and foot hunkered in a tight C-clamp. A quarter turn in the other direction, and the space at his center opens up so that we see in to the embrace of his arms and the focal point of a wound whose invisibility—no thorn mars the burnished bronze of his sole—lures the viewer into a deeper enigma. Of course, I had seen sculpture in the round before and had dutifully made the complete viewing circuit. I had circumnavigated Giordano Bruno and quoted Galileo's "*Eppur si muove!*" But how different it felt to stand in one place while the statue turned before me, as though I were watching a creature in metamorphosis. Finally, I executed the last quarter turn, which revealed a pure abstraction of line and curve that is also an irresistibly molded back continuing into the beginnings of a cleft between the boy's buttocks. That was enough museum for one afternoon.

Besides, I had a dinner date. In the big, noisy trattoria—such places are nowadays resolutely mediocre, but middle-class Romans flock to them because they are reminded of childhoods in some countryside they never inhabited—it took careful passive-aggressive behavior on my part to insure that I would be sitting face-to-face with Gabriele rather than set down randomly among the university chums who made up most of the company. If I fell for him—I mean something beyond being captivated by his good looks and his attentions to me—it was at this meal. He told a story about his first experiences in the Balkans. A thief broke into the house late at night. Gabriele, trying to summon up all of his two years of Macedonian to say the equivalent of "Help! Help!" came out instead with the equivalent of *"Buon appetito! Buon appetito!"* The punch line was miraculously timed with the arrival of a soggy scallopine main course at just the moment, strangely midway in the meal, when Italians finally wish each other a good appetite, as though the pasta course was just a warm-up.

Later he was explaining the importance of tree-of-life diagrams in Persian art when a fellow farther down the table—a sweet-faced man, who probably came closest to being my age—said quite seriously, "So you don't work for the post office?" Gabriele leaned over confidentially to me and said it takes so long to explain what he does that he is in the habit of saying he works for some branch of the civil service, a different one each day of the week. Sunday he delivered the mail.

The revelation that he had recently gotten a driver's license (which came as a great surprise to his old friends) produced an art show of identity cards sporting various photographs of

Gabriele. I said he was the *"uomo di mille facce"*; I thought how delicious he looked in all of them—perhaps better than in real life. Passing them around in one direction while dessert was being passed in the other, he shouted out captions for all of them. One, in which he was very serious but had a maze of tangled hair, was *"giovane communista"*; in another, looking bewildered inside some sort of floppy parka, he was *"nevrotico paracadutista"*; a third, shot from a low angle so that one looked at him up the line of his raincoat, was *"famigerato onanista"*—young Communist, neurotic parachutist, notorious masturbator: I couldn't get enough of those rhymes.

Now all I had to do was snaffle him loose from these riotous companions.

I started to understand something about the lure of the *Spinario*. Of course he had no name and no story. How do you make an icon out of a thorn puller when the thorn isn't even there? The boy focuses so intently on his foot, but the sculptor refuses him even the defect of a break in the skin. The *Spinario* has no reason, no meaning, no purpose except to be beautiful. If he is sexy, if you crave him, it's not because he is a hot boy who happens to be made of metal. It's because perfect shape makes perfect desire. Or maybe not. Would I feel the same way if he were the snakes that are strangling Laocoön, or if he were the dome of the Pantheon? As I keep remembering how he circled his way around through bronze and flesh and geometry, the truth is, I can't quite separate my sensations.

Dinner, finally, at my apartment, just the two of us. Things are not going well. Instead of hilarious anecdotes and knowing glances eye to eye, I am treated to a cultural monologue. He has racial theories, and in his life there are so many races—Jews and Armenians, Turks and Greeks, all can be explained by their nationality. He is contemptuous of the English language: how stupid that the present tense of the verb is *go* and the past tense *went*. (Never mind my struggles with forty-eight different endings for Italian verbs.) He hates all modern literature, particularly anything written by women.

I have barely started to put out olives and breadsticks when he announces that his girlfriend is going to join us shortly. *"Non ti dispiace?"* It displeases me mightily, but all I can think of for the moment is the terrible gaffe of my menu. For antipasto I have made two artichokes *alla romana* (braised, flavored with Roman mint, each served with its stem provocatively upright); for first course, two individual lasagnes layered with wild mushrooms inside ramekins; for main course, two butterflied medallions of pork tenderloin done slightly sweet with diced carrots and beets. Everything in pairs: it's a Noah's ark of feasts. Had I been that obvious in my menu planning without realizing it myself? And how could any of these twos be turned into threes?

The graver problem is that I do not have the Italian to deal with this. I cannot summon understatement, indirection, implication, irony. I don't have the conditionals and the subjunctives for "I would love to invite—what might her name be? Anna Maria?—if it were feasible; as it is, I couldn't possibly . . ." I'm left with saying, "No, she can't come." He makes a phone call, determines sullenly that he will join her after dinner. The banquet must, however, go on, and somehow my Italian becomes just sufficient to fight back on his theories of civilization. He is a Catholic Italian and I'm a Jewish American, but that hardly proves anything, I sputter. And besides that, some of my favorite writers are twentieth-century women.

While polishing off every morsel of food—with some very pretty compliments, it must be admitted—Gabriele grabs a sheet of my notepaper, pulls a red felt-tip marker from his pocket, and starts to sketch. Two bulbous interlocked human forms start to

emerge out of a single pen stroke. On the left, a more petite figure, his circular head described by ringlets and topped with a
wide-brimmed clerical hat worn at a jaunty slant; on the right, a
more corpulent personage with an earnest, angular face, his
jagged wisps of hair parted by the simple curvature of a skullcap.
Both seem enveloped in robes, both are bespectacled, but there
is a suggestion of decisive stylistic difference in these accou-
trements. Above the drawing, which is finished in moments, he
writes, "The rabbi and the Jesuit argue about Virginia Woolf."

We both go silent. I leave dessert in the refrigerator (two
chocolate truffles). I have forgotten my sociological counterclaims; I have stopped worrying about Anna Maria. I begin to
fall in love with this double image of two men who are made so
intimately out of a single line. Gabriele looks at me looking at
the drawing and promises that he will execute a proper painting
of this subject, and he will present it to me very soon as a gift.
With that, he goes off to his rendezvous. I'm satisfied: we are going to have a second date.

I spend research time in my apartment going through the
many artworks in which the *Spinario* is quoted. From about 1400
to 1600 he is everywhere, like some pre-modern Zelig, but he is
not just lurking in the back of a crowd. When Brunelleschi tries
to win the commission for the Florentine baptistry doors, a bent-
over boy with his upside-down foot in the air takes up as much
space as Isaac being sacrificed by Abraham. When the first frescoes decorate the Sistine Chapel, decades before Michelangelo,
in one picture a cross-legged muscleman seated on a stump up-
stages Moses, and in another, a slenderer youth in the same posture lures attention away from Christ being baptized. And is it a
joke that Signorelli's Madonna and Child share their landscape
with a naked *Spinario* who is as big as a cliff?

True, famous statues are copied everywhere; tracking things

like the *Belvedere Torso* or *Apollo*, art historians have played
Where's Waldo with the whole corpus of Renaissance art. But I
start to realize that the *Spinario* was different. Other figures get
integrated into stories. Laocoön becomes Christ or Vulcan or
Saint Lawrence, the Wounded Gaul turns into Adam reaching
for the apple, a Crouching Venus comes back as Bathsheba dry-
ing her hair—but the *Spinario* never gets a new name, never
joins in a story. He is always alone in the crowd, always the center of attention, but always staring at himself. He is the opposite
of Rilke's torso: you can look at him from all sides, but he'll
never look at you.

Long silence from Gabriele. I interrogate our few mutual acquaintances when I run into them. Some say he is in Milan; others say he is in Kabul. Once, in front of the fresh wild mushroom
stand in the Campo de' Fiori, I encounter the hostess who introduced us, and released into English, I discreetly vent my disappointment, focusing on not having received the promised
canvas. She says she hasn't heard from him in ages. But—can it
be a coincidence?—the very next day I find a strange document
loose in my letter box, a little folded piece of paper with a legend
all in caps:

I GIVE MY WORD OF HONOR THAT I WILL PAINT
FOR LEONARD BARKAN, RESIDENT IN PIAZZA DEI
SATIRI, ONE (1) PAINTING DEPICTING RABBI AND
JESUIT.

It is signed, in script, "the Jesuit," and the signer is represented
with a tiny profile self-portrait, wearing what has become a
fleshed-out form of the identifying headgear, now a sort of clerical sombrero. So he does deliver the mail after all.

But little else. More time goes by, and one quite quiet

evening in Satyr Square my doorbell rings. Looking out the window, I can make out in the twilight a familiar figure, hatless. As I aim the weighted key in his direction, he waves and screams, "No, no, you have to come down." In the piazza, I realize that he is standing by a car with the motor running. A young woman is sitting in the passenger seat. He hands me a sizable wrapped package, smiles radiantly at me, and says, "*Ci vediamo presto.*" See you soon.

Upstairs, I unwrap the picture. There, in the lower-right-hand corner, stand the two figures as in the sketch. Now, of course, they are multicolor: the Jesuit in a black gown, belted, hatted, beringed, and coiffed all in identical crimson; the rabbi gray in hair and robes (Gabriele has no idea how to dress a rabbi). The Jesuit—who *is* wearing a pince-nez—gazes into a vague middle distance; the rabbi looks distractedly upward. I think of Aristotle and Plato in *The School of Athens*. Of course, these two are no longer made of a single line, and they are dwarfed by a large expanse painted in beautiful sea blue-green. Most strangely of all, the empty spaces are entirely covered with Greek writing, first in horizontal lines and then, lower down, winding in snaky coils around the rabbi and the Jesuit. I have always been embarrassed by how little Greek I know. I find myself resenting this intrusion into our double portrait, and I start wondering how I am going to transport this two-by-three-foot object back to America when the time comes.

First epilogue. Years later, I discovered a piece of *Spinario* history that was completely unknown to me in Rome but was on its way to becoming a major hermeneutical plaything of the post-structuralists. It appeared in an essay called "On the Marionette Theater," but the title might as well have been *Paradise Lost*. It seems that Heinrich von Kleist—or some autobiographical persona of his—went swimming with a handsome young man. They had recently seen the *Spinario*. Now, as the young man was dry-ing himself off, he caught sight of his own image in the mirror and discovered that he had become the spontaneous and perfect replica of the sculpted boy. His older admirer realized it simulta-neously, and the young man—to turn him on? Kleist didn't say—tried to re-create the classic posture, three times, four times, ten times, but it was never the same. From that moment, the young man spent his life in front of the mirror in a vain effort to be-come the *Spinario*. As time went on, he lost all the freedom and naturalness of his body, and after a year all his charm was gone. "He had lost his innocence before my very eyes . . . and never found that paradise again."

Second epilogue. I saw Gabriele only one more time after the night he delivered the painting. It was many months later, when he was returning from his wedding trip with Anna Maria cruis-ing the Black Sea. He had brought back a vast contraband tin of beluga caviar, and there was so much of it—far more than two portions, clearly—that he invited a big crowd of his acquain-tances, myself included, to share the wealth.

But that's not the epilogue. I did manage to bring the paint-ing back to America with me. I hung it in a succession of dif-ferent houses, always in the same location: over the toilet. No disrespect intended, hard as that may be to believe. Perhaps it was the bright colors, or the half-childlike, half-medieval paint-ing style, or the sense that there was something a little arcane and narcissistic about it that relegated it to such a private spot, yet one where it would be regularly contemplated. Many years into this installation, I hosted a dinner party that included a Greek colleague. After having excused himself from the table, he returned with a beatific and patriotic smile, saying, "I love this house. It has Cavafy in the bathroom."

So far was I from having an idea about the winding script on

Gabriele's picture that at first I thought he was talking about some poetry anthology that had found its way into the lavatory. True, over the years I had made a small game out of deciphering isolated words in the canvas—something about the *Ionian*, possibly involving a *catastrophe* and *amorphous*. But only now did I discover that my painting contained a complete poetic artifact, a lyric entitled "On Board Ship." Two hours of conversation with my colleague about these twelve lines mostly told me how many ineffable meanings lurked in the poem's vocabulary, how impossible it was, in short, for me to comprehend it in my own language. I would never quite be able to understand in what way Cavafy was imagining a remembered sketch of a beautiful boy, whether the beauty was real, recollected, or painted. Mere English could never construe the many meanings of *aisthetikos*—beautiful, sensual, sickly. And what fool would even begin to tackle *psyche* or *pathos*?

Still, in recognition of a long-ago acquaintanceship, of a sketch, a contract, of brightly colored memories of things out of time and out of place, and of a mutual love of images that do not fade while bodies and memories do, I transcribe these lines—Cavafy's voice—rendered in my own vernacular:

> It's like him, of course,
> this little pencil portrait.
>
> Hurriedly sketched, on the ship's deck,
> the afternoon magical,
> the Ionian sea around us.
>
> It's like him. But I remember him as better-looking,
> He was almost pathologically sensitive,
> and this highlighted his expression.

He reveals himself more beautiful
Now that my soul brings him back, out of time.

Out of time. All these things are very old—
the sketch, the ship, the afternoon.

So Gabriele's message in a bottle finally washed up on my shore,
fifteen years later.

There was one misspelling in Gabriele's Greek. Not that I had
the skill to catch it; but once the poem had been expounded, I
realized that it was a providential error. "This highlighted his expression," is Cavafy's line as he remembers the sketch of the boy,
but Gabriele wrote "*ekphasi*" instead of "*ekphrasi*," for *expression*.
A trivial typo, yet if he had spelled it correctly, even with my
only fledgling Greek I would surely have been struck by the presence of a lifelong intellectual companion. *Ekphrasis*, the rhetorical term for a verbal description of an artistic image, like the
Shield of Achilles in the *Iliad*, or Keats's "Grecian Urn"—*speaking out*, in Greek, because such a description endows the silent
picture with a voice, just as Cavafy's lyric put poetic words to the
recollected sketch of the boy. But it is no surprise that where I
should have seen *speaking out*, I saw something like *out of phase*:
ekphrasis turns out to be the perpetual, recurring subject that
seemed always to be sneaking up on me, always catching me be-
latedly and in bemused retrospect.

A case in point. One spring day, a little before my move to
Rome, I was invited to lunch at the house of a colleague who
lived an hour up the Hudson from Manhattan; I offered a ride to
another guest, a former student with whom I had a pleasantly
droll rapport. Traffic was unexpectedly light, we found ourselves

about to arrive scandalously early, and I suggested that we kill time by making a detour to a nearby spot where I had spent childhood summers. As soon as we arrived inside this colony, which bears the absurd name Continental Village, I was flooded with memories, even though, as I explained to Brian, I hadn't seen the place since I was eleven. We drove to the large communal clubhouse, a rambling structure, part stone and part aluminum siding, that was very little changed from the 1950s, and all of a sudden I remembered that I had indeed been there once during the intervening time.

The summer before I was sixteen, I had taken part in a prep school film project, which required each member of the group to write and direct a movie. Brian was fascinated to hear of the precocity of such an enterprise. Or perhaps its pretentiousness, since he grew up in a different America, geographically and demographically, and his whole high-intelligence family had a brilliantly developed sense of irony toward self-congratulatory flights of East Coast achievement.

"So what was the film?" Brian asked.

"Well," I replied, "in German class I had read a Stefan Zweig short story called 'Die unsichtbare Sammlung,' and I decided it was perfect for a movie."

"What was it about?"

I explained. It was the story of an impoverished elderly couple—the husband is already totally blind—whose only remaining treasure is his collection of drawings by old masters. An art dealer, on the lookout for some valuable goods at a low price, journeys to the couple's remote abode in the provinces. His visit proves fruitless, however, since the wife gets desperately upset, begs him to leave, and promises to meet him at his hotel with an explanation. At that meeting—this was the scene for which we used the Continental Village clubhouse—she explains that in order to have the money to live, she has been selling off the collection one piece at a time. By now there is nothing left but blank sheets of paper. Her blind husband cannot, of course, tell the difference, but now that a dealer from the city has come calling, her cover is about to be blown.

Pressured by the old woman, the art dealer returns to the apartment and goes through the charade of looking at nonexistent Schongauers and Mantegnas and Rembrandts. Fully half of my movie consisted of the big final scene, in which the blind art collector, in possession of a captive audience, lovingly describes sheet after sheet of his invisible collection. At the climactic moment—when a flicker of doubt crosses the old man's face as he fingers a suspiciously smooth ersatz Dürer—the dealer is even prompted to invent some florid description of his own. Throughout, the camera relentlessly takes in the shiny emptiness of each page while the old man recounts a lifetime's familiarity with each artwork.

"So what you're telling me," Brian asked with just a trace of mockery in his voice, "is that at age fifteen you were a German *ekphrastic* filmmaker?"

"I never thought of it that way," I replied. It was, of course, in my class that Brian had learned about *ekphrasis*. He had quickly grasped something about the continuities of my life that was hidden from me.

Another case in point. One autumn day, a little after my move to Rome, I found myself heading north. I was alone in a train compartment with a German—the train's ultimate destination was Frankfurt—and each of us was presented with a simple breakfast snack. The reason we had a conversation at all is that I was very startled by what I was given to eat, and not in the way one might think. It happened that the crusty, malty, half-white, half-rye roll that the Deutsche Bahn offered gratis was so incredibly delicious that I realized after one bite that I had been gravely bread-deprived during my weeks in Rome. Coming from a city where artichokes and pork jowl and fresh tomatoes were an everyday pleasure, I had not expected to be captivated by a train snack carried down from across the Alps. Happy to have something nice to say to the man sitting opposite, I spruced up the residues of my German—datives and accusatives all in their proper places—and formulated a compliment.

From my impromptu ode on a *Semmel* he swiftly perceived that I was a food lover, and that impression was intensified when I told him that the purpose of my trip was wine tasting. I showed him a notebook with my past responses to the wines of Lazio. Did I do this for a living? he asked. No, I replied. I was a scholar doing a research project in Rome. On . . . ? I explained that I was a literary critic who had become interested in the visual arts, that I was documenting verbal responses to rediscovered ancient artworks (I had a notebook for that, too). I struggled to outline the concept of *ekphrasis*. The texts about images, I tried to explain, were not just unmediated efforts of accurate description; rather, they existed in a complicated relation to the image, partly comparative and partly competitive. Which meant that in the end, words and images were, as you might say, sentenced to being imperfect partners, loving and hating, mutually supportive and furiously jealous, eternally trapped in each other's company.

My new acquaintance listened to me talk about my research, buttered the second half of his roll, glanced at entries in my notebook like "cherry cinnamon nose, complex angular flavor, finish more Wagner than Rossini." Finally he said, "You know, it seems as though everything you do is based on the same problem: How can you use words to describe things that don't come in words?" I could see how right he was. Thinking about the "Invisible Collection," I wondered whether all these texts I was putting in place of pictures and wine weren't a little bit like my movie: the recurring shot of a shiny blank page, its contents lost or emptied or nonexistent, the whole thing filled in with a lot of made-up words.

And now, looking at the painted Greek text snaking its way between the rabbi and the Jesuit, I have to give Gabriele extra credit: even though it is misspelled, *ekphrasis* does seem to enter at my eye and spew out of my mouth. No wonder I never noticed it.

Never having studied Italian in the classroom, I missed out on practice sessions with the pen of my aunt and the table of my uncle. On the other hand, certain irresistible Mozartian rhythms, repeated in my own version of the language lab, had for years inculcated a swarm of paradigms that were suddenly begging to be released into my Roman conversation. Of course, *I seem to smell the odor of woman* wasn't going to be of much use; nor was it likely that I would soon caress someone's hand and murmur, *I feel as though I am touching cottage cheese and sniffing roses.* It was doubtful that even on a bad day I would accuse the devil of *opposing himself to my pleasurable progresses*, or on a good day declare *a more fertile talent than mine, no, no, there cannot be.* All these had been easy to sing along with but now proved difficult to say.

Who was I kidding? The best I could do mouthing the words of Don Giovanni himself was to stand in front of some museum with unpredictable visiting hours and intone *It's closed in there— how come?* even though in the opera it's not an *it* but a *he.* I would get further with paradigms from the hero's fascinated and victimized onlookers. *The villain believes with this deceit that he can hide his villainy* might just come in handy with a shipping company or a dry cleaner or a landlord. As for *So bright on the outside, so dark on the inside*, I enjoyed its sliding scale from metaphor to reality, its utility for both edifices and acquaintanceships. But that range of aptness was as nothing compared with *If the scene begins too sweetly, into bitterness soon it may turn*.

The truth is that there was plenty of the opera's vocabulary that screamed out for adoption. For one thing, the first ten minutes of the action contain enough thesaurus of abuse to unleash a lifetime's worth of repressed hostility, should one have such a thing. *Scellerato, sconsigliata, malandrino, indegno, misero, sciagurato*. Who needed the libretto's stilted English equivalents—*vile monster, ill-advised one, scoundrel*, etc.—for the universal language of these sounds? That still left room for some more extended epithets for me to dream of reworking, like *deviant, felon, nest of deceit*, or *yahoo, prick, dog mug*, and, just to get rid of the (hypothetical) louse, *Get lost, buffoon, you're pissing me off*. Then, as my studies became more advanced, I came to realize that there was a whole set of pronouns with no other purpose than disdain. Just call him *costui* or her *costei* or them *costoro*— roughly translated, *that &%;£$¢#*@! one over there*—and you are dealing out a vicious slight without even having to specify the grounds for your contempt. Every woman is *costei* when Don Giovanni is trying to get rid of her; in retaliation, they call him *costui*, and to any of the nobility, the peasants are always *costoro*. Now I knew how to insult people both to their faces and behind their backs.

Not that I did. What I relished was the vocabulary of sensations. On these wings of song, fear palpitates inside a heart, strange feelings awaken in a chest, a contrast of desires is born in a breast, indignation, rage, spite, and terror churn within a soul: it was like an anatomy lesson and a lexicon of the passions all in one. Just where the singers' bodies produce heroic tones, the characters they impersonate experience irrepressible emotion.

And not just suffering but also exuberance of joy. "*Viva la libertà, vivan le femmine, viva il buon vino*": that was easy. But after a few listenings you could go on to learn the syntax of *divertire*: "Now that I've spent my money, I want to enjoy myself." "Enjoy yourself! Cruel one, I know how you enjoy yourself!" And as for the verb *to laugh*, no massed repetitions in the schoolroom could do better than Leporello watching the Don manipulate Elvira: "If this goes on, *io rido, rido, rido, rido, rido, rido, rido, rido, rido, rido, rido*." This was the Italian-English dictionary of my dreams.

Or my nightmares. Never mind laughter and diversion: the two verbs whose forms *Don Giovanni* lacquered onto my consciousness were *volere* and *sapere*. *I want; I know*. Leporello: I *want* to play the gentleman; in winter he *wants* fat ones; in summer he *wants* thin ones. Masetto: I don't *want* to dance; I *want* to kill him. Don Giovanni to the Commendatore: Stay here if you *want* to die. And Leporello, when the Commendatore returns in stone: It *wants* to speak. Above all, Zerlina: I *would like* to, and I *would like not* to. But the real trick in the opera is *to know*. The victims are always in confusion: I don't know what to do or say; I don't know if I'm coming or going. To have power is to know: the Don knows how to get off clean, how to take Masetto's place, how to finish the job of seduction once Leporello has begun it. I want to know; I know I want: this is the combination that haunts the opera. When Masetto has been beaten and Zerlina offers him some mysterious remedy to everything that ails him— one that even druggists don't know how to make—she asks, in a moment sexier than anything Don Giovanni ever says, "Would you like to know where I keep it?" *Saper vorresti dove mi sta?*: a favorite Italian sentence to practice in my personal language lab.

I knew something about living life as a language lab: it was no surprise to me, making my way through Primo Levi's *Periodic Table* in those months, that the first chemical element in his table of contents turns quickly into a portrait of his family via the Jewish dialects they spoke. I knew nothing about *Il sistema periodico* when I chose it as a language workbook other than the renown of the author and the fact that it was divided into manageable chapters that seemed suitable to the intermediate student. But I was unprepared for lesson one, the book's epigraph:

> *Ibergekumene tsores iz gut tsu dertseyln.*
> (*È bello raccontare i guai passati.*)

For Levi, a proverb cited in a far-off East European patois, Italically transliterated—"It's good to remember past troubles"—serves as a fanciful entryway to the experience of the Piedmontese diaspora, which he goes on to quote in a vernacular of elaborately spelled-out sentences containing almost nothing recognizable as Italian. But to me, that foreign phrase was the least exotic part of his book. I struggled through the opening chapter, on argon, a gas that (if I understood correctly) was either inert because it was noble or noble because it was inert, all of which somehow equaled the Jews. I had trouble with the local dialect, with the sentence structure, and, especially, with the science. On the other hand, not only did some phrases from his family language jump out as more comprehensible to me than normal Italian—simple terms like *goyim* and *mamser*, plus an advanced vocabulary involving cattle, corpses, and lingering torment—but the whole business of life twisted among many tongues promised something very familiar. Italian through the interlinear of Yiddish seemed *haimish* to me.

If I was given the chance as a college freshman to spin *Don Giovanni* as I managed language lab turntables, it was owing to my own version of the linguistic diaspora. Practically every family story—and God knows, there were plenty of them—was a story about language. No: a story about languages. Never mind Levi's inert Judeo-aristocrats who moved confidently between a couple of local dialects; the shtetl dwellers of my ancestry navigated five or six distinct tongues as a matter of daily life. No wonder that adult conversation could be conducted aslant several layers of childproofing camouflage, from English to Yiddish to Polish to—God knows!—Ruthenian, depending on the ever-advancing comprehension of greedy young listeners. I probably learned the slipperiness of languages at the same time as I acquired language itself. I knew you could say things in different languages that were the same but not the same; I knew you could mix different languages in one sentence; I knew that the same sounds could mean something different in different languages.

I learned secrecy and defiance from my first attempt at reading, circa age three, in a language my parents wouldn't countenance, courtesy of a Hebrew grammar book clandestinely furnished by my pious grandmother in defiance of the self-congratulatory secularism that ruled our house. What I didn't learn, however, was Hebrew, since she could transliterate only into Cyrillic. Eventually the book was desiccated by its hiding place behind the playroom radiator, so that it took on the qualities of some sacred and undecipherable parchment. In the same years, I recall being dragged into a newly opened Madison Avenue dress shop, where I had to watch my mother's performance of hilarity and derision as she induced each poor salesgirl, by one stratagem after another, to repeat the name of the store, all because it had been unwarily christened Gay Cottons. The mirth had nothing to do with homosexuality, only with the name's sounding very like *gay kakn*, a standard Yiddish expression—like everything else, difficult to translate—that falls somewhere between "Fiddlesticks" and "Go fuck yourself!"

Our very pets were foreigners. My father used to tell a story about himself as a teenager making a delivery at an old lady's Lower East Side apartment; the parlor was empty, and as he attempted to penetrate farther, he was apprehended by a guardian parrot screeching out, *"Oy vay, a ganef!"* On special occasions, this reminiscence would be followed by a comparable tale, but of Chaucerian proportions. It seems that in the summer, which our family spent at a primitive lakeside cabin, my father would bring back a whole week's worth of meat on his return from the city each Friday night after everyone had gone to bed. Once, on the two-mile hike from the train, he was pursued all the way home by an insistent German shepherd. He eluded the beast, secured the goods in the icebox, took the unusual precaution of locking up the house, and went off to sleep himself. At the same time, unbeknownst to him, my tiresomely freeloading uncle, who had invited himself for the weekend, was on his way back from answering the call of nature in the outside privy. Barely settled into bed, my father heard telltale banging on the door, suspected the German shepherd, lurched across the small square footage, and screamed, "Get out of here, you dirty dog!" Whereupon the presumed animal replied, in perfect Yiddish, "Ben, what's the matter with you? Have you gone *meshuggah?*"

Before I knew any foreign languages that weren't among those spoken in the house, I knew there was a single set of sounds that in Spanish meant "Here is a table" and in Yiddish meant "A cow eats without a knife." Similarly, I knew that a slight vowel shift turned *voilà* into something Slavic for chicken wattles. When necessity arose, my mother would teasingly chant a long set of rhymes in Ukrainian that had the power to dissolve warts; I can still repeat it, though I do not know the meaning of a single word. I recall, similarly verbatim and uncomprehendingly, several verses of a song some family member had learned from a beloved aunt by marriage—a member of a couple always known via the none-too-complimentary rhyming names that my great-grandmother had given them, *Berel der shvartzer, Yossel der fartzer*. In this instance, I cannot even identify the language, though if I piece out the syllables, it sounds something like Portuguese, which might explain Berel's swarthiness.

Nowadays, this all sounds stylish, even glamorous. But half a century ago it was more shameful than chic. My family's brand of foreign migrated in one generation from gravely disabling to tediously bourgeois without ever passing through even a remote suburb of trendy. My parents were embarrassed because they were so different; in addition to that inheritance, I was embarrassed because I was so much the same. You could, of course, tell lies and try to pass: my mother spent years composing a never-to-be-published novel about a man who fashioned his own existence so that he would appear, in her too frequently repeated phrase, "to the manner born." Alternatively, you could take command of these inhibiting mortifications and make reality itself swerve. Invent your life by lying, or invent your life by steering it in the vaguely apprehended direction of your own fantasies.

Or a little of both. When *Saturday Night Live*'s immortal Coneheads find that their hydrocephalic shape or mechanized speech is about to betray extraterrestrial origin, they prevent discovery by immediately droning, "We are from France." All suspicion dissolves at once in the face of an identity that authorizes unlimited strangeness while also brandishing a sexy cachet. With scarcely more claim on this title than if I had come from planet Remulak, I spent my early years piecing together my own claim on France. A little bit was true, a larger bit was prevaricated, but the largest bit was my own hard work to absorb a culture I was scarcely born to. If I became a little French boy, then perhaps I could convert my family's citizenship retroactively. The work had to be covert so that the results would appear natural. Nasal vowels, irregular verbs, expressing seventy-two as sixty-twelve— these were easily mastered. But they were only the beginning of a private life spent absorbing the food and music, the politics and poetry of France. Indeed, so early and so effective was this self-invention that as an adult, my falsehood has become a kind of truth: I can quite authentically look back on a childhood spent with Tintin, Camembert, and the "Marseillaise."

Then, linguistically, I went into deeper cover. With Hebrew foreclosed, I threw myself into Latin. Later, I reached German and puberty around the same time. I must have looked forward to both as thrillingly, catastrophically alien—certainly both horrified my parents—but after a childhood of Yiddish, the German part of these terrors, at least, proved surprisingly unfrightening, strangely *heimisch*. In short, what enabled me to enter that language lab was the embrace of one culture that I had struggled to invent and another that I had mastered in spite of myself; what was to result was a tangle of interlanguages that put me perennially in the role of half-baked interpreter among foreign tongues and within myself. That was the starting point from which I was now developing Italian.

Not that all this proficiency was just a question of Ukrainian wart jingles and Mozartian flirtation. Learning a language, living a life, understanding a work of art: you can nail down the vocabulary, get used to the paradigms, even memorize a phrase book. But if you want to be more than a tourist, you have to figure out the underlying principles and speak your own speech. Give a man a dictionary, and he'll talk for a day; teach him the grammar, and he'll talk for a lifetime. The grammar of my childhood—fear and hilarity, bodily functions and estrangement—I can't set down so easily. Better to work on *Don Giovanni*, though it has its own difficulties. It's all very well to brandish a lexicon full of abuse and diversion, dastardly seduction and uproarious laughter. But is that the opera's true voice, or mine? The fact is, my first real step in comprehending the opera's Italian, or speaking my own, probably came when I could finally wield the subjunctive—the kind of verb that, instead of telling you what happens, teases you with what is anticipated, feared, hoped for, commanded, supplicated, or contrary to fact.

Sure, I wanted Don Giovanni to be the master criminal of love, and I wanted the opera to be one long exercise in unbridled passion. But so many subjunctives get in the way! Everyone's power is carefully qualified: *May the just heavens avenge . . . ; I would, if it weren't for the scandal . . . ; Every means shall be sought to find out . . .* Even the Don himself has to beg that he be permitted to eat, to urge that a search be dispatched, to hope that Elvira may succumb quickly; and when it's all over, the best Don Ottavio can do is to go into double negatives and pleonasms *as he does not doubt but that* Don Giovanni *be* the murderer. Most especially, from all of this, I absorbed contingency: *provided that* you act less jealous, *provided that* you don't talk about the killing, *provided that* they wear a skirt, you know what he does.

With these paradigms under my belt, at last I had sentence structures for the complications of my own existence: if I had, I would; if I were, I should; if I could, I might. These, finally, were the forms in which I could wield *volere* and *sapere*. Where had all this good stuff been when I needed it to forestall the arrival of Gabriele's girlfriend?

The lessons did, however, come in handy with the arrival of a new person in my life. My rented apartment came with a cleaning lady, and she turned up, fresh from arduous summer holiday travels, a few weeks after I had settled in. Giovanna was cheerful, self-assured, olive-skinned, opulent of physique and personality. In time, she would prove to be a partner—sometimes accomplice, accessory, coconspirator—of unwavering loyalty for everything in practical life. Merchants, government bureaucracies, neighbors nosy or noisy, and above all the landlords, who were her original employers: she had a creative proposal for every form of outside threat. But at the beginning, when our conversational topics rarely reached beyond the four walls inside which she cleaned, she was an exercise in language even more demanding than Primo Levi. In the first place, her own speech veered between dialect and an Italian that deformed its consonants following patterns I could not immediately discern. In the second place, my Italian needed to rise to a certain level of gracious indirection if I was not to appear to be ordering her around as though she were an indentured servant.

It starts right away with *you*—so simple in English, where God and the devil, masters and slaves, the one and the many can all be addressed alike. French, and *Don Giovanni*, had taught me that *you-all* was somehow more polite than *you-one*, but modern Italian went even further by calling every person, male or female, with whom one was on formal terms, *she*. Still, I could hardly say to Giovanna, She: clean under the refrigerator! Which is where the subjunctive came in. I'm sure I began badly, with "Let the underpants be bleached" and "May every salad bowl be dried by hand." But then I progressed to "It would please me were the hair to be removed from the shower drain, come what may." Then it developed, given the extraordinarily primitive electrical arrangements of the apartment (which Giovanna alone, of all people on the planet, understood), that she had a few contingencies for me to chew on. If you didn't unplug the hot-water heater before going into the bath, I learned, live current might get channeled through the showerhead; if you were to open the refrigerator while the vacuum was in use, a computer was liable to crash. The whole apartment operated on a vast grid of subjunctives.

Giovanna's life, as it turned out, was governed by far more dire hypotheticals than these—by life-and-death questions concerning Babylon, Armageddon, and the precise number of the anointed in the Heavenly Kingdom. I knew nothing of this at first. The closest I got was a series of rather confusing travel narratives. On her first visit to me, she had just returned from touring in a bus with (as I understood it) sixteen of her siblings. When I asked exactly how big her family was, she looked at me with affectionate superiority and explained that they were *spiritual* brothers and sisters. As for the place they had visited, where, she explained with deep compassion, everyone lived in the extremes of poverty, malnutrition, and political tyranny, I was astonished to hear that it was Bologna—famously prosperous, well governed, and gastronomic—but later, readjusting her consonants from voiced to unvoiced, I translated *Bologna* to *Polonia*. She'd gone to Poland.

None of this would have added up to Jehovah's Witness without a much larger episode of misunderstanding. Christmas was in the air. I pondered the decorum of a holiday bonus for Giovanna but decided that cash might seem too materialistic. A couple of weeks before the holiday, she admired a kettle I had bought to heat the water for tea. Carefully choosing one that was even more impressive, I presented her with the brightly wrapped package in mid-December. Her response was polite, confused, embarrassed, incoherent—who knew that Jehovah's Witnesses were stern disbelievers in Christmas?—and she remained uncharacteristically taciturn the whole cleaning day. The following week, however, she returned with her usual cheery demeanor, and scarcely pausing in her ritual of donning an allover apron to cover quite elegant street clothes, she handed me a package.

Only now did the penny drop. It was a book with no dust jacket, no author, no cover art, just block gilt lettering that read (in Italian simple enough even for me) *Life—How did it get here?* and an imprint from the Watchtower Society. "It's scientific," said Giovanna, perhaps catching some sign of alarm in my face, "and it has beautiful pictures." I flipped through the heavily illustrated pages, images of apes and human craniums passing before my eyes as I wondered how to respond to the gift of an antievolution tract that clearly represented Giovanna's deepest spiritual commitment.

I can't quite explain what happened next, except on the grounds that I had fallen into some abyss of social and verbal confusion, the pandemonium of my life as an interlanguage. Of course, I was going to tell lies; the only questions were, how many, how big, and how well I would do in a foreign tongue. Perhaps it was the heritage of my self-invented childhood: if I was going to make up stories, they may as well have to do with family history. I decided to say that a scientific book was the perfect gift because my father was a chemist. The truth is, my father wasn't a chemist, not in the American sense, anyway (British was another language I had labored to master); when he wasn't hearing animals speak Yiddish, he was running a drugstore. And perhaps it was this jagged leap that threw me back from my newly minted, imperfect Italian to the more assured—if also fabricated—universe of my French. Whatever the reason, the words I carefully framed in my head were Mon père faisait la chimie. And I proceeded to translate them literally, or rather phonically, into Italian: "Mio padre faceva la scimmia." Unfortunately, what I had just said in Italian was, "My father was a monkey."

After a moment of silence, Giovanna smiled a little more guardedly than usual and asked, "In what sense?"

I was on a roll. Why stop inventing? "In a laboratory," I replied.

We had many more conversations, Giovanna and I, but never about my family.

———

"Provided that she's wearing a skirt . . ." That was the expression that really trained my ear in the subjunctive, partly, I suppose, because the rest of the Italian—"You know what he does"—is so easy, and partly because each segment of the sentence gets severally repeated in a wonderful rising sequence of descending notes. But mostly because it is the climactic gesture in my favorite aria of all, the earliest bit of the libretto that I came to know effortlessly by heart, the piece that I soonest grew unable to resist singing along with, even in the opera house.

Poor Donna Elvira has been fobbed off with Leporello, who is supposed to give her the "strong reasons" why she was abandoned. The nonsense about a square not being a circle having failed, he fulfills his task in a backward sort of way. Instead of inventing more excuses for Don Giovanni, he tells the truth about his master's innumerable (specifically, 2,064) conquests. Elvira, in other words, is the victim not of accident, but of necessity, of inevitability. And Leporello establishes this by sharing with her his logbook of the Don's loves.

There were, to be sure, some upper-brain reasons why I was possessed by the catalogue aria. It was about sex but didn't mention sex, a century-and-a-half-older sibling of Cole Porter's "Let's Do It." Here, however, the operative verb is *amò*—another language-learning Everest to climb, the *passato rimoto*, for action in the past that is completely finished and done with—meaning, roughly, "the ladies whom my master loved once, only once, and never will love again." Then, too, over the years I grew fascinated with the opera's strange doubling between master and servant. Later they exchange identities. Here they operate in a more traditional symbiosis: one performs actions; the other chronicles them. In the long run, since we depend on chroniclers to know the past at all, who is to say which are the greater heroes?

But this is all after the fact, product of more mature musings.
The reason I was struck from the beginning by Leporello's aria is
that I have spent my life obsessed with lists. A glimpse from
childhood: a picture of the family huddled around the Dumont's
twelve-inch screen, my parents in attitudes of anger and fear I
have never seen before, as a not-very-clean-shaven man with
lopsided slitty eyes brandishes some sheets of paper, saying, "I
have in my hand here a list of 205 card-carrying Communists . . ."
(Of course, I don't remember the exact number; neither did he,
as it turned out.) Or another glimpse: My mother repeating a
poem, always from memory, about Abou Ben Adhem "(may his
tribe increase!)." An angel is writing down the names of all who
loved God, and when Abou discovers that he is not on the list,
he rather saucily demands to be put down instead among those
who care about other people; the next night, the angel returns
with a new list, of those "whom love of God had blessed, / And,
lo! Ben Adhem's name led all the rest!" I suppose the recital of
this wretched jingle represented a bumbling attempt to inculcate
some god-free social religion. At the time, though, I was as
frightened by Abou Ben Adhem as my parents were by the image
on television. Did they have a Communist past that inscribed
them on McCarthy's terrible roster? Was my name on the list of
"those who loved their fellow men"?

In time, I recovered from these fears but not from the mag-
netism of the list. I remember my great leap forward in learning
the French of everyday life when, in my early twenties, I moved
into a cabin in Provence and was given a ten-page inventory of
every domestic article in the place—insurance against the possibility that I might abscond with tongs, brush, or plunger when
my month's occupancy was ended. Both the text and the objects
became, in fact, a sacred trust, not to say fetish; I relished the
knowledge that three seemingly identical food mills, or four

dishrags distinguishable only by the cabinet in which they were placed, bore completely different French names. A few years later I delighted in the opportunity to prance around the stage as the Lord High Executioner in *The Mikado*, singing, "As someday it may happen that a victim must be found, I've got a little list . . . ," perhaps because it promulgated the notion that autograph hounds and peppermint eaters, female novelists and unprincipled politicians should be subject to an undifferentiated code of capital punishment. Shakespeare, too, got into the act. I struggled to help an undergraduate actor with ten lines of verse in *Romeo and Juliet* that consist of nothing more than a list of people invited to the Capulet ball; the techniques came in handy later with a similar list of the dead in *Henry V*. Was there some strange kinship in Shakespeare's mind, some common effect of leveling and becoming generic, between going to a party and dying at Agincourt?

Rome presented itself as no less list-heavy than any other passage in my life. It had started with the disastrous circulation of my book inventory, which led the Italian customs office to sequester my possessions. Nor was that the only list in my luggage. Ahead-of-time informants had furnished me with whole catalogues of goods and service providers, some more useful than others. Favorite barbers, computer repairmen, and Vatican insiders would come in handy; rosters of the best places to look through a telescope, get your formal wear dry-cleaned, or buy marrons glacés, less so. And it is probably a sign of failure in all this early preparedness that I was soon sending home desperate registers of things that visiting friends from the States should bring me, including antihistamines, Lapsang souchong, and an Itty Bitty Book Light.

The most challenging of the lists I brought with me—the hope and bane of many a well-networked traveler—were friends of friends, every one of them wise and gregarious, profound and accessible, who, though previously unknown to me, would become my best pals if I wasted no time in looking them up as soon as I arrived in the city. Their alluring profiles live in my memory still. Perpetual American art-history graduate student gone recklessly native inside seventeenth-century Rome; urbane Jewish Italian essayist on everything fashionable in contemporary culture; ex-Californian gay couple of high musical sophistication occupying a penthouse atop the most beautiful street in the old city. In all cases, I awaited a response to my letters, worded in a careful mixture of self-promotion and coquetry, in vain.

And, let's face it, the lists that really count are lists of people. Which is, perhaps, why Leporello finds it imperative to *count* them. And Don Giovanni certainly has good numbers—far better than McCarthy's:

> In Italy, six hundred and forty,
> In Germany, two hundred and thirty-one,
> A hundred in France, in Turkey ninety,
> But in Spain, there are already one thousand and three.

It's not only the quantity of seductions, it's the precision of the tally. And what are we to make of such wide fluctuations in this erotic version of the GNP? Granted, he lives in Spain, which gives him more opportunities (one thousand and three, *and counting*, Leporello suggests), and Turkey is far away, which would account for his relatively poor showing there. But perhaps other factors impinge. After all, in France, just over the border, he hardly manages to outdo his lackluster Turkish performance. Is there a graph lurking behind these numbers that charts the relative easy-ness of girls from Seville to Constantinople, or is it rather a measure of the Don's tastes for different complexions or native costumes? And why should nationalities be the prime categories under which Leporello files his data? By comparison, the division by social class—"peasant girls, / chambermaids, city girls, / countesses, baronesses, / marquesses, princesses"—produces nothing but a statistically unspecific jumble.

"In Italy, six hundred and forty": I had a long way to go in making friends around the peninsula. True, I did have a baroness. A visiting English friend, obscurely connected to the grand lady via a sister-in-law, received permission that I tag along to a luncheon. The baroness's vast apartment and its spread of terraces looked out over the Spanish Steps, almost as good a view as I had enjoyed, a few weeks earlier, desperately lurching over the Quirinal to find action at the railroad station. The family name was sufficiently ancient to merit gruesome punishment in Dante's *Inferno*; the footmen wore white gloves; the lady was aged, petite, all-seeing, and immaculate. Her command over English was so perfect that it even permitted her to stumble occasionally, so that she could flatter me by appealing for my help in a translation from the Italian.

That first occasion, with its several courses of food and wine, might have continued to rigidify into the most adamantine of formalities were it not for a piece of good fortune. It had seemed only correct to bring some tiny hostess present to lunch, except that, with the press of multiple servants, we had forgotten to present it on our arrival. As the visit was drawing to a close and coffee was being served, I remembered the little box of chocolates I had gone to some trouble to procure—pursuant, of course, to one of my lists of Rome's premium purveyors. When I handed the countess the handsomely wrapped parcel, I saw a new look in her eyes. She expressed amazement that after only a few weeks in Rome I knew about the tiny hole-in-the-wall chocolatier buried within the Colonna palaces. Instead of being moved toward the

door, we were ushered onto a west-facing terrace. With the afternoon sun and St. Peter's in our eyes, the conversation went
something like:

THE BARONESS: I know your friend is returning to England to-
    morrow, but perhaps you'd like to come to luncheon again
    next week.
ME: I'd be delighted.
THE BARONESS: What shall I have the cook prepare?
ME: Anything, really . . . Perhaps a risotto?
THE BARONESS: What kind of risotto?
ME: Porcini mushrooms?
THE BARONESS: I shall pick them myself, at the weekend.

For a little while, I became something of a regular in the house.

A poetess, whose charm might be traced to her mood swings,
could also be added to my list, once I had tagged along with
American friends who'd been invited to a pre-holiday festivity at
her vast, ramshackle apartment overlooking one of Rome's least
heralded and sweetest food markets. Rough going, at first. Neither
she nor her even more unreadable companion, both having
made their names with savage mastery of avant-garde aesthetics,
seemed responsive to literary conversation with a professional
scholar. This time, it wasn't my gift—I had come empty-handed,
not being able to gauge the decorum of this social set—but someone else's that did the trick. Where these gems came from I never
knew, but the dining table groaned with rare white Burgundies of
grand vintages, a thing unheard of in the ethnocentric wine universe of Italy in those days. Whoever the fairy godperson may
have been, no one undertook to celebrate these marvels as they
deserved. I must have witnessed an imminent sacrilege—perhaps
someone tried to mix two wines in one glass or add a spritz of

mineral water—which, however slender my rights to be there, forced me center stage in the conversation. Whereupon I allowed myself to paint a verbal picture of the whole *terroir* from Chassagne to Puligny to Meursault to Corton, explaining the differences among *grand cru*, *premier cru*, and *lieu dit*, and perhaps even touching on malolactic fermentation and the use of the *barrique*.

Who would have guessed that this insufferable party pooping was the way to my hostess's heart? After a quarter of an hour or so, her companion called for the attention of the whole company and declared that she had never heard the poetess sit so patiently listening to anyone in her life as she sat listening to me talk about wine. Or perhaps it wasn't the way to her heart: I never saw the inside of that apartment again, but I did quite regularly run into my poetess hostess when I passed through the little market outside their windows. With no wines to discuss, or drink, we always seemed a little starved for conversation.

Then, some time later, I came across a poem she had written about Saturday afternoon at the market in front of her apartment, when the few wilted remains of greens herald the long, silent closure that is a Roman weekend. Looking out the window, she decides she doesn't need to buy anything, but she is attracted to the street nonetheless.

> When I went downstairs, it was already late
> among the piles of artichoke leaves
> and faded tomatoes, where a hunched old woman
> ran greedily to reclaim some apple halves,
> or some peppers that were three-quarters good.
> But I wasn't after fruit, rotten or fresh,
> I wanted only certainty
> of a week that is ending,
> of opportunity lost.

It became the ode for one segment of my every week in Rome, the approaching time when even the casual contact with shop-keepers would get suspended. I could not have guessed, on such little acquaintance, by what chronometer the author of these lines measured out her life. But a full-time poet may well be something like a professor on sabbatical. I, too, was learning the habit of clocking the day and the week by the shreds of un-bought produce on the ground and by the emptiness of the street scene when Saturday afternoon rolled around. We had, it seems, more in common than Burgundy.

My list also included the urbanologist. I first met her when she breezed into my apartment with an international crowd of people among whom I had a few tenuous connections. They had been dining near the Piazza dei Satiri when the early winter weather turned nasty—and decided to seek refuge in my tower. With her dazzling smile, resplendent wardrobe, and impassioned attentiveness, it was no surprise to me that several ex-boyfriends were in her orbit. All I could do was listen in on dramas about her ex-husband, her daughter, the abstract expressionist murals she was commissioning for her apartment, and the two or three pretenders to her current favors who were in attendance at that very moment—one of them, as I recall, a sad-faced Jew named Christian. Certainly, this crowd had no need of my expertise. They all seemed to have just flown in from Paris with a few kilos of foie gras and a Matisse drawing wrapped up in their suitcases. My bedtime long past, I was relieved when the throng moved on, and only the next morning did I discover a note on my desk: "You'll telephone me to come see sunset from my terrace?"

I never knew what I had done to deserve this, but before long I was a little epicycle in this woman's orbit, and I became quite expert on the ambient anxieties concerning her past loves and the hopes of others to become part of her future. There were quite a few sunsets over the Colosseum to be witnessed, and many parties. Even when she was passing through Rome on her way from Dakar to Brooklyn Heights, enough smoked salmon and champagne for twelve would be rustled up from the fridge without any help from me. Late that night—again, bedtime long past—I was given a lift home by the current, soon-to-be-former, boyfriend. He said he was a hydraulic engineer, and I had no idea what that meant (perhaps nothing more than plumber), but I was fascinated by his elegant literary conversation and the fact that he spoke the most beautiful Italian I had ever heard. When we arrived as near my apartment as it was practical for an automobile to penetrate, I said good night and expected to see him drive away. Instead, he got out of the car, embraced me, and said—I think—"You are a treasure." I did not know what I had done to deserve this.

A few more possibilities might be eked out. There was an Amazonian lexicographer who tried me and found me wanting for a small private salon she ran in her Trastevere apartment, and a Sicilian-German psychoanalyst who addressed me as though she were my English nanny. That's one who didn't make it to my list and one whose nationality was unclassifiable. Terrible numbers, of course, but then who wants to be a Don Juan, stuffing individuals into the ignominy of the roster? "Women of every rank, every shape, every age," *purche porti la gonnella*: it's the same mentality as McCarthy's Communists or the dead bodies in the Hundred Years' War.

Except that the more I listened to Leporello's aria, the more I started hearing a counter-story. Sure, it is ominous to hear him say, "In winter he likes them plump, in summer he likes them slender," which sounds as though Don Giovanni is doing seasonal menu planning. And it is even more troubling to know that "he makes conquests of the old ones just for the pleasure of putting them on the list," which suggests the catalogue is becoming an end in itself—not a record of pleasure but a substitute for it. But after Leporello has told us several times that his master likes women of every kind indiscriminately, suddenly there is a pause, a double bar, and a big rhythm shift, from a stern and booming 4/4 to a sweet insinuating 3/4:

> With a blonde he's in the habit of praising her kindness,
> With a dark one, her constancy,
> With a fair one, her sweetness.

They're not all the same, then. And in recognizing the differences, Leporello praises each woman's internal qualities. But this just prepares us for a bigger change. As he finishes the phrase about courting the old women just to put them on the list, the music goes through a multiple metamorphosis, from sharps to flats, majors to minors, tonics to dominants, then just as suddenly back to where it started. The four-bar roller-coaster ride accompanies the words "his predominating passion is the young beginner." When the harmonics go normal again, it returns to the familiar business of libertinism and list making—he doesn't care if she's rich or poor, beautiful or ugly, provided that she is wearing a skirt, et cetera, et cetera. In that dizzying interval, however, we have seen something real, personal, differentiated.

Maybe I shouldn't make too many claims on behalf of Mozart's sexual politics—though I'm confident that the point of *Così fan tutte* is, precisely, that women don't all do it the same way. But listening to the swings and roundabouts of the catalogue aria, I began to see something different about lists. Yes, in one way, the French kitchen equipment and the Agincourt fatalities and Don Giovanni's women got chopped down to uniform size when they appeared in an inventory. But in another way, putting them on a list is a kind of precondition for separating out their differences. Put a few hundred supposed Communists on a list, and if you're lucky, the idea that they're all the same starts to unravel. Read the invitation roster for the Capulet party carefully—Mercutio, Rosaline, Tybalt—and you can pick out all the fine articulations of the drama that is to follow. And of course, the joke about the Lord High Executioner's victims in *The Mikado* is that they don't all belong on the same death row.

The real lesson for me was that my whole research project was about a list, or something like it. In ancient Rome's glory days, statues of marble and bronze existed as parts of a complete culture, rich in contexts and connective tissue. A thousand years of ruin go by, and what the Renaissance looks at is a kind of underground warehouse with an inventory of bits and pieces. My job was to look at that inventory not like Leporello's catalogue list, but in a way that would make them live and breathe again. Mozart was only part of the necessary training, though. When my German acquaintance on the train saw from my notebook that I had recently tasted fifty Chiantis during one evening in Siena, he asked me, "How could you possibly tell the difference between them?" I replied, "It was tasting all fifty that taught me to tell the difference," which, I suppose, is what separates me from Don Giovanni.

•   •   •

LB to DS, December 1987:

Somehow solitude was not, after the first couple of weeks, anyway, a gut-wrenching problem. I have been spending lots of my life alone at home enjoying doing nothing in my funky apartment. But most of it is that I love being in Rome. I was lonely for a while; then I became happy in my isolation because I fell so in love with the city itself. I'm embarrassed to be typing this, but all these fragments are becoming my friends. The big marble monuments of the Vatican are just so much uninviting rock; but the lame, the mutilated, the chatty broken statues in the street—there's something about how ruined they are that makes me want to talk to them.

•

Looking at the statue head-on in the street, I see a faceless, turbaned, armed figure in semi-profile, with strangely broad shoulders swiveling his upper body and an almost freakish amount of lap. Turn the corner from the Governo Vecchio toward Piazza Navona, and suddenly the stony mass cleaves in two. What was lap is now the lower torso of a second, equally robust figure, defined by belly button, hank of pubic hair, and the imprint of a hand. Whose hand? Not his own. Vestige of an embrace that extended from the long-effaced arm of his companion, enveloping his once recumbent, now truncated form.

Who are these people? Epic protagonists engaged in noble combat. Allies? Adversaries? Perhaps some more pleasurable kind of struggle. *Symplegma* is the official term for statues of two men wrestling, or making love. Achilles, Alexander, Hercules— all of them had engaged in ferocious exploits of both sex and war. Then why does this statue go by such a vernacular diminutive name as Pasquino? Is it another history of misidentified sculpture, like the Apollo who became a *Hermaphrodite* and then turned into a *Venus*? But at least those were all gods; this great composite hero has been metamorphosed into some Roman-in-the-street with a cutesy moniker.

•

Pliny says that in his day Rome had two populations, one of living human beings and the other of marble statues . . . But what would Pliny have said, seeing such a large population of marble in the time of Emperor Vespasian, if he had been able to travel to the future of many other succeeding emperors, who brought infinitely more statues to the city? . . . I'm sure he would have said that in Rome there was one population of human beings and ten of marble statues.

—Pirro Ligorio, 1570

•

Two sixteenth-century stories explain why the statue got named Pasquino. (1) Pasquino was a grammar teacher who encouraged correct Latin by having pupils post witty verses all around the sculpture. (2) Pasquino was a barber or a tailor in whose nearby shop clever, seditious talk against popes and cardinals could be freely entertained. When highly placed individuals wanted to evade responsibility for what they had said, they blamed it on Pasquino—first the tradesman, then the statue. In time, these utterances became literary productions— pasquinades—that exercised citywide, and then worldwide, satirical terror. A pair of classical titans became a ruin, the ruin became a citizen, the citizen learned eloquence, and stone grew a voice.

•

As conquering heroes might expect
To celebrate the triumphs that they earned
For just one single day were then returned
Just as before, wretched and abject,

So with me, on shabby Roman street marooned
I suffer rain and hail, corrosive decay
throughout the year, but then one single day
In honorific sacredly festooned.

Varying forms with visage half-divine
I body forth, and then, my godliness unborn,
The name Pasquino I re-acknowledge mine.

And in that way, though prey to hate and scorn,
For a time, at least, I feel much better off
Than all you bums who look at me and scoff.
                                        —Pasquinade, 1515

•

It turns out that Pasquino is the senior member of the Confraternity of the Sharp-Tongued, all six of whom have been chattering among themselves and with the Romans for centuries. I developed a new itinerary for my walks in the city: the circuit of the Speaking Statues. Collect a full set, win a cool prize. Marforio was, evidently, the most high-class of the lot—a vast, muscular, reclining divinity, his huge head wholly encompassed with shaggy curls. Like others, he had been shuttled from place to place—the Forum, San Marco, the Capitoline, where he now reposes—but unlike them, he has been famous in his own right for eight hundred years. Again there are problems figuring out exactly who he is. Possibly king of the gods, and since he is reclining on a bed of lumpy spheres, he must be Jupiter the Baker, supreme divinity of breadrolls. Others have tried to make sense out of his name: Was he from a Forum of Mars, even though there was no Forum of Mars? Or was he Nar Fluvius, the river god representing a Tiber tributary? He's too big to be a mere tributary: he must be the Rhine or the Danube, or even Oceanus, who surrounds the whole world's landmass. Whatever his identity, he is Pasquino's most intimate conversation partner, his crosstown buddy and favorite interlocutor.

•

Listening to Pasquino. Pasquinades. Sharp and salacious, unsigned and abusive, these lampooning assaults on authority have a half-millennium history of circulating in the marketplace of Roman conversation. In the Renaissance, Pasquino had his own festival day; he would get elaborately costumed, as Saturn or Jupiter, Minerva or Venus, Mars or Mourning. In the course of twenty-four hours, via some sort of vast humanist conspiracy, the annual identity would be declared, his broken trunk would be restored into something like an elaborate carnival float, dozens of poems would be composed in his voice and in the voices of those in conversation with him. Then, just as suddenly, the whole structure would be violently demolished, the children of the neighborhood bashing him back into his wonted condition of mutilation. He managed to live in multiple worlds—classical masterpiece, modern ruin, dress-up dummy for the fantasies of a culture in love with its past and frightened of the future. He was an image that had words pinned on him. With barely a body, or two bodies, he possessed triumphant powers of speech. He was a travesty, and *travesti*.

•

MARFORIO: Dear friend Pasquino, dish me all the dirt
on how Pope Leo died, and please be frank,
did they poison him or wreck his heart,
or was it too much drink or too much wank?

PASQUINO: Marforio, you're mad to want to know—
state secrets such as these had best stay hushed,
But if you will insist, I'll whisper low:
he was fucking the ass of his boy toy too much.

MARFORIO: Do I dare to believe what you're telling me?
Are vows of abstinence so sacred all forgone?

PASQUINO: Suspended by pontifical decree.

MARFORIO: Yet who'd have thought the Pope still gets it on?

PASQUINO: I'll tell you how this story came to light:
Tired in the midst of his flagrant delight
He called his physician in darkness of night.
As he neared the Pope's bedside, the myopic doc
Instead of his arm grabbed hold of his cock
As he searched for a pulse, he was in for a shock.
Neither odor nor color struck him as legit,
So he shrieked, "Holy Father, you or I'd better quit
Or both our reputes will be covered in shit."
—Pasquinade attached to the statue, 1521

•

My third acquaintance among the sharp-tongued Confraternity, Facchino, is a quieter type, more a doer than a talker. His name means "porter," and they called him that after a real-life Roman street porter. When you come upon him in the Via del Corso, he looks more like a water carrier, though. His own body recedes into a niche, while his barrel pushes forward like some kind of detachable cylindrical paunch, complete with an umbilicus from which a little fountain piddles forward. A pompous inscription refers to his "coronation," which—do I have the Latin right?— consists in having been slapped on the ass by his fellow porters when he came on the job. His real problem, it turns out, was not heavy water, but heavy drinking; he was done in by some mixture of water-barrel carrying and wine-barrel emptying. Worse yet, he was said to resemble Martin Luther—no compliment in Rome.

•

Of burdens he'd never tire,
Long life was his deepest desire,
But, determined to lift ever higher,
The effect on his body was dire,
Now he hauls for the heavenly choir.
—Facchino epitaph, ca. 1850, now removed

With what kind face, o courteous peasant
You offer the parched your welcome present
Of sweetest waters unsurpassed.
And yet with wonder I stand aghast:
Since you seem so alive, I marvel why
You keep your own lips forever dry.
Either H$_2$O is not your shtick, or
You're saving yourself for higher-proof liquor.
     —Gian Battista Marino to Facchino, ca. 1619

•

Wedded bliss among the sharp-tongued: Madama Lucrezia, a.k.a.
Mrs. Pasquino, is a great big lady—her bust alone must be three
or four feet high—swathed in gorgeous draping but almost completely without a face. Probably a priestess of Isis, but she gets
her name from a Renaissance ingenue and femme fatale who at
the age of eighteen won the heart of the older and married King
Alfonso of Aragon when he ritually offered her a bag of gold
pieces called *alfonsini* and she replied coyly that just one Alfon-
sino would be enough for her. In Piazza Venezia, she has a long
history of being dolled up on special holidays in the latest styles
of makeup and millinery, her vast, featureless head beribboned
with onion clusters while strangely matched couples of codgers
and cripples dance parodic obeisance around her. Her labors of
eloquence in the fifteenth century seem to have left her a little
quieter lately, though in times of trial she is known to offer up
unwelcome truths. Pope Gregory XIV, who fell gravely ill after
only a few months in office, tried to forestall the inevitable by
having a vast set of barricades built around his bedroom. Lucrezia's response when the pontiff passed on: "Death can pick
any lock."

•

Pasquino I am, in hardest rock engraved
To others' talk I listen but stay quiet

On Saint Mark's feast, my vow of silence waived,
I'm honored by a celebratory riot.
On that one day, with neither fear nor favor,
Of others' speech the happy fruits I savor
Whether prose or rhyme they choose to utter,
The words are theirs but mine the imprimatur.
—Pasquinade, 1516

•

Pasquino has been a fortune-teller, a social critic, a practitioner of good Latin, an oracle, a sexologist; he has orated with the voice of a god and the body of a castrato, or two bodies in intimate contact. He was a vehicle for cardinals who sent each other coded messages, but in the vernacular he was permitted to speak obscenities to power. It was no coincidence that his neighborhood of Parione was Rome's center for stationers, copyists, and (once Gutenberg's technology traveled south) printers. Pasquino became the very principle of publication. He sent words out into the world that carried all the weight of his authority, and yet once they traveled from the center, they developed a life and authority of their own, shaped and shared by all who spoke or heard them.

Did any of this explain, perversely, why I was having so much trouble writing about him? Instead of producing my own version of publication, all I kept doing—shades of the language lab—was doodle my way toward English-language renderings of pasquinades. I kept thinking of Dante and the five-man Dead Poets' Society (Virgil, Homer, Ovid, Horace, Lucan) that he converses with in Limbo. He talked to the glorious literary dead, while I was listening in on the smart-alecky remarks of some foulmouthed slabs of marble. He wrote an epic for the new ages; I dreamed up smutty rhymes. Again, it entered through my eye and spewed out of my mouth. I'm still so far from the *Apollo*

Belvedere, from all that noble grandeur; this glory won't stay quiet.

•

Tell the artist, once he's sketched the rest of me,
To give me back my testicles—the best of me.

—Pasquino in Latin, 1515

•

More of the Confraternity. Abate Luigi, perched flat against the wall of a church practically within view of my apartment, didn't start life as an abbot. From the look of him—miles of toga but not much personality—he seems a relatively uninspired piece of late Roman carving meant to represent some generic senator. It doesn't help that he is forearmless and that his craggy head is a few sizes too small. He became an abbot by misguided association with a notoriously sarcastic neighborhood churchman who had the misfortune to resemble him. Luigi inherited the talent for satirical social commentary, which was mostly exercised in responding to a cruel destiny of dislocations. He lived on the street, then was briefly protected in the courtyard of the grandiose Palazzo Colonna, then was back on the street, then sequestered in the Palazzo Vidoni, then returned to the street. The public showed its gratitude by continually breaking off his head. Solemn records of decapitations in 1889, 1970, 1984, 1985 (accelerating pattern?); each time the repairs were accompanied by reassurances that the civic authorities had a warehouse full of replacement parts at the ready. One of Luigi's own responses:

> Whoever left my neckline this flat
> Better give me my noggin back stat
> 'Cause the reward for decapitation
> Is urban administration,
> And I'd rather be landfill than that.

•

Babuino, similar case. He looks like Whistler's mother as a balding, bearded monkey wearing BVDs made of moss. Not a monkey to begin with, but some sort of rustic pagan divinity. When
Gregory XIII attached him to a little bathtub fountain in 1576
and placed him on the street to which he ultimately gave his
name, the Romans took one look and demoted him from deity to
baboon. Around the same time, a noble Spanish cardinal—variously described as nearsighted and hard of hearing—evidently
developed a blurry fondness for Babuino, imagining him to be a
saint, possibly Jerome in the wilderness. His Eminence got in the
habit of tipping his hat to the statue; Romans responded by turning Babuino into a bitter simian oracle. This one is no joker.
Terrifying empty stare, eyeless but savage, like Beelzebub in a
gracefully recumbent posture. He is wedged in between a newspaper stand and a flower kiosk, the wall behind him covered
with ominous, not always decipherable, signs and symbols of political rage.

•

No camouflage could hide you, you could dye
your beard or rise up from your reclining posture
or dress up double-breasted—
disguise yourself at will,
you will always be you, Babuino,
object of attention and distraction,
upper-case/lower-case, persona/personage,
symbol visible and invisible, speaking or silenced,
inclined to tragedy or comedy,
creator of words and of silences,
torpor and magic, reflection and incubus,
acceptance and repugnancy, prison and free passageway.
You are fixed rock and swift shudder,

calm sea at sundown and gale force at midnight,
soliloquy and dialogue and whispered secrecy,
Babuino of prohibitions and unforeseeable accesses,
the narrow strait of experiences and the open sea
of an infinite consciousness.

You are nothing but a construct
of earth and of words,
your form has no content but those.
Visible image, on the street
filled with questions
you walk the line,
trampling interrogatives.

> —Elio Filippo Accrocca,
> two poems from *Recliner in Stone*, 1980

•

Not to be forgotten: Pasquino also does time as some kind
of schoolboy dirty joke. Is there a persistent connection between grammar and sex? Is there a double meaning in the
1521 pasquinade that urges more Latin instruction in the passive voice? Also: "Whoever in the city is hot for pretty boys
can't stop longing for Pasquino Day," one poet declared, al-
luding to Virgil—only in the *Aeneid* it has to do with the joy
young men feel if they die in front of their fathers while defend-
ing Troy. Another Latin rhyme, less epic in its field of reference,
suggested a high level of competition in producing the annual
poems:

> Young pupil tries his hand at writing Latin text,
> But when the Muse withholds her stimulus, alas,
> The boy's obliging master, always oversexed,
> Exchanges pasquinades for passes up his ass.

Plagiarism and penetration—though the original is far more specific about the hydraulics. A far cry from the haunting, disembodied hand I keep noticing on Pasquino's sideways torso.

•

Pasquin, those many guises through which you pass,
on top of all the ruins time has wrought,
would make the sculptor say, "Ah me, alas
So much work of chisel all for naught."
O populace dull-witted through and through
Sightless, heedless, ignorant hoi polloi
who cover you in paper, chalk, and glue,
compelled, it seems, your features to destroy.
Farewell that ancient shape so lively, so odd,
perhaps by Phidias or Praxiteles.
Today's forms come from tailors, not from God,
No more statues left but dummies now, and these
assaults by fools each year produce debris
Where Hercules almighty used to be.

—To Pasquino, 1516

•

The author of *Pasquino statua parlante* asks the completely dead-pan question why Pasquino should have chosen Marforio as his best friend. After all, he writes, they lived at opposite ends of the town. Maybe it was that luxurious drapery, which gave Marforio a certain charisma.

I know something about choosing a best friend. I also know about the fantasy of living in a vast space filled with aleatoric and yet intimate conversation. Again and again in *Don Giovanni* the opera gives up on actually plotting encounters among differ-ent characters and just has them magically run into one another. More than divinity or morality or the heroic efforts of those endowed with virtue, what protects the world from lustful predators is, essentially, urban convergence. The Don is about to score with Zerlina—she has gone past *vorrei* and *non vorrei* into *voglio*—when his earlier victim, Donna Anna, materializes. No sooner has she gone through a brief bout of her customary vocal trapeze act and removed herself and Zerlina from the Don's grip, than who should Mozart conjure up in the same space but the other suffering heroine, followed by her tenor protector? Not to worry: they haven't recognized him as the attempted rapist, but the hero's sigh of relief is cut short when, abracadabra, Donna Elvira returns to denounce him as her betrayer. A complexity for four voices. Is he a scoundrel? Is she crazy? Can persons of such noble standing and elegant manners as either one of them possibly be in the wrong? The ambiguities are perfect for an intricate quartet, at the end of which the Don once again escapes scot-free.

Not quite, though. Something in his very voice of reassurance—"Pardon me, most beautiful Donna Anna, if I can serve you, I await you at my home"—tips her off, and the opera arrives at one of its most musically fearful moments, all irrational leaps and diminished chords, when she realizes that Don Giovanni, far from being her chivalric protector, is in fact the monster she needed protection from. Only now can she reveal the details of his nocturnal assault, which left her nearly ravished and her father dead. The opera seems to swing between private spaces where dangerous private passions get enacted, and public spaces where citizens, circling in their elliptical tangled orbits, try for equilibrium. Don Giovanni, radical hero and villain, tries to subvert the whole system when he stages deliberate multiple encounters—dinner parties, essentially—in his own space. But that will be his undoing, and another story.

•   •   •

If you're making history out of archaeology, you end up telling your story backward, pivoting off vestiges in the present toward the retrospect of the past. Or at least you do your time travel in two directions at once. So it was with my inventory of ancient sculptures that were reborn in the fifteenth or reimagined in the twentieth century; so it is with my own traces.

A few months after my arrival in the Piazza dei Satiri, I found myself for the first time deep in the countryside beyond the city limits of Rome. The place is a hilltop in Tuscany, the time late afternoon. I am in the midst of one of the most nearly perfect moments my life has known. I am surrounded by the pentangles of a medieval castle, once clearly a military stronghold designed to command the big valley below, now a vantage point from which the crowded mosaic of the town's roofs in the foreground gives way to an almost infinite landscape of gorgeously tended hillsides beyond. The castle is in mint condition and marvelously navigable: towers and dungeons, keeps and battlements are unguardedly available to the visitor, and there is almost no one else in sight. You can walk the vertiginous ramparts, but you can also sit comfortably among olive trees warmed by the sun as it radiates off high, encompassing walls.

There is some delicious childhood pleasure in circulating within this space. My favorite grade school history lessons were about medieval citadels; and I believe, as I move through these enclosures, that I can actually identify barbican and parapet and machicolation because of my careful attention to homework in the fifth grade. But mere picture-postcard architecture would not likely have produced such a moment as this one. There was something in the air, literally. On a late autumn harvesttime afternoon in central Italy, hue, saturation, brightness—every property of color—is dependably set on maximum. But this day, some climatic inversion, or perhaps even a quite habitual process of

Tuscan sundown rarely glimpsed by foreigners, seemed to erase all the vibrancy of brown and green, the baked panorama of hillsides covered in olive and cypress framed with gold. Instead, chill winds blew a palette of pearl and ash into these guarded enclosures, transforming them into temporary ruins. The sun became invisible, temperature dropped, dark birds started to circle; it was as though there were a whole culture shift—from a scene where being and thinking were wordless and indistinguishable to a scene that provoked enigma and demanded relentless searches for meaning. As though one had traveled instantaneously from Eden to Elsinore.

Then, just as suddenly, the prevailing miserly color scheme brought another recollection—not fifth grade this time, but twelfth—of getting lost, ecstatically, inside the subterranean ruins under some hilltop acropolis in Provence. I was thousands of miles from my family, and for the first time. When, by accident or on purpose, I strayed from the tour group, I experienced one of my first memorable instants of fathomless, contentless introspection—*I am I, I am singular, I am myself*—and I returned to the bus covered in the pallor of limestone dust but blissed out. This time in Italy, though, I was not alone. I was with my best friend—my own version of Montaigne's "I loved him because he was he, because I was I"—and his wife.

When I met David, not so many years earlier, my love life had for some time been more or less a blank. Long, long before, on the same twelfth-grade trip that witnessed my chalky epiphany about selfhood—probably no coincidence there—I had discovered what it meant to fall in love passionately, wanting and wanting to be someone else, simultaneously discovering that in my life such a person was likely to be a boy. Through the years, and over and over again, it had become ever easier to turn these objects of desire—smart, funny, good-looking, and talented in their various and dizzying permutations—into friends. Indeed, to redefine what friendship meant in their lives and mine, so that it remained always dangerously, thrillingly on the brink of something more. But never, or let's say on no more than a couple of intoxicated occasions, had I gone over that brink. I was the Don Giovanni of platonic love.

And, like the Don, I developed a list: "In winter he likes them plump, in summer he likes them slender." When I was young, I looked for older brothers; as I grew mature, I looked for younger brothers. And at the time David entered my life, it was with my students that I would perform the opera. My list was pretty much drawn from my class lists. As Leporello says to Donna Elvira, "Observe, read it with me."

Andy—overbite, acne not yet cleared up, the best student in my seminar—divulging everything he knows about the colorful private life of the other class star, Rick—tall, dark, and brooding, brilliant when he takes the trouble to turn in assignments. Rick, it turned out, had been unsuccessfully chasing Jeremy—long, curly hair, perfect body, a sexy angel, his papers abstruse and incompetently written—declaring him the most beautiful boy he'd ever seen. Or so Jeremy told me: he sat somewhere in the far mists of my lecture course but imposed himself with twice-weekly visits to my office hours, where our teacher-student relation eventually metamorphosed into a perilous friendship, full of philosophical fights, erotic indirection, and belly laughs.

Jeremy was as unavailable to me as he was to Rick. But then, I was also fascinated with Ethan—Jewish male model, long, straight hair that bounced in the breeze as he maneuvered his athletic body with careless energy, assiduous but uninspired at literary criticism—whom I chased obstinately and with intermittent encouragement; his very existence was anchored in sexual tease, both as perpetrator and as victim. Lecturing to this group about Shakespearean comedy, I watched Joanne lust after Ethan, as he lusted—under all sorts of asexual, metaphorical cover stories—after Fred, who in turn wanted a date with Joanne.

This was no way for a man on the brink of middle age to live. Then I met David, who was about halfway closer to my own age. What first struck me, watching him alone and a little awkward at a party, was neither beauty nor brains, but conviction. Every muscle in his five-and-a-half-foot frame, all the brightness in his dark almond eyes, each sinew in his tennis player's trim build, was at the service of a solitary attack on a Rubik's Cube. Forget Yeats; David, who is filled with passionate intensity, is one of the best. He is a man of ferocity, and his fiercest, favorite subject is love. In the few months before he was to move a thousand miles away, the two of us spent long Chicago evenings in fervent discovery: careers, his just beginning, mine faltering; families, mine nearly extinguished, his continuing to grip tightly, while the sweetest topic of all, us, gave me what the rest of my lovelorn existence denied—the knowledge that *we* could be a topic.

A boy I had loved in graduate school had been far too grudging in acknowledging this topic, or even in spending time with me. He wore his watch on the inside of his wrist—some macho allusion to hard labor that he had never performed?—and I grew to recognize the signal that our minutes together were drawing to a close when he would tighten his hand and turn his arm inside out so as to read the time. That sensation, of a fist drilling into my insignificance, is what David delivered me from. How did it happen that the pairing of a straight boy and a gay boy, usually fatal, was as magnetic, as full of the thrills of difference as that more orthodox union of opposites—a man and a woman? Because he was he, because I was I.

Plus one other thing. Through the years that followed—his marriage and children, my changes of job and geography and loves—we have been each other's cheerleaders and scourges; we have confided terrible secrets and engaged in long, searing silences; we have lived at the brink between unconditional love and indefinable desire, where it is possible to say everything one day and then either hopeless or needless to say anything the next. Through it all, the bond that never fails us, the still center where thinking and feeling and longing converge, is food and drink.

We met at a wine tasting—Zinfandels in the dead of a Chicago winter, spicy with untamed blackberry fruit and high alcohol, as though one were indulging in binge drinking and the soothing medicine to cure it at the same time. From there, I lured him to my apartment, where the temperature was so low that a freeze had taken hold among my Mosels: it was now or never to consume these barely thawed explosions of sweet pear and tart apple, and I struggled to find the foods—pork and prunes, smoky cheeses—that would accompany them and make the right impression on him. He replied with a thrilling, ghastly amateur exploit in his own kitchen: duck with canned cherries and homemade bread that, never having been kneaded, never rose.

Soon, however, we were cooking together. One memorable evening his seashore New England heritage united with my cultivated French formation in a mussel bisque. After one sip, David said, "You know, people would pay for this." And thus into our lives, starved for wine spending money, there was born Cuisine Chez Vous, a two-man catering enterprise that had a certain desultory flourishing among our friends. We were good at fresh artichoke lasagne—I discovered I could clean thirty-six of the prickly little cacti while listening to the first three sides of *The Marriage of Figaro*—but terrible at producing a decent cup of coffee. Filtering with paper towels, we learned, doesn't work.

Every milestone in our lives was, or was made, gastronomic. I celebrated his thirtieth birthday with Louis Roederer Cristal and Imogen Cunningham's photograph of a fennel bulb; my fortieth was the occasion for the rarest Trockenbeerenauslese to be found in all of Bernkastel. We consulted on menus for his wedding and on the correct Bordeaux to lay down for children born in 1988 and 1992. We christened new houses in Massachusetts and Connecticut and Michigan and New York with Volnay and Barbaresco and Tokaji Essencia and truffle oil; then we worked together in each of those kitchens, learning how to flip the pop tab of soft-shell crabs or to bone a whole duck without breaking the skin or to make egg whites provide all the lift for a genoise. A crisis of belief in the whole balance among our divergences of age and taste erupted over the differential handling of seafoods in a bouillabaisse; I compounded my error, sometime later, with the faint praise I offered to a sugary, one-note California Merlot that he offered as a banquet's pièce de résistance. Through it all, there remains, timelessly, a picture I once took of David. As he holds out a glass of deep garnet wine—in the background a label dimly legible, 1966 NUITS ST GEORGES LES ST GEORGES— his look toward the photographer is an expression of pure love. Was he thinking of the grapes?

No surprise, then, that it was wine and not just scenery that brought us to the Tuscan hilltop. David and his wife, Adrienne, expecting their first child, were paying me a visit. It was, and wasn't, our first time there together. By whatever mix of motives—better not to know—they had earlier chosen Rome as their honeymoon site. In honor of that occasion, I had produced a specially annotated copy of Georgina Masson's *Companion Guide to Rome*, including a system of marginalia in which the necessity of visiting individual sights was hierarchically signaled as *Must!*, *Must!Must!!*, and *Must!Must!!Must!!!* Both parties reported back a relentless, passionate, codependent compulsion to fulfill all my written mandates, from a mere one *Must!*, like Borromini's little statue in trick perspective at Palazzo Spada, to such crowning three *Must!*s as the fourth-century grape mosaics at Santa Costanza, which almost make you believe that Christian art could have gone pagan if only the Byzantines had been kept out of it. In short, Italy was triangulated among us.

And so, on this October afternoon, we were paying our respects to the birthplace of Tuscany's most acclaimed wine. Picturesque as these environs may be, the castle's real claim to fame is as a vast civic tasting room. We have climbed the mountain at Montalcino so as to sample as many Brunellos as is consistent with being able to find our way back down again. Granted, Brunello is not altogether pilgrimage material. Up in the Piedmont, Barolo was born in the Middle Ages, Chianti is sufficiently ancient so that by 1750 they're already complaining that it isn't as good as it used to be, and even lowly Vernaccia gets serious ink as far back as Dante and Michelangelo. Brunello, on the other hand, was essentially concocted and promoted in the late nineteenth century. And it bears the traces of corporate invention. Most of the world's aristocracy of great wines are a no-pain-no-gain operation, produced by centuries-long struggles against inhospitable conditions. Montalcino, on the other hand, basks in a perfect mix of soil and weather: the grapes attain ideal balanced ripeness just by being born there. The upshot is that Brunello often misses out on the glamorous poetry of man against the elements; it's like your rich, talented, beautiful friend who has never had to work a day in his life.

But maybe this is all just sour grapes. The biggest problem with Brunello is that I can't afford it. Which means that I had little experience with it and that this opportunity needed to be rigorously savored. The 1982s had appeared after several years' dearth of good vintages and were already rumored to be great. So many wineries, so little time. I plunged into a name I knew, and the three of us huddled over the shared glass. Costanti starts slowly, with a few spices—cinnamon, maybe nutmeg—in the nose. Then, when it hits the mouth, it's like cherry trifle with blackberries and orange peel. After that, it goes all tannic, as though your tongue were growing hair, and just when you think that it's gone into vulgar registers of overripe fruit, something happens at the back of your throat, some kind of fitting together into multiple harmonies, and you realize that it is crowned by elegance. Lush, blowsy, heavy-breathing elegance, but elegance nonetheless.

Then David remembers that he liked a Lisini Brunello some years back, so we divide up a glass of it. This one comes as a shock after the Costanti. Adrienne—pregnant, she gets the smallest portion—declares that it stinks. But then this smell, of dirt or dank or mustiness, starts to resolve itself into mushrooms and mint, leather and cedar. It's as though the grape weren't a fruit at all but a sort of wax tablet on which the forest and the barnyard left their impressions. We keep feeding each other lines about how nasty this wine is, but we keep grabbing the glass for more. There is something mesmerizing about its restraint from pleasure, about the way it hits all the bitterness receptors. It seems to be pushing some envelope toward nonfood, inspiring a counter-evolutionary tendency to consume what is bad for us.

That glass having been cleaned dry, the plump, seraphic man doing the pouring, with no other customers around, takes a benevolent, extralinguistic interest in us. Perhaps he senses that the Lisini had pushed us a little over the top. For whatever reason, he takes the initiative and pours us a glass of Caparzo, which turns out to be quite a bit under the top. All smooth and streamlined, fragrant with oak, charmingly full of fresh, ripe red fruits, no bit of tannin that isn't immediately soothed with velvety sweetness, no hint of earth that isn't soon cultivated with violets and gardenias. All right, I think, so the three of us might be rookies, but why patronize us?

There, too, our host may have read our minds or understood our English. He disappears, perhaps into the cellar-dungeon, and after a few minutes he returns not with a bottle or a glass, but rather with three glasses—Adrienne's, cunningly, a half portion—and grandly suggests that this round is on him. Now that each of us is equipped with a private allotment, the experience becomes more intimate, or more reclusive; one could, in short, stick one's nose deep into the drink without trespassing on communal space. Maybe that's what, at first anyway, makes this wine stand out. More likely it is the thing itself. Adrienne, as she sniffs, lets out a long "wow." David starts to babble expletives, some not easily transcribed. I recall the history of great Italian wines I have tasted, back to an ur-high-altitude Nebbiolo (1971, maybe) in front of which, in the language David and I developed for these situations, I had seen God.

We try to talk about this latest Brunello, but words fail. All my first impressions are negations. It is not exactly earthy-dirty, but certainly not scrubbed clean, either. There is fruit, lots and lots of it, but I can't identify whether plums or cherries or blackberries, and it certainly isn't one of those tutti-frutti concoctions of overextended ripeness that signal a too clever winemaker. There is also non-fruit—edgy, fascinating mixtures that aren't quite meat and aren't quite smoke and aren't quite animal hide.

I am under that strangely graying sky when I have my little revelation. It is something about alcohol. All of a sudden I understand what it means, deep inside one's taste buds, that fermentation is natural magic, that Dionysus is a god. There is some ritual sorcery in the relation between the perfume of this wine and the way alcohol becomes the angelic messenger of every-thing that earth and sun and soil have given to the grape. But what is really happening with the Brunello now in our glasses is that the wine first displays and then withholds all these ecstatic constituents. It is in every sense volatile: unstable, explosive, evanescent. All the other Brunellos have offered riches, luxury, joy; only this one seems to travel through the glorious colors of the sunlit mountain and then change its own weather, only this one turns deep inward. In this company, under these constraints, of course I see God in this bottle.

Returning to earth and requesting that the bottle itself be produced, I remain sufficiently in possession of my senses to no-tice that this wine is twice as expensive as any of the others. I have never heard of it. Case Basse, it is called. Low houses, I think, which we are tasting on a high mountain—and from 1982, the year David and I met. Brunello, by ritual and by law, goes through a long series of mandated procedures from the har-vest to the bottling, intervals of ferment and repose, efflores-cence and maturation. If the groundwork is properly laid, it can live almost forever. During this hiatus in the opening weeks of my Roman solitude, I am happy to embrace those same corny metaphors for friendship.

—And his wife.

La moglie. I couldn't have learned the word from *Don Gio-vanni*, since no wife turns up in *Don Giovanni* and the word *wife* occurs only once. On the other hand, for a hapax legomenon she packs a big wallop.

The excitement begins when Leporello and the Don switch costumes. There's no reason, or too many reasons, for this turn in the plot. Giovanni wants to escape Elvira's relentless stalking, or to spice up new conquests with variety, or to have a better chance at chambermaids who are said to be suspicious of men in fancy clothes. No matter why: the fact that the two men spend a notable portion of the evening transformed into each other has always excited me. I enjoy the idea of Don Giovanni being enlisted to kill Don Giovanni. I enjoy Leporello's inept and overblown versions of the great lover: he calls Elvira "beautiful snout," and when she orgasmically exclaims that she is all on fire for him, he replies, "And I'm all ashes." I congratulate myself for noticing, too, that the music gets exchanged along with the costumes. The Don picks up a lowborn operetta habit of rhyming patter, while Leporello goes from his former servile monotone to dizzying aristocratic intervals. And I delight in the complex mini-denouement—war of all against all—when all six of the opera's characters minus the hero try to sort out the confusion of what Leporello did as Leporello, what the Don did as the Don, and what the two of them did as each other.

But it isn't just about plotting and scoring. If master and servant are interchangeable, then I can sing along with anybody. Being Leporello, after all, is not enough. I love the catalogue aria; and the challenge of finding, and doubling, Leporello's bass part in the midst of all Don Giovanni's seductions is even more fun. But I wouldn't exactly say that I "identify" with him. Sure, he's the clever and yet hapless observer who stands halfway between the drama and the audience, but the real excitement is that the opera doesn't really let you separate sidekick from hero. At the end of the first act, Don Giovanni preposterously trots out Leporello as the would-be rapist of Zerlina. At the end of the second act, the hero safely deposited in hell, Leporello concludes the opera with the coolly expressed intention of replacing Don Giovanni. In between they imitate and ventriloquize and parody each other. Masters require servants; servants require masters. Come the revolution, who is who?

Here, it operates by antitheticals. There is a moment of inter-lock when the two men, with each other's costumes in place, be-gin a composite seduction of Elvira. As usual in this opera, it's hard to see but easy to hear. Don Giovanni lends his voice—"My idol, you are the one my soul adores, I'll kill myself if you don't love me"—while Leporello, dressed in the Don's clothes, plays the front man. But instead of mouthing his boss's amorous rheto-ric, he keeps repeating, "I'm laughing, laughing, laughing, laugh-ing." That was the trick: to be the one who makes love and the one who laughs at the same time.

When I first met David, there was no wife, just a lazy trail of unraveled romances. I recall a glamorous working-class girl who had a hole in her heart, a drab girl he bitterly regretted casting aside, an affectionate girl who called him "Babe," which meant that no one could ever call him that again. Never, not even at the height of all the laughter and pleasure that accompanied our mussel-shucking or drinking defrosted wine, not even at those moments when he would say, "If only you were a hot girl . . . ," and his voice would trail off, never did I think I could have David. Was there a chance of full-time employment as his Le-porello? Would he ever become the sidekick to my amours? "Be-cause I was I, because he was he"? No, Montaigne's formula is a little too fixed and settled. Because I was he, because he was I, because both of us could become someone else together.

Don Ottavio, ever pursuing an Anna who is just beyond his reach, appeals to her in a pathetic little downward phrase, "Spouse!" and then instantly downgrades from unresolved domi-nant to secure tonic: "Friend!"

Sposo. Amico. Wife is what causes the trouble in the opera, too. The real climax of the identity swap comes when Don Gio-vanni narrates an offstage experience—one of many, he sug-gests—in the borrowed clothes. He met a lovely young thing on the street, approached her, seized her hand. At first she resisted,

but then, mistaking him for Leporello, she became highly responsive. He took advantage of the confusion—it's exquisitely
unclear what exactly that means—when suddenly she realized
her error. She cried out for help, and he fled over the wall into
the churchyard, where we are now seeing him. Leporello for
once becomes openly critical: "How can you tell me this so casu-
ally?" And he continues with one of the opera's most potent subjunctives:

> *Ma se fosse costei stata mia moglie?*
> And if that one had been my wife?

To which Don Giovanni replies, "Better still!" And he begins to
laugh, and laugh, and laugh.

That's the beginning of the end. It's that laugh which causes
the dead father to reveal himself as a statue in this very graveyard. To the Don's hilarity, the statue responds, in a melody of
terrifying monotone with a bass line of vertiginous references to
the uncanny chords of the overture, "You will have finished
laughing come the dawn." What's so funny? Does Leporello have
a wife or not? With that past subjunctive, who knows? Is it a joke
that Leporello might have a wife? Why is this joke the one that
turns the whole opera from the plains of Spain to the infernal
realm of death? The tables are turned: Who is the lover, who is
the joker, who is the joke on? *Rido, rido, rido, rido, rido, rido, rido.*

Except that we don't go to hell just yet. While the stony
voice from beyond drones on about netherworld and eschatol-
ogy, the Don reveals other plans: he invites the statue to dinner.
And that, you could say, put to rest all my problems of identification. The truth is, there is another character behind all this, the
puppet master of Don Giovanni, of Leporello, indeed of everybody except Mozart. Lorenzo da Ponte—I had devoured his

translated memoirs shortly after acquiring that first record of *Don Giovanni*—was not just Mozart's librettist. He was a coconspirator in Casanova's amorous adventures, a celebrated wag at several central European courts, a brilliant schemer with a continent-wide reputation for trickery and sedition. Before him, Mozart's operas were derivative mixtures of farce and sentimentality; afterward they became witty and profound, erotic and revolutionary. He was a Jew. He lived the final twenty years of his life in New York. He was Don Giovanni and Leporello, lover and joker. He knew how to put words to things that didn't come in words: laughter, desire, Mozart.

Not only that; he knew enough about dinner to go professional in later life. Da Ponte didn't travel first-class to America on the coattails of theatrical triumph; he escaped two steps ahead of the law. And like many Italian immigrants who followed, he eked out a living in the grocery business. He ran a commissary wagon along the Susquehanna River. He went upmarket by creating Venetian brandy in his back room and then aspired to import Parmesan, salami, and olive seeds. Having gained a little status in early-nineteenth-century Manhattan, he introduced spaghetti to America—or so he boasted. And even when he put foodstuffs behind him for the loftier profession of bookseller (on his way to becoming professor!), he couldn't stop himself from comparing Italian literature to candy and wine and pasta.

Of course *Don Giovanni* climaxes in banquets. Long before inviting the statue to dinner, the hero has already stocked up for the first-act gala, where he hopes to detach Zerlina from her peasant companions. "*Cioccolata, caffe, vini, prosciutti!*"—sounds like the precursor to da Ponte's traveling inventory—all confected expertly to dazzle the unwary and addle their senses. "So that from wine, their heads will overheat, let a grand feast be prepared": the Don's orders to Leporello are usually performed as the giddy "champagne aria" (though no such wine is mentioned), but the truth is that he is pursuing a steel-trap gastronomic strategy. No luck, though. The Don's social equals, who crash the party in order to rescue the girl, are less impressed with the menu, and all sweetmeats are forgotten in a rush of vengeance interruptus.

So, at the end of the second act, Giovanni goes to considerably more trouble with his guest from the next world. This time, to be sure, no proles are invited. Pheasant is on the menu, accompanied by a strange, bittersweet, slightly sparkling wine—swanky in Mozart's day but now strictly for a few dowdy tipplers in the Veneto—called Marzemino. The Don is in high form. "Now that I've spent my money, I want to have a good time," he exults, and we have it on Leporello's authority that he is downing the bird in huge bites. In fact, the servant begins the party by stealing nibbles of poultry and commenting on the musical parodies of rival operas. He, of course, doesn't get to sit down; with all this comic business, it takes us a while to notice that in spite of the 2,064 conquests, there is only one place set at this table.

Maybe that's why my autumnal listenings to the opera were so full of clumsy efforts at thinking my own way onstage. From the heights of Montalcino and Case Basse, of the companionship of David and his wife—I suppose I should mention the all-night asthma attack in a Tuscan hotel on the eve of their departure, assuaged only partly by the speed-reading of two helter-skelter David Lodge novels—it was a long way down to Rome and renewed solitary residence in the Piazza dei Satiri as winter approached. Scholarship awaited me there, the week spent on the road having come just when I was on the verge of committing myself to paper, but there was also the brotherhood of da Ponte and Mozart, and of course, there was the continuing daily adventure of planning the perfect dinner. Call it the ghost of the grocer: it was just at this time that my culinary life met a little conversion experience of its own.

A bit of laughing in the graveyard, too, or at least being deflected from the Beyond. In lieu of facing the archive, the note card, or (most terrifying of all) the empty sheet of paper, I decided one late afternoon to explore two contrasting but contiguous Roman burial sites. On the left, the colossal mortuary self-promotion of the first-century tribune Gaius Cestius, who built himself a vast pyramid in the newly fashionable Ptolemy style; on the right, the melancholy beauties of the Protestant Cemetery, where Keats and a host of romantic foreigners in love with the city got interred some millennia later. But I never got there. Indeed, I have never yet visited these wonders of Rome, since any subsequent visits to their neighborhood, and there have been many, could spare no time from celebration at the shrine I first encountered that day.

The store window exhibited herrings in four states of dress; perfectly caparisoned tiny horses carved out of pecorino guarded some great bulbous master cheese whose mold dripped into an oversize parfait glass; scarlet mini-peppers swam in pale, congealing olive oil under the title "Little Buttons of Fire." As the door opened, a pheromonal aroma of freshly dug white truffles—it was their high season—canceled all the miscellaneous odors of the street. Before the portal could shut, I was inside. A seraphic man was the eponymous shopkeeper, whose ekphrastic powers regarding foodstuffs, I soon discovered, were heroic. There were unlimited tastes (from eyes to mouth indeed!), many lire changed hands, time raced or stood still, and one could not count the number of visits or their frequency or the distinctions among them. I heard about one cheese that got deep-sixed under cement for a hundred days and another that let out a cry of pain when it was cut. I tasted pure lard: fatback cured in the marble caves of Carrara, taking on their color and texture. I got to know some nasty-looking wild onion or lily or hyacinth, prepared, as they call it, "in purgatory," to which aphrodisiac powers, unproved by me, are ascribed. I was taught the special way to cut a certain salami—diagonally, in slices exactly the thickness of a peppercorn—whose name mistakenly made me believe it was made from cats. I learned, as I munched on samples of them, how to pronounce *saouseusse* and *Teteun*, the one an innocent-looking pork sausage, the other a densely packed scrapple made of udder.

Not that eating a few outlandish fauna and flora, or hearing stories about them, makes a conversion. Like the old joke— What did the Dalai Lama say to the hot dog vendor? Make me one with everything—I was realizing that cuisine did not have to be what I could cleverly concoct in my kitchen. It could be what I harvested from the great works of anonymous, deathless, immemorial others. Not that it had been a sin to reduce guinea-fowl broth or gift-wrap fennel in dried meat; it's just that I needed to heed those serene, stoic lessons I taught from Shakespeare about mastery, striving, and control. The readiness is all. And, at last, I was ready. Ready for *gavoi* and *ciauscolo* and elixir of *zibibbo*, ready to let the peninsula do its work.

And so it came to pass, some little time after David and his wife returned to the States, that I planned another solitary feast for myself. Solitary but, like Don Giovanni's last meal, not without dialogue. To begin with, I had his meal to accompany mine. The comedy of stolen bits of pheasant and Mozart's self-quotations to disparaging comment from Leporello is abruptly over when Donna Elvira storms into the banquet scene for one last showdown. But all Giovanni can think of is dinner: "*Viva il buon vino!* Let me eat, and if you like, feel free to join me." But she curses his filthy, stinking existence. "What do you want from me?" he asks, and she replies in a quite challenging bit of bel canto, "That you change your life."

In fact, I did make something of a discovery about my apartment and my life that evening, the sort of breakthrough that had been staring me uselessly in the face since my first days in Rome. It concerned the room where I spent most of my time. On one side were the meager cupboards and appliances that qualified as kitchen; opposite it in one direction was the cramped folding table, always covered in books and notes, where I did my work; at a third remove was the long walnut refectory table where I enjoyed my meals. Perhaps it was because my little desk was becoming impossible to navigate, or perhaps because bringing home ready-made delicacies from the *gastronomia* reclaimed time that I had earlier spent cooking. Whatever the reason, that night I crossed the great divide. I undid one of those fundamental binaries that anthropologists place at the heart of primitive existence. I spread out both my work and my meal along the broad, knotty surface of the dining table. In another life—even another of my own lives—this might have been a step backward, a choice against pleasure and a collapse into a heedless labor ethic. At that moment in Satyr Square, however, dinner, the overdue beginnings of *Unearthing the Past*, and Mozart all belonged together.

The meal began with *culatello*—ham of the ass, essentially, but sweeter, less sinewy, the fat more integrated than in prosciutto. As I fanned out three or four slices on a big dinner plate, it seemed only appropriate to set the table as well with a few of my most promising note cards, each containing a story about a piece of ancient sculpture that was somehow heroically, but accidentally, rediscovered around 1500.

Meanwhile, things are getting worse for the Don. Elvira gives up on him, rushes out, and emits a terrible shriek from offstage. The music goes minor and becomes full of chromatics and accidentals. The terrors of the overture return; the trombonists finally get their moment. It seems that the statue is, in fact, coming to dinner. In a rush of tritones—the augmented fourth, irrational midpoint of the octave, *diabolus in musica*—the sculpted Commendatore strides onstage and confronts Giovanni. Still, all they talk about is eating. "Leporello, set another place at the table" (more welcoming than he was with Elvira!). "I've come up to your dinner; now you come down to mine."

Time for something a little spicier. Calabria is the Italian homeland of the hot pepper, among the strangest of whose manifestations is a condiment of infinitesimal fetal sardines, smelts, and mullets bound in a fiery red sauce. Placed atop pasta with a touch of garlic, oil, and parsley, it creates a dish called Spaghetti with the Newborn. I made myself a generous portion, but there was still plenty of room at the table. I could spread out some of the most evocative images from Renaissance archaeology: fragments of colossal hands and feet and heads, but also grand and complete statues barely disinterred in grottoes, as well as monumental papal installations of newly discovered masterpieces staged as though they were the figureheads of ancient Roman triumphs.

All talk of dinner chez Don Giovanni comes to an end when the Commendatore declares,

> *Non si pasce di cibo mortale*
> *Chi si pasce di cibo celeste.*

> No one who is nourished by celestial food
> will find nourishment in mortal food.

And that's when the eerie scale passages, going up half step by half step, begin their terrible accompaniment. If the two men are not to meet at this earthly table, there is only one other dining option. The Commendatore repeats his infernal invitation in muscular octave-long leaps. Don Giovanni, defying cowardice, accepts the statue's ice-cold handshake and embraces his own damnation. Only then does the Commendatore offer another possibility: "Repent. Change your life. It is your final moment."

Where had I heard this before? Why were statues so interested in life change? From Rilke's headless torso to Mozart's undead. *Du mußt dein Leben ändern.* Too late for the Don. He burns in his very vitals, hell being the antitype of lust. And much as he is suffering now, the last thing he hears from the chorus of demons just before he disappears into the blaze that celebrates and annihilates him—the same fire out of which romanticism will be born—is "An evil still worse awaits you there."

If not my life, I could at least change my course. My meal ended with *burrata.* Imagine that fresh mozzarella has been formed like a piñata, wrapped on the outside in leaves of asphodel (speaking of romanticism!) and, on the inside, guarding its treasure of pure cream. As I open the molten, swimming package and garnish it with a few grains of salt and a fine thread of deep green olive oil, all distinction between *cibo celeste* and *cibo mortale* seems to be erased. No need for repentance, no need to cross the room so that I could compartmentalize pleasure and labor. I just took a pencil and a blank sheet and wrote, "The *Apollo Belvedere* reentered the world around 1490 unannounced—at least in any document that comes down to us . . ."

One more life change. The picture I have painted, of eating an elaborate dinner and writing the first page of a book, isn't quite right. Not that it's inaccurate, just that something is missing. By what historical scruple I cannot say, but I have a long-term aversion to drinking alone. I have taken many meals by myself, in houses equipped with enviable cellars, and I have, most of the time, never so much as lifted a corkscrew. And so on that November evening, my fetal fish and posterior ham and my weeping cheese remained unaccompanied. Indeed, had they been partnered—let's say with a young blackberry-scented and subtly effervescent Sangiovese di Romagna—that first page, and for all I know the whole book, might have never been written. Further into my stay in Rome, the scruple against wine consumed in solitude relented its grip somewhat, with the result, now that I think of it, that the big breakthrough of simultaneous dining and working rather fizzled.

But this is about steps forward, not steps back. The Spanish Steps, to be exact. The day after my compositional breakthrough, when I had finished dutifully checking some facts in the Monster Mouth library, found me in that neighborhood—at once elegant, honky-tonk, and blowsy—in a mental condition known universally to be Italian: *dolce far niente*. Sweet doing nothing.

I passed a wine store, rather nondescript on the outside—nothing like the ecstatic sidewalk scene-painting offered by my newly discovered *gastronomia* across town—and it struck a memory chord from a visit nearly a decade earlier when I had wandered through Rome with a much beloved cousin and we had happened on a primitive bottle shop where we were surprised to discover blockbuster Tuscan reds from great sixties vintages. We duly purchased them, drank some in the hotel room, and carried others back home. Their individual tastes, and prices, remained in my head. The corner shop in front of which I stood seemed that it was, and wasn't, the same place. It no longer said VINO OLIO outside—sure sign of a place where you could bring a jug or a crock and have it filled with passable wine or oil respectively—but now proclaimed ENOTECA. Inside, the decor seemed on a threshold between decay and luxury. A vast marble bar, but a cracked mirror behind it. Elegant displays of champagne flutes, but a beggar polishing off a glass of red wine by the stockroom door. A complete disorder of inventory, but some remarkable names on the hazardously perched wooden cases.

A glamorous young woman looked up as I entered, her hair of some painterly color, her smile somewhere between generous and practiced. There was a bit of to-and-fro between her jagged English and my uneven Italian; by tacit consent, it appeared I was the better linguist, and we proceeded to communicate in her language. The shop was largely empty; she seemed bored; we continued a conversation whose long pauses might have been linguistic or erotic or just lethargic. I tried to convey my earlier memories of the place—if it was the place—and by naming so precisely the wines I had bought there years earlier, I suppose I was already brandishing my credentials as a customer who deserved special attention.

We stood by a once grand breakfront with broad walnut doors and thick glass panes, not all of which were still intact. Inside was a careless assortment of recent Brunellos. I pointed to them and said that I had recently been on a trip to Montalcino. Perhaps I thought it would make me sound like a professional colleague from across the sea. But I worked no magic with this gambit; in fact, I couldn't quite tell whether she was really interested in wine at all.

No matter, I went on to drop a few more names: Amarone, Erbaluce, Gattinara, Gavi di Gavi. They had a certain music, yet it was a miscellaneous, naive, dilettantish roster, as I would learn before long. The young woman seemed to become less interested, and she busied herself with what appeared to be useless efforts at organizing bits of chaos around the shop. I smiled and turned toward a precarious arrangement of wines from the swamps of the Maremma. I picked up something affordable and turned to the little register cage, where an elderly gentleman, who would be Dickensian if he were not Italian, was writing numbers in a ledger. I was counting out a few thousand lire when the young woman called out to me from the side of the big walnut cabinet.

"Montalcino?" she said. "Did you try the '82 Brunellos?"

"Yes."

"Which one did you like best?"

I caught sight of the display case in all its faded grandeur. Nothing like the array we had seen atop the mountain, but still I made out several familiar names. Big boisterous Costanti, tough-love Lisini, Caparzo too eager to please: they were easy enough tastes to remember at a few days' distance. Others I recognized, but only from reading their names on labels. Something was missing.

"To speak truth, Signorina," I said, opting for short sentences with verbs all in the indicative mood, "I don't see here my favorite. It was one I had never heard of before. Maybe it doesn't travel this far. It was called Case Basse."

She paused and directed much more attention my way than I had previously merited.

"You know, Signore . . ." Another pause, a dazzling, quite authentic smile. "We have little private tastings here every Wednesday night after the store closes. You perhaps would like to become a member of the group?"

3

THE COMMUNIST
GOURMET CLUB

Too early. Customers—they can't *all* be members of the exclusive tasting group—are milling around Clara's shop, buying bottles or sipping at the counter. I notice with some satisfaction a deeper recess of the room, which is fitted out with a sleek marble table and ranks of brightly polished crystal glasses, far more elegant than anything I had previously noted in the public space. As I re-peruse the Brunello cupboard, Clara emerges and, ever so gracefully, takes up a position by the door, where she begins the double work of speeding the browsers out of the shop and shooing away hoi polloi on the sidewalk, mere street clientele who wish to conduct workaday vinous transactions. So, the glittering sanctum will indeed be reserved for those on the inside.

Yet life on the inside has a distinctly un-Roman look, at first. The group assembles slowly, mingling with the undifferentiated common shoppers and in no haste to take up its place of honor. Earliest to distinguish himself is a burly, grinning frat boy. My suspicions about his nationality are confirmed when he greets the second arrival, an Amazon with flaming red hair who responds in a deep Scots brogue. At once they launch into comparative gossip as between his workplace, the American embassy, and hers, the British.

No sooner have I registered this anomaly than another taster emerges from the deeper back room. No fraternizing with the public for him. "I'd call that the second-best Ontario Beerenauslese of all time, eh, Jeffrey?" he is exclaiming over his shoulder.

A long pause before the entrance of his interlocutor—grayfaced, priestly, dressed in an Ivy League garb some decades out of fashion—who materializes with a decanter in each hand and a Mona Lisa smile on his lips. He could have been thirty-five, he could have been sixty, but nothing in between. About Canadian late harvest Jeffrey says nothing, but he greets the arrivals in an unlocalizable, but distinctly American, English. I will soon learn that this leader of the group is a Jew from Savannah who has lived in Rome for thirty years.

Worst-case scenario: the tasting group is nothing but a bunch of foreigners like me. Best-case scenario (and the truth): I am sharing this lifeboat with Anglo-Saxons at the appointed hour not because Romans have been excluded from the group, but because they are nowhere near as punctual.

Twenty minutes later, synchronized to their own clock, the Italians arrive in a wave. Clara introduces me en masse; names and identities blur. A handsome thirty-something, natty dresser, prematurely bald, embraces the redhead; I am given to understand that they are the group's rainbow couple, the giantess from Glasgow, the gnome from Palermo. Then, separately, two gorgeous, swarthy figures arrive, paired only by their look: a youngish woman all in haute couture black, a man of my own age styled in chic informality and with a sexy five-o'clock shadow. Both sport unnecessary dark glasses; she doffs her shades to reveal piercingly attentive eyes, while his lenses soon clear up on their own, exposing a smile that seems to take possession of the room. I do memory work on the names that are being thrown at me. Ian must be the Canadian, Marian the Scot. But I am undone by the last arriving trio, another kaleidoscope of physical types, who seem to be called Big John, Little John, and (this one in English) Long John.

Assigned seats, almost. A tidy little corner spot is left for me. A primitively xeroxed sheet with a title and six thematically chosen wines is passed around, commented on from varying degrees of expertise.

Heard on one side of me, the Canadian, with theatricalized exasperation: "But why the '83 of that one? The '79, '82, and '85 are *so* much better."

Heard on the other side of me, Little John, with an anxious smile while scanning other faces for approval: "Are these whites or reds?"

The drill was the international one for wine tastings. Masked labels, rules of silence, spit buckets, all sense receptors alerted toward nose, flavor, and finish, a thesaurus of metaphors waiting to be released. I was accustomed to this labile turf, halfway between laboratory and orgy room. Despite admonitions not to speak (and the language we weren't speaking was Italian, which Scots and Dixiecrats suppressed with equally daunting fluency), there were muttered attempts at the parlor trick of identifying each wine from color variation alone.

Jeffrey circled the table repeatedly, pouring doles from a separate decanter into each of our six glasses. Simultaneously, like a man who could definitely walk and chew gum at the same time, he delivered an impromptu lecture in an Italian that was textually perfect but with an accent that made it comically indistinguishable from American English. It was like aphasia, listening to the sounds of my native language but, tortured between poles of vocabulary and pronunciation, understanding only intermittent phrases.

"Calcareous soil . . . cooling the must . . . massive onetime investment . . . autochthonous varietals . . ."

When the several dozens of glasses were filled, it was at last permissible to sniff—but only wine number one. I committed furtive infractions and settled into the pleasure of some familiar olfaction across the board: coffee beans, vanilla, violets, mushrooms. Here at last was the language that those whose company I was now enjoying knew how to speak.

Once each specimen had made the circuit from smelling to swirling to spewing, the conversation that had been forbidden became mandatory. As I sat in cautious silence, I heard a chaos of impressions (perhaps it wasn't such a universal language, after all): bitter, sweet, salt, sour, chocolate, tobacco, green pepper, custard—in short, a nasty diet. Then, after a couple of rounds, I began to see that this was a story about the people as much as about the wine. Everything was dictated by the fact that Jeffrey knew which wine was which and the rest of us didn't. Called upon to judge the qualities of one's latest sip—Was it more like blackberries or more like plums? Were its tannins astringent or velvety? Was it not yet in its prime or, contrariwise, over the hill?—each member of the group exhibited a divided loyalty between the wine itself and the thrill of pleasing the teacher.

Some sought the way to Jeffrey's heart by being able to taste the geography. "No mistaking the place: where Tuscany meets the sea!"

Or the agriculture. "High-density planting, low yield—you can't miss it!"

Or the technology. "Cold maceration, all the way!"

Others tried to capture his benevolence with the plenitude of their emotion: there were wines that made people laugh or cry or get angry or remember their childhood.

Then there were the more intricate responses—call it meta-criticism. "You always know what pleases me, Jeffrey. You tell *me* if this is the one I like best."

As the arc of the evening came around, I could tell that we were players in a drama of several acts. First, exposition: Jeffrey's slightly too schoolmasterish introduction to the evening's theme; next, peripeteia, in which six periods of regulated silence were followed by six anarchic bursts of general discussion, our leader all the while maintaining exquisite deadpan; then climax, when, one by one and in secret ballot, every taster produced a ranking from best to worst; finally, anagnorisis, when decanters were reunited with bottles, and catharsis, when all identities were revealed and each of us was implicitly judged by the wisdom of our choices.

If I stayed a bit on the sidelines that night, it wasn't just the language, it was the wine. How can I convey exactly what it meant to have gained entry to this sanctuary by uttering the magic word "Brunello," only to find the altar profaned with six bottles of Italian Cabernet Sauvignon? Mind you, they weren't stiffing us. These wines were expensive, staggeringly so in some cases. And they weren't badly made or passé, neither unsalable nor flavorless. *Au contraire.* They were just—what other word can I use?—vulgar. To pluck a single grape variety out of what has been for centuries a complex recipe, to move that grape at will across the boundaries of commonwealths, continents, and hemispheres, to choose a grape that struts its stuff with everything vegetal, tannic, and alcoholic: as I looked at this list (aggregate cost equal to a middle-class worker's weekly wage), as I scented eucalyptus where I wished for plums, as I gnawed on leather where I wanted steak, I thought, How foreign this crowd of Italians is, how arriviste their tastes!

On the other hand, I was a foreigner, I had just arrived, and as it turned out, I could benefit from a bit of vulgar. When it was time to vote, I reviewed my choices: Big Blackberry versus Mighty Oak, with a sentimental leaning toward String of Licorice. Then there was that strange last wine, all amber and perfume. It seemed to be constructed of caramel and cedar and potpourri, but a long time ago, in another age. I've been to many tastings; I know that when one wine is radically different, it always gets voted best or worst. This time it captured nearly all the first places, including mine—but with one dissenting voice.

The wine turned out to be from vintage 1968, a year generally as inglorious for wine as it was glorious for the Revolution, and those innocent digits brought one of the participants to a prominence that he never again relinquished. Giorgio, of the chameleon-tinted lenses, had proved himself transgressive at every turn. Some of his moves were diversionary. Instead of wine comparisons, he interjected cross-disciplinary allusions to Marlon Brando or Count Basie or Edward Hopper. And just when I started to notice that his field of reference was exclusively American, I also noticed that each of these gambits was accompanied by a dazzling grin in my direction.

Other moves challenged the management more openly, introducing uncanonical opinions, daring to speak the unspeakable. Already Giorgio was teaching me a lexicon of expressions—"if I may be permitted to say" or "in my most humble opinion"—that seemed servile but were in fact defiant. But the phrase he wielded with greatest elegance was "according to me," so irresistibly absurd in English, where it seems like a case of solipsistic schizophrenia, creating oneself as the guiding authority for oneself.

Now that the group has voted, Giorgio wishes to distance himself drastically. Never mind that we have just been treated to a legendary rarity, that we should consider ourselves blessed by the munificence of Clara and the connoisseurship of Jeffrey.

"*Secondo me*," he began, "this wine is a disgrace to 1968." Whereupon he traveled through Paris and Berkeley, Durkheim and Marcuse, overripe grapes and oxygenated barrels, skipping through fields of reference where I could not follow and ending with something about bad sex.

But the crowd paid little attention to Giorgio's rhetorical climax and started scattering homeward. As Clara unlocked the front door, I remarked that a heavy rain was suddenly falling. Then, all at once, we were outside, the door was shut behind us, and there was no one there but Giorgio. Unfazed by the need to huddle on the threshold, he spoke unhurriedly. Perhaps he was accommodating the limits of my comprehension. Not enough, though: groping through some unfamiliar vocabulary, all I managed to glean was that he had a wife and a five-year-old and that he loved cooking for them. "*E tu?*" he continued without a pause.

I loved the familiar pronoun but wasn't sure whether he was asking about my marital status or my kitchen habits. No matter. I had in readiness an appropriate (and more or less accurate) formula, though I had never before tried it in Italian.

"*Molti anni fa*, I had a girlfriend who taught me to love cooking. Then I started to love cooking more than she did. Then I started to love cooking more than I loved her." I was proud of myself: I had just mastered the difference between *più che* and *più di*.

The rain was abating, but, as though needing to keep dry, he swayed a little closer—I could smell damp tweed and a little bit of cologne—and in the midst of what appeared an academic discourse he spoke one sentence that I fully understood. "This is all that counts in life: *buon vino, buona cucina, buona letteratura, buon sesso.*" And he was gone.

The walk home from the Spanish Steps had become one of

my favorite Roman itineraries, made even more picturesque by the glow of flickering lights on the damp cobblestones. Normally I would spend as little of the route as possible on the unlovely but dependably linear Via del Corso, but I had just learned about its long history as the site of a Roman carnival tradition known as the Horse Race of the Jews. Fortified by the delights of my first evening in real society and by the prospect of spaghetti with eggplant, which I had already prepared against my return, there was a certain pleasurable safety in following the path of those Counter-Reformation unfortunates who had to run naked the whole length of the Corso while the crowd shouted "Christ Killer" at them. Even so, I veered off—it was a quicker route to the Piazza dei Satiri anyway—before reaching the end point of the event at the Capitoline, where the chief rabbi was made to kiss a pig or where, under the more enlightened conditions of later centuries, he merely had to endure a kick in the butt while the senior magistrate shouted, "Go! For this one year we'll tolerate you!"

Which was all I was asking, I suppose. But the evening had raised the stakes; perhaps I could hope for more than toleration. *Buon vino, buona cucina, buon sesso.* Sure, I thought, but why put *buona letteratura* in that company? Making my way past the ponderous parliament buildings and the half-classical, half-Bauhaus portico of the stock exchange, I sifted through my scant recall of Giorgio's monologue, only to realize that the expression he had kept repeating, which I could not modulate into any known piece of Italian vocabulary, was the name Raymond Carver. So "good literature" turned out to be a quite specific reading list. Not a new assignment this time, like de Man or Bukowski, but a body of savagely exquisite short stories that I knew well and could hardly imagine Italians would have heard of, let alone taken to heart. A universe of secretive, eroded, inarticulate souls, it seems, was being promoted in a place where everything appeared joyous, oratorical, extroverted. Only now did bits of Giorgio's vocabulary—*cryptic, uncanny, deracinated*—make sense to me. They weren't about food or wine or sex after all.

But which kind of Carver experience was I living? The stories where groups of people sit around talking but never understanding each other, or the ones where a moment of unrecapturable bliss is glimpsed through a veil of loss, or the ones where an utterly quotidian existence intersects with inexplicable violence? The tasting group, my stay in Rome, the Jewish Kentucky Derby: anything was possible. As I passed the Church of the Magdalen and there rose before me the indelible sight of the Pantheon, with its mind-bending geometries of cube and sphere, I remembered another kind of Carver story, in which all the bitter gloom of ordinary life is annihilated by something transcendent, spectacular, symbolic. Like the one where a mean-spirited narrator, a bigot, suddenly finds himself explaining cathedrals to a blind man while the two of them hold hands, tracing Gothic patterns on a shopping bag. It pleased me, as I climbed my staircase, to fantasize that Giorgio was insinuating one of these experiences, or all of them, onto me. How fortunate that the Sicilian in the market had given me a sprig of wild oregano along with the eggplant: it tasted like something from an unclassifiable world.

Such dinners alone started to become less frequent, however. The first to issue invitations—who would have expected?—were, separately, Giovannone and Giovannino. Both seventyish widowers, they were otherwise polar opposites. Big John insisted on chauffeuring me up to Monteverde (though I was already adept at choosing among the 44, the 75, and the 710 buses for the tortuous climb) in the flashy, high-horsepower Lancia that he managed to pilot into the minuscule Piazza dei Satiri, where, in all my time at the windows there, I never saw a vehicle larger than his. Little John left me instructionless, with a mere scribbled address somewhere in Parioli. Big John had concluded a career selling furniture, and dinner consisted of a progression through one space or another within his sprawling, lugubrious apartment, each room dominated by what I took to be the gaudiest unsold chiffoniers from the recently liquidated business. Little John had sold diamonds; in his house, we never moved from inside a tiny frescoed solarium. The menus, on the other hand, were paradoxical: Big John served tiny morsels of sculpted hors d'oeuvres centering on vol-au-vents and quail eggs. Little John delivered to the table one ungarnished huge roasted pork leg, from which the whole evening was spent chiseling slabs. What the two men had in common, though, was a very small gift for conversation. At this rate, I might never reach intermediate Italian.

Fortunately, I had already made provision for advancement. With a second Wednesday still far off, I returned one afternoon to the wine store, mingling with the ordinary clients but with the excuse of confirming my ongoing invitation. Clara promptly scampered over to greet me, laughed conspiratorially, and started interrogating me. Not about wine, but about Jeffrey. I was an American; I was a professor; I was just like him; I could explain him. The questions flooded out. Was Jeffrey as old as I was? Is it true that he used to be a rabbi? What had he done to get shipped away from university and sent to Rome? Did he grow up on a plantation, like the people in *Gone With the Wind*? It was the trailer, as things developed, for a long-running doppelgänger sitcom, with Jeffrey and me so inter-identified that in some Roman circles our first names became randomly exchangeable, even though we never had trouble telling them apart.

But there was no time for me to betray ignorance or commit indiscretion, since, out of nowhere, the object of our secret conversation appeared, pushing a cart with bottles and glasses. Except Clara didn't treat the talk as secret at all. She giggled—had I realized before this moment that the budding high priestess of my Roman temple was barely more than a teenager? It was she, and not Jeffrey, who needed explaining—and promptly repeated her final question. Geography seemed, fortunately, the least perilous region of inquiry, though it registered clearly enough on Jeffrey's wary countenance. After a pause and, I suppose, with his and my future in the balance, I summoned up the necessary vocabulary to say, "But certainly, Clara, the Goldfarbs lived right next door to Scarlett and Rhett. Go ahead, Jeffrey, say something in Tara."

"Gavi di Gavi," he responded.

Rather than demonstrate mastery of Deep South dialect, Jeffrey was about to undertake the trial of several ambitious efforts at reviving the fame of this once glorious name in Piedmontese white wine. As if I had always belonged there—and as if I weren't being enlisted in some lethal gossip against him—he had brought out tasting glasses for three. Each of us went through the first few wines and spit them out. In the face of an almost overwhelming desire, I was maintaining what I took to be the rule of silence when, sample by sample, adjectives started to fly.

"*Insipido*," said Jeffrey.

"*Pallido*," said Clara.

"*Inerto*," said Jeffrey.

"*Acquoso*," I hazarded.

"*Scialbo*," said Clara. We had gotten past the limits of my vapidity vocabulary.

"*Scipito*."

"*Sfatto*."

"*Sciocco*."

"*Svanito*."

It was like the anti–*Don Giovanni*, a thesaurus of dullness.

There was nothing exactly insipid about my next invitation, nor did it require an interpreter. In the final analysis, I suppose you'd have to classify Long John—pale and monumental, a sculptor who looked like a sculpture, say, the *Dying Gaul* minus Village People mustache—as Drinking Buddy. Big John drove a Lancia; Long John drove the tiniest of Fiats. No surprise that he could navigate my square, but how did he navigate his own body into the car? John's drives were more unpredictable than Giovannone's. He might turn up with the motor running under my window, eager for an impromptu excursion to a raucous drinkfest at a bar so nearby that I'd rather have walked, or alternatively, he'd cancel a long-planned jaunt to a harvesting orgy in Frascati by leaving a note in my mailbox, without even ringing the doorbell. Somehow I never felt offended, partly, I suppose, because John was so devoid of guile or coyness or narcissism, so artlessly generous, so indiscriminatingly attentive, that his presence seemed to neutralize all distress.

More than that, though, was the joyful recollection of my very first escapade in his company. It was early morning on the second Wednesday ("Great Reds from 1979"). I heard the doorbell, scampered down from my sleeping loft, and looked out the window. Two gray masses, one vertical, one horizontal, resolved themselves into the sight of a large person next to a small car. I was about to throw down the tasseled key when John said, "I gotta go to work, but you wanna see some 'ruins' later?"

Even from on high I could hear the gentle provocation of irony in his voice. I had explained my research project when I met him, and he had replied that it was his job as a restorer of antiquities to make sure ruins didn't get any more ruined. If he'd been around a few centuries earlier, he said, I would have had nothing to write about.

"Ruins?" I said. "Anytime."

The time was chosen, and later that day I found myself squeezed into the minute vehicle on the way to Long John's jobsite. The Arch of Constantine, which had been completely covered up throughout my time in Rome, would probably not excite me so much if I were a real ancient-art historian and cared less about backstories. To wit: Constantine, with the Christian God newly enlisted on his side, wanted to sell himself as the culmination of all the best emperors, so he did some subliminal advertising by building his own arch and covering it with bits of art stolen from much earlier monuments to Hadrian and Trajan and Marcus Aurelius. Good for publicity but bad for textbooks that are dedicated to the notion that art comes in discrete periods. Still, for someone interested in the messy ways that objects move through time, how their materials change, and also how eyesight itself changes, the Arch of Constantine—collage, bricolage, hodgepodge—is like a monument to the shiftiness of the past.

And then there's the Raphael connection. A few months before his death, the artist had been appointed as protector of antiquities, and there remains in the archive a report to the pope written by him, or at least in his name. As a document, it's madly unreliable—it cites, just for starters, as supreme authority on ancient architecture an author who was somebody else's typographical error—but it always meant a great deal to me, partly because it's a kind of prose poem about historical loss and partly because whoever wrote it was able to see by looking at the Arch of Constantine the story I was trying to tell almost five hundred years later.

As our car weaves through traffic against oncoming dusk, the remains of the Forum to our right, the shell of Trajan's Market to our left, the broken circle of the Colosseum dead ahead, I have these phrases from 1520 running through my head: "queen of the world so wretchedly ruined as to be almost a corpse . . . famous works burned and destroyed by the brutal rage of men wicked as beasts . . . there remains only the skeleton of those things, the bones of the body without the flesh . . ." I also keep thinking about what the Arch of Constantine, with all its bits and pieces, enabled Raphael to see. He loved the architecture and hated the sculpture. And with that perception—miraculous, given the kind of awe that antiquities held for the men and women of his time—he recognized historical difference. He saw that the past was not a monolith, that there was such a thing as different pasts with different styles; and when I look at Raphael looking at the Arch of Constantine, I see how history enters through the eyes.

John's car possesses miraculous access, it appears, as he drives up and across the cobbled pavement between the Colosseum and the vast plywood box protecting the arch. While bewildered tourists scatter, he extricates himself and ushers me through a door that leads into the dimly lit interior.

"We don't need to bother with the hard hats, but here, throw this on so you don't get your clothes dirty," he says, enveloping me in a baggy smock—I'm feeling classical already—without donning one himself.

"No hard hat?" I ask nervously. Danger had not occurred to me.

"The good stuff is at the top," he says, pointing to a steep, winding staircase whose limits were barely visible—approximately the vertical distance, I judged, of my Satyr Square entranceway, but less substantially constructed. Now, I like to think I'm a man of moral courage, though I'm not sure the proposition has ever been tested; but I know I'm not a man of physical courage. Climbing to me is basically a synonym for falling, and so I've lived a life pretty much without diving into swimming pools, hiking the Rockies, or frescoing ceilings.

No time for reflection, though; John is ahead of me and almost out of sight. I do my best on the narrow stair treads, until I reach a landing faintly illuminated by a couple of work lights. I hear John urging me on to the top while there's still some day-light, but suddenly I see directly above me a perfectly horizontal floating angel. Stern and square-jawed, she (he?) is doing a sort of midair belly flop. Once I get past the amazement of being up against a conga line of two-thousand-year-old military little peo-ple, I'm struck by the rigid, flat uniformity of all the soldiers to-ward whom she is bringing, presumably, victory. I try to imagine this through sixteenth-century eyes: yes, it must have looked blandly medieval, not like magical antiquity at all.

But John is returning toward me. "Forget the Constantine crap. You gotta see Marcus Aurelius." I obediently return to the climb, and suddenly I'm inside another picture. Now there are fewer people, there's space, there's perspective. I see what's left of a couple of horses and a few figures in histrionic postures, their togas in lush folds. I actually lean over a gap in the scaffolding to find myself exactly toe-to-toe, and toga-to-toga, with some head-less Roman orator. But my guide is summoning me aloft once more. "Never mind Hadrian. That stuff really is in ruins down there. Nothing to be done with it."

I can hear him. I can almost see him. But as I try to climb, I come to what appears to be an absolute ceiling. The arch itself, with its wide expanse of dentellated molding, blocks my way. There is no more stairway. Then I notice a tiny space between broken bits of the frieze into which a narrow ladder has been wedged. I'm fifty feet off the ground, and I'm supposed to make the rest of the trip clinging to a few sticks of two-by-four? I'm pretty much frozen at the point of having one foot on the second rung, when John appears above me. At once his broad arms are enmeshed in the folds of my protective garment. Surely he can't pick me up by the canvas, I think. But then, quite suddenly, my feet are climbing, my shoulders are ascending, and John is delivering me to a broad, secure platform.

From here I can see everything: the work lights are in full force, the sky is open, and there's a cranberry sunset behind me. The emperor, in stylish short tunic and surmounted by banners waving in the breeze, is looking down at me from his rostrum. At the back I glimpse a crowd of—what?—barbarians, each with a different physiognomy and in some state of anguish. Exactly in my posture, facing the crowd but with his body turned in reverence toward the ruler, stands a grizzled old soldier, muscular and clad in many layers of articulated armor. I feel as though I have just been admitted to the citizenry of Rome in the glory days. What am I to think about Raphael now? *Sciocchissime*, supremely vapid, he called the reliefs on the arch—like a superlative of Gavi di Gavi. By looking at these sculptures, he succeeded in distancing himself from the past; when I look, I seem to be *joining* the past. He needed to do what he needed to do; I need to do what I need to do. Raphael, again: "On the one hand, this knowledge of so many excellent things has given me the greatest pleasure, on the other hand, the greatest grief." Of course, he didn't have the blessings of a scaffolding and a brawny angel to bring him face-to-face with Marcus Aurelius.

"Funny," says my guide, pointing to an intricately sculpted spot between the leggings of my double, the soldier. "I've been working all week on this guy's long johns."

It was almost time for the weekly tasting. We said little on the way back through the evening rush-hour traffic, but we established a sporadic practice of visiting some imperfect art site on Wednesday afternoons. None of them ever quite equaled the Arch of Constantine, except maybe the trip to Hadrian's villa. "I'm like 007 down there," John said, joking about his legendary powers of entrée. And he possessed full authority, as it turned out, to unleash the imperial rococo waterworks; even an hour later, as we drove up to Clara's for an evening of Jeffrey's 1983 Supertuscans, we were both soaking wet.

It didn't take long for me to hazard my own voice at the tastings. Probably as some sort of penance for my (unspoken) recalcitrance in the face of Italian Cabernet, my maiden effort at extensive speechmaking was dedicated to commending—how could this be happening?—what turned out to be a Chardonnay from Lombardy.

"Rich, ripe, deep, but acidic, Burgundy but not Burgundy," I managed to declare. Soon thereafter, I composed a bumpy little ode to a Tuscan Merlot: "Like celestial fat of animals in Coca-Cola."

Then, looking around the room nervously, I added, *"Secondo me."* Betraying, I suppose, some of my real intentions. If I had diagnosed my fellow tasters as possessing divided loyalties, between judging the wine and pleasing Jeffrey, I was developing my own agendas. Sure, Merlots can taste like soft drinks. But why such specific product placement? Every week, I had been watching Giorgio amid the *anglosassoni*, and every week there had been new fields of American reference. Woody Allen, Mel Tormé, Andy Warhol; could it be that once, I saw him wink at me and say, "Adlai Stevenson"?

But these were such perilous seas of nationalism and desire. Granted, I had my eyes on Giorgio. I wanted in on his list of *buone cose*, and even in the sidebars of conversation during those first weeks, there were tantalizing references to specific experiences with all of them. Was sharing possible? I had come to Italy to be a little bit less of an American. Yet here I was, on some skewed map where the Spanish Steps lay equidistant between the Mississippi River and the Strait of Messina, fumbling with the expression of my own passionate opinions about grapes and the soil where they belong.

The unraveling of these delicate balances began with my

proud little discourse on behalf of the Chardonnay. During the catharsis phase of our ritual, once the wines' identities were revealed, sparks flew, mostly over my head, between our twin leaders. Jeffrey, I noticed, had winced at my speech, but whether it was the content or the grammar, I didn't at first know. Only now was it possible for him to come clean.

"Chardonnay!" he sputtered. "Every hectare they plant with Chardonnay, they pull up Garganega and Malvasia. They stop making the great traditional whites of Lombardy; they stop making Lugano and Moscato and Riesling Italico." He started in on a philology of Lombard grape varieties since medieval times, then segued into a litany of other bastardizing enormities—Syrah in Tuscany, Pinot Noir in Liguria, Zinfandel in Lazio. I lost track.

"Excuse me, Jeffrey," Clara replied with some hesitation, looking around the table for support. "But the 'great traditional whites of Lombardy' are *una porcheria*." She colored ever so slightly at her own liberty of expression, though she had said nothing worse than "pig swill"; she was a very well-brought-up girl. I was just thinking, How perfect: the Georgia boy is all for keeping the Italians Italian, the Roman girl wants to go international, when she turned to me and said, "*E tu?* What do you think about all this?"

I knew what I thought. For all my laboriously expressed enthusiasm about the results of recent experimentation, I was one of those foreign sentimental nativists. I had already become the group's most acute skeptic about product names, the scourge of neologism. The magic of the grape is the magic of place; the whole scheme of wine is the utopia of being rooted on a certain hillside since forever. If you go weak at the knees when you hear words like Chambertin or Montalcino, it's hard to face a hundred-dollar price tag on some confection whose name is a jokey Piedmontese corruption of the French *c'est dommage*. Now I could see that it wasn't just about names, it was about things.

C'est dommage indeed, but was the *nouveau arrivé* going to be lecturing this mongrel assemblage on the virtues of staying put forever in your natal soil? Worse yet, what about my indigenous Roman friend, the hedonist with the radiant smile behind those metamorphic sunshades, the intimate whisper in the rain, and the bottomless treasury of foreign references? Which side was Mr. Barolo–as–Eleanor Roosevelt going to be on?

I didn't have long to wait for my rescue. As I began to blunder through some formulas of "on the one hand . . . on the other hand," Giorgio rose, picked up his chair, and sat down at my side, knee to knee.

"*Povero professore.*" He laughed and put his arm around my shoulder. "Wandering Jew, *ebreo newyorkese*, cultural attaché from the Great Empire in the West who has shipped himself down here to the unruly provinces. It's not for you to settle all our racisms. It's not your job to decide whether we should be quaint or modern, whether it's better to stay with Michelangelo in the sixteenth century or struggle with the twentieth when we can't even deliver the mail." A shocked silence through the room. Well, I thought, he pretty much has me covered.

Almost in the same breath, as the group rose to say its goodbyes, Giorgio smiled broadly, looked at his watch, and said, "You hungry?"

"Almost always," I answered. Hastily throwing his and my overcoat on our respective shoulders as though they were swashbucklers' capes, he pulled me down one street and into another until we were in sight of the majestic cobbled spaces of the Piazza del Popolo. Two famous cafés, both ancient, both trendy—I knew all this vicariously—bookend the twin churches which themselves frame the spaces between the three grand boulevards that fan out from Rome's ancient city gate. But if I had visions of gastronomy as well as companionship, they would be disappointed, at least this time. In fact, we found ourselves at a pizza-by-the-slice stand-up joint. The place gave off fumes hot with burning lard, but as we leaned in the doorway, we could look out at the obelisk and the fountain, and Giorgio wanted to talk.

"You know, before you came to that group," Giorgio began, handing me a slice of potato pizza, a starch-on-starch concoction that was only the first of his autocratic choices for this repast, "it was a dictatorship. No one ever contradicted Jeffrey."

"I don't recall any decisive acts of resistance," I replied cautiously, though hesitant to dispel my aura.

"Ah," said Giorgio. "*L'*understatement *anglosassone.*" It took me a moment to recognize the English inside the Italian. "But, you know," he continued, *"sei il grande trasgressivo."*

"I'm a great transgressor?" Did I have that right?

"Ma certo che sei." Now it was a slice covered in what looked like a slab of Crisco that he put in my hand. I kept looking at his impeccably rippling camel-hair coat, unmarked by the slightest sign of pizza contamination, while a fresh grease spot was already wicking on the front of my parka. For an instant we both stared at my telltale stain, but he laughed and continued. "I've been watching over you these last couple of weeks."

And he proceeded with a complete blueprint of my tasting behaviors. I was the first to realize, he said, that Jeffrey's high-minded ritual of the secret ballot was a farce. After an open discussion of each wine, were the tasters really voting their consciences, or were they trying to get on the winning side?

"Then," he continued, "there is your masterpiece. You figured out that Jeffrey always placed in the number six position—after all, he's not exactly an avant-garde dramatist—the wine he expected to come in first."

"Well, it did dawn on me after a while . . ."

"But then you passed from *theoria* to *praxis*." Another slice, with something dark and burnt, maybe eggplant, maybe lunch meat. "You began to subvert the plan. That's what was so brilliant when you made *il grande elogio* in favor of that dreadful *pisciacqua* Chardonnay."

I thought it better not to protest.

"And of course, you really got him when we did the Burgundies. You, after all, are a citizen of the world, not like us provincials. You know how to taste French wine." The truth is that I did see behind Jeffrey's habits here. Of course, he had placed Olympian Romanée Conti in the climactic spot, but I had hammered home the peppers and plums of the penultimate candidate—Richebourg, as it turned out—until my colleagues were beaten into submission.

"You know, Giorgio, when I tasted them afterward, I kind of thought the Grands Echézeaux was better than either one of them."

He threw up his hands, as though this last move on my part confirmed everything. "You are the great Oedipus of the back door." That was the way I translated in my head, anyway. "I sense *un grande feeling* between us." He was leaving in the direction of his bus, Colosseum-ward, and I was walking homeward in the opposite, Pantheon, direction. *Un feeling.* More vocabulary to learn.

Our meetings became more frequent, though not always so auspicious as pizza night. A somewhat malign destiny, at first anyway, attended upon efforts to be entertained at each other's homes. One afternoon, a few weeks into the season of Jeffrey's tastings, somewhere between "Great Reds of the South" and "Spumante Foreign and Domestic," I was in my apartment looking at images by Maerten van Heemskerck, a Dutch painter who spent part of the 1530s in Rome and my all-time favorite sketcher of antiquities in the Renaissance. Foreign artists who did this kind of work—and strangely, they were almost always foreign—often wanted to make the fragments look good, so they "finished" them, adding the necessary arms or legs or noses to what were, after all, highly segmented pieces of art. Not Heemskerck: he delighted in ruin and often intensified it, played games with it. A Venus is shown in three profiles so we can see just how many parts are missing; a dog is extracted from one relief carving, becomes "real," and is pointing at another (broken) relief carving as though it were his quarry; a sculpted sandal is displayed in a foreground so that it is just as big as the gigantic Portico of Octavia that sits vividly behind it. Is this the triumph of perspective, or its parody? I was planning to pursue this question by walking the few blocks over to the Portico and the Theater of Marcellus that lay behind it. Of course, that sandal wouldn't be there any longer, but I wanted to imagine the vantage point where Heemskerck stood, to see through his eyes. As usual, part scholarship, part necromancy.

But the phone rang—still a somewhat unusual event in my house—and it was Giorgio saying that *potrebbe essere possibile* that I come to his house for dinner that very evening. The conditional was easier for me than the subjunctive, and more promising, I thought. Conveniently, the route to the Giorgio bus lay directly past the Theater of Marcellus, and so, with xeroxes in hand, I set off with two pleasures in anticipation. The sandal and the portico were the first disappointment. I did not have the same freedom of access, what with high-speed-bus routes and iron gates, that Heemskerck had. But even when I could approach the kinds of hilly and tortuous vistas that were in his sight lines, no reality could compare with Heemskerck's vision.

Leaving the scene, what I saw through my own eyes was Giorgio, looming incommensurately large across the landscape of ruins—not at home, where I was supposed to find him, but at the bus stop where I was going to begin my journey. He was wearing a completely new sort of stylish outfit, vaguely country, involving tattersalls and plaids. As I approached, he sent out signs of distress or embarrassment visible from afar.

"*Scusami, scusami.* Something came up, very complicated. So I decided to come here and wait for you. Sabina . . . Giulia . . . we'll talk about it later," he said. That expression—*ne parleremo dopo*—was to become almost a mantra of evasions and missed opportunities; on subsequent occasions I often heard him use it with his five-year-old daughter. "But not to worry. We'll have a *dolce* together," with which he pulled me off to a café that featured enormous custard-filled pastries.

Now, I didn't like being done out of my dinner, and I didn't want, or want to be, a cream puff. But I was far from being able to negotiate the difference between my disappointment about dinner and my distaste for big, sloppy sweet things. While Giorgio was concocting long sentences about his evening's contingencies and other plans we might, conditionally, make for an upcoming rendezvous, I was unleashing my refusal to eat a pastry in terms that were, doubtless, out of all proportion to the matter at hand. He stopped, held me at arm's length, looked into my face, paused, and read the scene.

"You don't like sweets. You know what your trouble is? Not enough mother love." He was dead serious, doctorly, but also indulgently affectionate.

"Or too much," I replied.

"*Ne parleremo dopo.*" He shrugged and let go of me.

At my house, the first time, all we managed was the opposite end of the meal. A Thursday afternoon, a spontaneous phone call: he is in my neighborhood with a bottle of wine, we will taste it together, and *magari*, I'll make a little snack to go with it. Two necessary pieces of interlinear. First, Thursday afternoon was for me the nexus of all the unfathomable mysteries governing the Roman shopping schedule. Stores were shut down for about three hours in the middle of every day; they were also closed either Monday morning or Thursday afternoon, except in the warmer months, when Saturday afternoon might be substituted for or added to the other closures. Food stores, however, had different schedules, in regard to both the hours and the days of operation; outdoor markets were open only in the morning; Sunday, *nothing* was open. Second, the meaning of *magari*, whose presence in conversation was almost as unpredictable as shop closure. It could be something quite innocent, like "maybe even" or "perhaps also"; on the other hand, its etymological origins lay in the mysterious wills of divinities such as the *magi*. More to the point, used all by itself in response to a hypothetical assertion, it could mean either "If only . . . ," in a tone of fervent hopefulness, or, in the negative, something more like "Yeah, right!" Giorgio seemed to fit somewhere in those wide-open optative spaces.

Now, at any rate, I needed to determine whether I could shop for food, so that I might *possibly even, perhaps as well* produce an irresistible munchie. No time to climb down the stairs and find stores closed; better to raid the pantry, such as it was. An *insalata caprese* was in prospect for the evening: while it was far too much of a cliché to propose in my maiden voyage with Giorgio's taste buds, some of its modules might be disassembled. I also had some leftover roasted eggplant slices and a few little half-red, half-green tomatoes that were uncannily lush and acidic at once. Yes, something could be managed.

The greeting was warm and tactile, the Gewurztraminer from the German-speaking border territory was a suitably exotic mix of crisp and tropical, and for the first time, Giorgio offered bits of autobiography. He was a philosopher, but not at the university.

"People like you in Italy, university professors," he said, "are *orrori*." He shuddered in onomatopoeic horror through all those trilled r's. When I asked what kind of philosophy he practiced and where, he free-associated away from any specific responsibilities and narrated a long involvement with psychoanalysis.

"You know, Otto Rank . . . Erich Fromm . . . Wittgenstein . . ."

The high-level name-dropping was not comfortable territory for either one of us, and I sensed it deteriorating as each citation was made. On the one hand, I felt inadequate to this roster of eminences; on the other, I was wondering what this man could possibly do for a living that would leave him so free to wander around Rome on a Thursday afternoon with an open bottle of wine. I brought out the snack. A platter with a perfect foursquare of toast points, each rubbed with a little olive oil and garlic, each with a layer of roasted eggplant, a fine dice of tomatoes carefully deseeded, a thin slice of buffalo mozzarella that had been passed briefly under the broiler, and finally a latticework grid of freshly chiffonaded basil, the small-leaf kind. It produced a gratifying expression of awe.

"Che bontà," he said. What generosity. Taking note of the ingredients, he went on to give me good marks for originality within a familiar theme, for both surprise and aptness of interrelated flavors. A ruminative pause, full of promise, while we tasted food and wine together. A pleasurable murmur, a swallow, the dabbing of a napkin. Then a sharp turn in my direction, accompanied by an obliging smile.

"But, excuse me. Basilico! It's out of season." He hunched his broad frame over the platter and proceeded to pluck the garnish off all fourteen remaining crostini. I began to think of Giorgio as a gastronomic Carver character, capable of obsessive concentration and sudden acts of violence.

A very different scene played out a few days later, when I was invited spontaneously to Giulia's sixth birthday party, for which the family had commandeered a picturesque tiny valley on the

Celian Hill. With cypresses swaying in the breeze under a starkly changing sky, the intermittently visible broken arches of the Colosseum, and a dozen kids costumed fantastically in yardages of muslin, it looked like a slightly lurid pagan festival of babies, with one jovial presiding deity. No cuisine to speak of, just plat-ters of multicolored jelly rolls that went under the name *merenda*. Both the object and the name—uncomfortably close to *merda*—kept me, once again, off sweets.

But I wasn't permitted to be more generally aloof. "Come with me," Giorgio said, opening a small trunk filled with swatches of brightly colored fabric. He wrapped a piece of purple brocade around his shoulders and threw a long stretch of green velour on me. "*Vieni, vieni,*" he said, running toward the two ta-bles where the kids were picking at the *merenda*. I held back, hes-itating to embark on some unscripted ritual. Perhaps Giorgio could read childhood memories on my face, or perhaps it was merely impulse that made him turn back toward me, readjust my ponderous stole, and say very quietly, "*Devi lasciarti andare.*" He repeated it louder. "*Devi lasciarti andare.*" You have to let yourself go.

Little Giulia can't have heard, and still less understood, this admonition, but at that moment she detached herself from her fellow revelers, ran over in our direction, looked me in the eyes, and said, "*Zio Leo, devi giocare con noi!*" She knew my name, I had become her honorary uncle, she called me *tu*: no resisting all that. Now when Giorgio tugged, I came along. And the game, it seemed, was that each of us adults, metamorphosed by the im-promptu costumes, would run under the tables that contained the food, precipitating a gleeful hysteria of fear, in which all par-ticipants would shriek—I heard the phrase screamed enough times so that I could finally parse it—"*Lo gnomo della festa! Lo gnomo della festa!*"

Since no anthropology for this figure was ever provided, I am not sure if the "gnome of the party" was to be Apollo or Dionysus, boogeyman or messiah. It was clear, though, that the under-the-table performance, especially if I added extra huffing and puffing, produced triumphant excitement, with bits of cake flying everywhere, no matter how many times we tried it. Nor was the excitement limited to the six-year-olds. Just before our first emergence from hiding, there was a split second when Giorgio and I were nose to nose, lips to lips, where no one could see us. I recalled one hallucinatory evening a decade earlier, when a much desired, ever unattainable friend, at the end of a dinner party and with his wife noisily loading the dishwasher in the next room, had maneuvered his soft Italian loafer into just the right place between my legs. The whole performance—and he stared expressionlessly into my eyes until it was over—was, as now, concealed by a heavily laden dining table.

No such outcome this time, though. Giorgio, after provoking one last sequence of howls, wearied of the game. As he defrocked me and quite carefully folded up our garments (for next year's gnome?), he took in the whole landscape of children and gave me the day's final piece of earnest advice: *"Devi fare un figlio."*

You have to let yourself go. You have to play with us. You have to make a baby.

It was getting dark; the party was breaking up; I started walking down the hill. Giorgio shouted, *"Baci, bacioni!"*—kisses, big kisses—and soon ran after me to administer them directly and in plain sight. From that day, with whatever jagged logic, Giorgio was some part of my life. Cooking for each other, eating in each other's houses, if not regularly scheduled, were at least patterned. Sometimes our harmonies were deft. I impressed him by inventing an artichoke dish (it was by now early spring and the artichokes safely in season) that played on the *carciofi alla romana*

that I had concocted for my tête-à-tête with Gabriele, but now I
was prepared to improvise. I used shallots and spearmint instead
of garlic and parsley, and after the artichokes were cooked, I set
them stems-up on plates and placed in the cavity, so that it appeared as a surprise when you cut the artichoke, a little prize
scoop of salmon caviar. Giorgio was then inspired to create another new artichoke dish—raw slices of artichoke heart with tiny
fresh shrimp, almost raw, seviche style.

More often, the counterpoint had a large share of dissonance.
A grandly planned meal at his house was quite suddenly, and on
vague grounds—*ne parleremo dopo*—transferred to my house, and
three children were added to the guest list. His sublime veal
broth with tiny meatballs wasn't perhaps perfectly in tune with
my warm salad of duck and sweetbreads; his perfect, light-as-air
gnocchi were a shade underserved by the garnish of a smoked
salmon whose deficiencies were less evident to an Italian than to
someone who had been reared on an all-lox diet.

None of this would ever have come into discussion were it
not that Giorgio eventually entered a phase where, for didactic
purposes, he desired instant postmortems on the quality of the
meals. He found it easy to criticize; I found it impossible. The
best I could do was offer occasional lukewarm reviews of wines
he chose, which seemed safe since he hadn't, after all, *made* the
wine; but that distinction flew beneath his philosophical radar.
For his part, having delivered some broadside, after the obligatory *secondo me*, about my mushroom lasagne—what was I thinking of when I stripped the prosciutto of its fat and when I used
Parmesan on every layer instead of just the top?—he would then
treat me to a barrage of apologetic phone calls over the next
forty-eight hours, assuring me that he loved the lasagne, that
Sabina loved the lasagne, that Giulia took a doggie bag of
lasagne to school the next day, where it was hailed by students
and teachers alike.

Even when there was no need for damage control, the post-mortem phone call became Giorgio's signature gesture, and an irresistible one. After we left each other's houses or parted at a restaurant, there was always something he had to assess, footnote, provoke, or confirm. And these were the occasions when his language was most passionate but also, to the still intermediate student of Italian, most demanding. Who cared? He was thinking about me after I left him. Yet how exactly was I to understand *bellissimo* and *carissimo* and *amore mio* when applied to me? What level of metaphor was involved, especially on the phone, when he said, "I give you the strongest embrace"? Not to mention the phone call after one of Jeffrey's tastings—"Surprising Whites of Calabria"—at which I was teased into exceptional quantities of pontification and was, perhaps, unusually inattentive to Giorgio.

"*Sento una piccola crisi nella nostra storia.*" I feel a little crisis in our *storia*.

"*La nostra storia?*" I replied. So we had a history? A story? Something else?

"Come now, you're not going to deny that we're having a kind of *storia*."

Were we? *Magari*.

But I am telling the story without its pivotal personage. The first time I entered Giorgio and Sabina's home, besides the aroma of a stockpot with several kilos of shallots slow cooking, I was struck by what was even for Rome an exceptionally golden light. Windows, half covered with multiple layers of antique sheer curtains, gave out on courtyards facing mulberry-colored tenements, and the light from dim reading lamps never quite penetrated to the tall ceilings, leaving the many bookshelves and artifacts in jagged shadow: it was an atmosphere apart, painterly.

And not just any painter, but one who had been dominating my domestic space. The apartment in the Piazza dei Satiri, in addition to being a shrine for Charles Bukowski and Paul de Man, lodged a third household god. Everywhere I turned within its tight spaces, books, pamphlets, and postcards advertised Modigliani. Whether this domestic trinity was of a piece or not—whether, in other words, I was to construe the painter as a revolutionary socialist cosmopolite or, as I had previously thought, as the apostle of hard-partying Modernism Lite—I could never quite decide. Such taxonomies are in any event futile, and there was something in the daily contact I had with those portraits, something about the burnished color schemes, the faces that seemed simultaneously Mediterranean and Polynesian, the eros that was both estranged and mystical, that soon bypassed the critical faculty to reach an embarrassing spot where I was perilously close to getting in touch with my imaginary Italian-Jewish soul.

Now that I was making my first crossing of Giorgio's threshold, I turned a corner just as Sabina was rising from a threadbare maroon settee, and I believed I was in the presence of Modigliani's Zborowska. The almond skin in a frame of jet black, the filigreed features placed almost aslant on the grandly serene field of her face, the watchfulness. What really struck me, though, was that Sabina and Zborowska, though individually odd-looking, quirky, even plain, made each other beautiful in mutual reflection. In time, scholar that I am, I did a little research on this doubling of identity, and I started to notice that all the Modigliani subjects whom he defined as *wives* shared something of Sabina, and indeed, the likeness of Jacques and Berthe Lipchitz, their jaunty faces aslant as their bodies barely nestle together, could pretty much serve as a family portrait in this apartment.

A Modigliani wife? It probably doesn't bear thinking on, especially given the suicide of the painter's companion on the day after his death. No: that's quite the wrong note to strike. Sabina was no mere silent follower; no chance that she would throw herself on Giorgio's funeral pyre. When I think of her inside my life with Giorgio, it's always one particular often repeated speech act that comes to mind. For example: One day Giorgio turns up completely unexpected in the Piazza dei Satiri. Both he and Sabina are due for dinner at my house the next evening. To-night, I am hoping to work on a little foreword I've been asked to write for a book on Renaissance sex—but this is another story—and more to the point, I plan on completing the *pâté en croûte* that will wow them both on the following day. Right at the moment, duck bones and forcemeat and flour are strewn over half my house; I don't want any visitors. And there is Giorgio ringing my bell and waiting for me to throw down the key.

Instead of complying, I take the unprecedented step of coming down the stairs myself. As I descend, I wonder, had there been a misunderstanding about the day of the event? I recall a little dispute about schedule, and I wonder if this was Giorgio's way of resolving it in his favor. By the time I get there, Sabina has joined him, and I can tell from the embarrassment on her face that there has been no mistake, that Giorgio has simply elected to be spontaneous.

"You're not inviting us inside?" he says with a big laugh. "Yes, it was supposed to be tomorrow, but something came up—*ne parleremo dopo*—so here we are. If you can't make us dinner, *va bene*, let's go and have coffee in a bar."

My mouth was probably open. There was a long moment of silence. Sabina took charge.

"Perhaps Leo was thinking that he wanted this evening to himself," she said quite simply.

And that became the formula: *perhaps Leo was thinking . . .*

On this occasion, there was a negotiated peace. No spontaneous coffee, but dinner postponed until the day after tomorrow; the pâté would only improve. Other situations were more complex. The three of us were dining in a restaurant, and Giorgio, sitting between us, spent thirty consecutive minutes, his body turned away from both of us while he flirted with a teenage waitress; as a result, no other conversations were possible. Sabina: "Perhaps Leo was thinking that it's time to tell us about his trip to New York." Or a weird sudden argument over yet another dinner about the literary merits of *Gone With the Wind*, which Giorgio extravagantly praised, and when I neither contradicted nor concurred, I provoked a lecture about aesthetic snobbism. I continued silent. Sabina: "Perhaps Leo was thinking that other novels are better."

The truth is that I needed Sabina around quite a lot to tell Giorgio, and me, what I was thinking. One day he took me for a long walk on the Esquiline Hill, shuttling in the parkland spaces between Michelangelo's *Moses*, ostentatiously on display in the church of San Pietro in Vincoli, and the remains of Nero's great palace, the Golden House, long buried beneath the soil.

"It will be a little program for you," he began as we climbed the church steps and caught sight of the statue's massive head. "The prophet of your people, then the subterranean secret life of the empire. You and Freud both. You find yourself somewhere between the two, no?"

Before I had a chance to decide whether these reflections contained more, or less, than met the eye, he sprawled us out on a bench in view of an opening, now enshrined in pseudo-classical brick, from which Renaissance artists had lowered themselves on ropes to catch their first sight of ancient painting, deep in the bowels of Nero's palace. Then, leaving my underground for his, he began a long narrative about a dalliance he had had with a nineteen-year-old girl, whom he had pleasured, he said, with no diminution on account of his greater age. Perhaps Leo was thinking . . . Why am I having to listen to this? Perhaps Leo was thinking . . . Am I supposed to take this as an invitation? Perhaps Leo was thinking . . . Can Giorgio tell the difference between reality and fantasy, between story and history?

The subject soon changed, however. "I've organized a *dopo cena* tonight at my house. It's time you met other intellectuals. *Secondo me*, the crowd at Clara's is just riffraff. *Andiamo.*"

"An after-dinner party? But I haven't had dinner yet." He laughed but was already leading me toward the bus. "And what do you mean, 'riffraff'? Silvia is a great photographer, no? And Vito is a brilliant journalist. Mi *piace* Silvia. Mi *piace* Vito."

"*Ti piace?*" He burst out laughing. "Both of them?" The laugh became a little cynical. "You're not going a little *bisessuale* now, are you?" By this time we were on the bus, where conversation needed to be more guarded. A glitch in my elementary Italian training. If something—say, *il vino* or *la città—mi piace*, it means "it pleases me" or "I like it." Apparently, it wasn't the same if Vito or Silvia *mi piace*.

The *dopo cena* was either exquisitely stage-managed or else subject to remarkably happy accident. For most of the evening and across the whole room there seemed to be only three topics of conversation: gay people, Jews, and Americans. In the first category I was not alone, though I felt no special bond with the pair of middle-aged men holding hands whose fingernails were dyed the identical shade of aqua. As for the other predicates, strictly third-person testimony was on offer—rapturously positive, to be sure. I had entered a time and space (so hard to foresee in the days of Vietnam, so hard to reconstruct in the days of Iraq) in which clever, engaged, liberal Italians found themselves drawn to certain glamorous minorities and equally mesmerized by American culture. And somehow their own mythic histories of political transgression could be seamlessly folded in. For a brief historical moment, I had it all. But there was so much smoke that evening, and so much posturing, the social analysis was so simple, its data so thoroughly furnished by MGM and Motown, that I seemed to have little choice but to withdraw from the universal gaze just when I might have provided a less mediated vision for all my charming new acquaintances.

All the same, I chose—or was constrained—to say nothing. I was learning, at this first outing amid the intelligentsia, that their parties never reached a conclusion, that there was no consensual hour of terminus, no Cinderella carriage at midnight, no combination of signals, whether among guests or hosts, to convey unmistakably that it was time to go home. I could, of course, have acted unilaterally, but both the tact and the logistics of such a move were problematic. Just as well, it turned out, because as breakfast loomed ever closer, there appeared out of the night a fresh, chubby-faced, giggly, beneficent art historian called Cecilia, who redeemed the evening for me. Quite unlike the other guests, she offered hardly any declarative statements; she observed, and she asked questions.

"You just got here a few months ago?" she asked, confirming what I had explained in response to her questions about my research work. "But you've been here before, no?"

"Yes . . ." I was about to recount my years of faithful tourism in Rome.

"Because you've obviously known Giorgio and Sabina for years." Her gaze followed the row of our three faces and then back again.

I laughed and started to speak.

"Certainly, he has," Giorgio interposed. "We first met twelve years ago. I was leaving my apartment, and Leo happened to be coming down the street looking at everything, just like a tourist. He stopped me and asked me to recommend a place to eat, since he was new in town. I suggested . . ." He named the trattoria where, independent of any connection to him, I had been a regular patron since I first visited Rome twelve years earlier. "The next day he rang my doorbell, saying, 'Excuse me, you may not remember me, but I'm the American you sent to the Grappolo d'Oro, and I just wanted to thank you in person. It was great.' And we've been *affezionati* ever since."

Now it was my turn to stare at face after face. Shrewd observer though she may have been, Cecilia wasn't quick enough to pick up the flaws in the story—for instance, Georgio lives in a big building with a lot of doorbells. You can't blame her, though. The delivery was as sincere as it was spontaneous. And in this instance at least, in contradistinction to so many other occasions of his fabulation—ranging from excuses for missed appointments to whole paragraphs of opprobrium that had supposedly been heaped on me by Jeffrey or Silvia or Giovannino—I was more than willing to grant Giorgio the privilege to a truth that was higher than lies.

Still, the evening wasn't quite over. Cecilia gave me a ride home, I bade her goodnight and trudged up the many stairs, and as I opened the door, the phone began to ring. Not a surprise.

"Leo." Giorgio began without preliminaries. "Excuse all the politics tonight. I know you were bored." I started to protest. "It doesn't matter. I had to telephone you. You were so cute all evening. *Ti voglio bene.* Sweet dreams." He hung up.

I want you well? Dawn was breaking over the Piazza dei Satiri, and I was reaching my linguistic breaking point. Before leaving the States, I had been given a joke present, a little lexicon called *When in Rome: 101 Ways to Say I Love You to Italians.* It was now or never to avail myself of this research tool. I went through the book, noting every useful expression that might decode my so very undefinable life. It started satisfactorily enough:

affezionarsi con qualcuno: to be attached to someone

c'è un **feeling** tra di noi: there is a certain attraction between us

piacere a qualcuno; mi **piaci**: to be sexually attractive to someone; I find you sexually attractive

Well and good. Now, an encouraging discovery:

una **storia**: a love affair

And, on the other hand, a maddening one:

ti **voglio bene**: I love you (in a Platonic or romantic way)

There was only so much a dictionary could do for me. But that had always been clear.

The dictionary work might serve as a multitasking exercise if I decided to write that foreword about Renaissance sex. What better way to ambush readers of such a book than to give them, in the very opening pages, not the thing itself, but the *words* for the thing? How did the Renaissance say *love* or, for that matter, *fuck*? Clever, unexpected, instructional. Or possibly, disappointing, smart-ass, and all too familiar a move in my own life and work.

Better to travel in the opposite direction, away from words and toward pictures. They were about as close to the real thing as I could get. And that meant revisiting the Villa Farnesina. Lots of things could be said about Agostino Chigi's exquisite little pleasure palace along the Tiber: Raphael, Amor, Psyche, frescoes; open to the public for free every morning and completely empty of tourists. But my interest was concentrated on one spot within a vast loggia covered in narrative painting. Vasari, writing in 1550, tipped me off:

> Above the figure of a Mercury who is flying, the artist made to represent Priapus, a gourd entwined in bind-weed, which has for testicles two eggplants, and near the flower of the gourd he depicted a cluster of large purple figs, within one of which, over-ripe and bursting open, the point of the gourd with the flower is entering.

Is Vasari disturbed by these X-rated vegetables? Not in the least: "The conceit is rendered with such grace, that no one could imagine anything better. *Ma che più?*" Why say more?

I did want to say more. Why—in the middle of painting a story about Love and the Soul, Cupid and Psyche, where desire drags its poor spiritual victim through hell to heaven—why insert the most beautiful dirty picture ever painted? Why should the left hand of Mercury—always the pointer god—be gesturing to the gorgeous and alarming spot where a rigid, helmet-headed squash invades the much smaller space of the fig while a little milk-white flower issues out from below? Not an easy question to answer; all I could do was go and see for myself.

The first thing you realize when you get there is that you're standing in a dining room. Chigi was famous for his feasts, notably a celebration for Pope Leo X at the beginning of the sixteenth century in which the magnificent gold and silver vessels were thrown into the Tiber at the conclusion of each course—a grand gesture mitigated by the fact that nets had been placed in the water in order that divers-in-waiting might retrieve the valuables. On the walls of the room, Psyche moves from the torments of desire in hell through all her trials until she is sufficiently purified so as to take up permanent residence among the Olympian heavenly bodies. At that point she qualifies to be on the ceiling, where the artist depicts the soul's paradise in the best terms the Renaissance knew for ecstatic perfection: dinner. Immortality is bestowed on Psyche as she drinks the cup of nectar; with that sip, she fully enters upon her divine status at the celestial feast.

Then you realize that everywhere you turn in this giant complex, the walls are completely covered in food—and not just smutty food—every scene festooned with the tastiest possible produce. Venus looks down from Olympus inside a surround of apples and carrots. When Psyche triumphantly floats to heaven, her feet are framed by ears of corn and a pair of spiky cucumbers. The muscular kiss that Jupiter plants so mesmerizingly straight on the lips of Cupid plays itself out amid pumpkins and pears and a leeringly open pomegranate.

I don't know whether dinner is the sublimation of sex or sex is the sublimation of dinner, but I do know that the people who dreamed up and admired these picture ensembles had been trained in a lubricious Platonism, which offered them a happy nirvana where pleasure—*buon vino, buona cucina, buona letteratura, buon sesso*—was undifferentiated. After all, the whole thing started with Plato's *Symposium*, and that just means drinking party.

This was not really material for scholarship, though. The foreword never got written, but I did insert a new port of call in my Roman itinerary. Once a week or so, on the trek between Satyr Square and the top of the Janiculum, I could make a mini-pilgrimage in perfect solitude of the good kind. Not the kind when my apartment telephone goes dead precisely three days before and three days after my birthday. But the kind where, as if by compensation in the midst of that same period, Bramante's perfectly circular Renaissance temple, generally shuttered inside its courtyard halfway up the Janiculum, not only proves approachable but turns out to have its doors wide open, allowing me inside, where I stretch my arms almost far enough to touch its opposite walls, dance a little private hora, and feel as though I am Leonardo's Vitruvian Man in the flesh.

The truth is, I had a practical destination atop the Janiculum and needed some fortification to reach it. Psyche's heaven, or Bramante's for that matter, was a far cry from the paradise at the top of the hill, the academy of my countrymen, where scholars and artists conducted their own utopia. To this gracious facility I had occasional—on the whole impersonal—access. The Academy's tranquil library offered scarcely more camaraderie than did the Germans at their more centrally located mountaintop. Yet from time to time the Americans did invite me to dinner.

Large communal tables, general conversation. The topic is a recently published scholarly volume. My interlocutor, very intense, a little older, multiple marriages and children, rumored to have a boyfriend half her age somewhere back in the Texas Panhandle, likes the book better than I do and demands that I give an account of my opinion. In fact, I am trying to peel a pear with a dull knife. I attempt some generalities about the book's shaky hold on detail and its methodological uncertainties.

"I don't understand a thing you're saying. I'm going to open a page at random and you're going to tell me exactly what's wrong with it."

My knife slips a little. "I usually get paid for these seminars."

"Fuck you."

Another dinner, a different interlocutor, speaking with an enigmatic laugh: "You know, you ruined my life."

"How is that?"

"I had eight months mapped out to write a book on Ovid.

Halfway through it you published practically the same book. So I quit."

"You got off easy. It took me twelve years."

Or the complementary pronouncement from another fellow scholar: "Why are you writing a book about ancient statues in the Renaissance? I already covered that in a footnote." Someone from the opposite end of the table, not previously part of the conversation: "Besides, they're so ugly!"

Only once—after an evening of typically execrable cuisine, when a higher official in the Academy befriended me, stole a bottle of brandy from the bar, and took me to his apartment, where we attempted a dreadful breakneck impromptu performance of Schubert's four-handed Fantasy in F Minor—only for those few minutes could I move in this academic space and imagine that it was better to be in company among my fellow professionals than by myself at one of the Academy's neighboring paradises, either in the perfect cosmic circle of Bramante's Tempietto or at the dinner table of the Olympians in the Villa Farnesina.

The comparisons themselves are academic, as my own cosmic circle was about to expand. The prelude was a particularly solitary evening: I attended a concert alone, the hall was in a remote part of the city, and when it was time to return home, I stumbled in the wee hours through a complete bewilderment of alarmingly high-numbered bus routes. Then, the next morning, in the course of a stroll through the far oblong cross section of Piazza Navona, undertaken for no loftier purpose than changing money, I lived my urban village differently.

In front of those enigmatic grisailles on the Palazzo Massimo, I caught sight of Mauro, a quiet, late-coming, slightly marginal member of the Wednesday night tasting group who had mostly impressed me with the glow of his dense mustache and the fragmentariness of his speech. Our connections had been so tenuous that I was hardly expecting him to recognize me at such a far radius from Clara's, when at once he called out my name loudly, took my arm, pulled me a little away from the fountain, and said enigmatically, "You know, I've just come from Trastevere. Hundred thousand lire. I'm being unfaithful to Jeffrey. Don't say a word. But if you want the information, here . . ." He put a calling card in my hand with elaborate, presumably facetious, circumspection and went off in another direction.

Moments later, peering out from the Four Rivers, I discovered Cecilia, Giorgio's credulous friend of the late-night *dopo cena*. Almost before I had recognized her, she whooped and said, "I was just thinking of you!"

"Of me?"

"You know that I'm on the recreational committee of the Party, no?" I didn't, but at least I could figure out which party she meant. "Well," she added with a laugh that might have been sarcastic or might have been triumphant, "they're going gourmet."

"The Party? Gourmet?"

"*Ma certo*. Eno-gastronomy indoctrination." I was face-to-face with Euro-Communist irony. "No, really. They're doing it every week at some high-class restaurant in Trastevere. You and Giorgio have to join. Unless you're worried about what those *fascisti* are going to do to you when you get back to America."

Finally, as I entered the labyrinth of my bank at the upper end of the piazza, I found myself face-to-face with yet another recent acquaintance, though from a different set. Born Italian, educated French, married English, Dario was the dashing *jeune premier* inside a little academic circle that had begun to overlap with my sparse native scholarly contacts. The members of Dario's intermittent seminar, all either trained in Paris or wishing they had been, read one another's papers on the history of *things*.

Not Big Important Things, like revolutions and battles and edicts, but little material things, like calendars or dissection pictures or astrologers' charts; and since I was myself working on *things*, I enjoyed their occasional company.

It was a different kind of thing, though, that Dario wanted to talk about. He had always seemed the most cultivated, coiffed, and aesthetically deviant among the members of his slightly humorless cohort.

"*Tu ne le croiras pas mais le vin français est sur le point d'envahir la terre italienne!*" Over a memorable outdoor lunch of Roman innards some time earlier, we had judged our several capacities and made a solemn choice of lingua franca. By now it was a little outdated and artificial; still, we kept to it.

"A wine invasion?" I replied. "Reporting for duty, *mon capitaine*." I saluted.

"*Oui. Contre l'armée rouge.*" And he reported what he had heard from his Parisian academic gastronome support staff—that for the first time Burgundy, Bordeaux, and the rest were going to be celebrated publicly, with serious political backing, across the Alps from their homeland.

Granted, this wasn't the only topic among my three acquaintances that morning—Mauro wanted to show me his new physics lab at the university, Cecilia invited me to a contemporary art opening, and Dario was scheduling an Etruscan-ruin-cum-Tuscan-barbecue excursion in the Maremma—but it was nonetheless the case that at the completion of this five-hundred-meter errand I was able to deduce that the Communists were organizing tastings of French wines in Rome and that, if I chose, I might be able to join the party.

Good thing that I had pocketed Mauro's card. Three phone calls later, each of them something of a linguistic ordeal, I had confirmed that there was indeed a set of seminars, to begin the following week, that would lead fifty fortunate souls through the panoply of "Great Wines of France." It was to inaugurate a whole program in pan-European gastronomic appreciation. Forty-eight seats were already subscribed. But if I brought my cash directly this evening to a restaurant in Trastevere where the leader of the seminars was the esteemed sommelier, I had a chance of gaining admittance—that is, if I could catch him while on break from the rigors of wine service.

The only problem: I was cooking dinner for Giorgio that night. And occasions like this did not admit of interruption, certainly not the kind initiated by me. Solution: the high moral road. I would propose to Giorgio that we both enroll in the French wine seminars, and since he had been showering me with strange little gifts lately, I would even make the tuition cost into my treat.

I planned impeccably. Multiple finger foods, gently fried and requiring permutations of dips, followed by an intricate pasta involving a single raviolo with a single egg inside it, garnished by a few slices of black truffle that would moot a certain French ambiance: these would occupy all of our attention. At that point it would be appropriate to undertake a palate-clearing stroll to accomplish the errand across the river; our places in the seminars assured, we could return to Satyr Square, where, with no further mess or bother, there would be a *torta di carciofi*, best made earlier in the day and served at room temperature.

And it all worked, up to a point. Giorgio was thrilled, though a little surprised, to be the recipient rather than the donor of a gift. And everything about the seminars pleased him, both the politics and the comedy of the politics, the sense of something foreign that was slightly ahead of the curve, the large-scale fellowship of fifty simultaneous tasters. Nor was there anything but praise for my menu. In fact, by the time the truffle was exuding its musky scent over the raviolo filling, he was in high pontificating mode.

"These are the elemental flavors of life! The earth and the egg!" I had been on the point of apologizing for serving truffles from a can, but he had left gastronomic fundamentalism behind him. I was actually called upon to produce a second raviolo—fortunately, there was more pasta, more egg, and a few scraps from the truffle can—and as soon as this had been slowly digested, Giorgio raised both large arms in a theatrical gesture of fatigue and said, "Now it is time to rest." With both Trastevere and my main course still to come, I was not sure what this meant.

"Why don't you just relax a minute on the sofa?" I said. But suddenly he was passing through the dining room and climbing the ladder to my sleeping loft. What exactly was the alcohol content, I wondered, of that Pinot Bianco that Giorgio had been drinking twice as fast as I? I had an inspiration. "*Bene, bene.* You take a little snooze, and I'll go enroll us in the seminars."

"*Dai! Vieni su pure te.*" You come upstairs with me.

He was on the topmost rung of the ladder, one hand already on the mattress.

"Giorgio, there are only two places left in the seminars. We have to give them the money tonight."

I was attempting to reason with him from ground level. We were like some antic upside-down Romeo and Juliet.

"*Dopo. Dopo.*" Afterward. After what? By this time we were both upstairs. Nothing had prepared me for this quandary: French wine, artichoke pie, Giorgio and I attempting to occupy the narrow space of my sleeping pallet. Suddenly, with greatly sober care, he was unlacing his carefully shined shoes and then methodically removing his socks. Uncertain, I waited for more. But that was the end of it. Far from disrobing further, he sat up, grasped his tweed jacket tighter, turned so that our faces, again, were nearly touching—was this our foreplay?—and said, "Rub my feet."

I didn't move. I entertained some hope that I had misunderstood the Italian; then I thought of pretending I had misunderstood. It wasn't prudery, exactly. I had handled worse than feet. Back in simpler and safer times, I had long frequented an urban pleasure palace called the Bijou, where I had embraced a gradual initiation, beginning with the outer circle, which consisted of a mere nondescript porn theater, to an even more nondescript back room, to a vertiginous spiral stairway that led, finally, to a massive tangle of booths, doubtless the work of a demented gay architect, some cubicles wholly private, some wholly exposed, the majority plotted with an intricate maze of juxtaposition that enabled occupants to perform in hexagons and octagons of contiguity, both visible and shielded from each other. Not to mention other kinds of spaces, including a little chapel of pulpits, each with a view of movie screens, each with a little hidden kneeling space under the lectern.

In uncanny resemblance to the sodomites of the *Inferno*—had Dante cruised?—who look at one another like tailors threading a needle by the light of the new moon, we moved at the Bijou squinting greedily through space illuminated by the dim glare of the cinema bulb into darker, ever more labyrinthine vistas, where cigarettes and sweat, strobe light and poppers, either deadened or intensified transgression and desire, depending on one's tastes. There's a Boccaccio monk who convinces an innocent girl to have sex with him by telling her that they are putting the devil in hell. The Bijou was that hell. To do, to watch, to do while watching, to watch while doing, Panopticon meets Pandemonium: no place else in my life did time stop so still as it did within this labyrinth, where, as the hours went insensibly by, it seemed ever possible to chalk up one more abjection, one

more violation of taboo, one more act for mental replay as soon
as I had exchanged this form of solitude for that of my bedroom.

To this day, the maze, whether it belongs to the Minotaur or
to Henry VIII, is my personal sign of thrilling, perilous, transi-
tory license. But Giorgio and I inhabited another kind of maze. If
not feet, what did I want? Perhaps to stroke his almost bearded
face, or to lay my head on his broad, sheltering, cello-shaped
chest. I wanted pleasure, yes, but the kind of pleasure that signi-
fied the end of solitude. He had his fetishes, I had mine.

I did nothing. "And then?"

"What do you mean, 'and then'?"

"After I play with your feet, what then?"

"I don't understand."

I looked carefully at his feet. "It's time for me to go to Trastevere."

"*Vabbe'*." He was pulling his socks back on. I had forfeited
my chance. "You'd never be able to match any decent wine with
that *torta* you're trying to serve me." He was wrong about that.
Two days later I was discovering on my own the remarkable
properties of Friulian sauvignon in conjunction with artichokes.
But I had kept my word: Giorgio and I were numbers forty-nine
and fifty on the list of soon-to-be French wine initiates.

Not that there weren't hitches and glitches along the way.
Cautiously entering the dining room at Rome's fanciest fish
restaurant—neither twenty minutes of fresh air, nor the crossing
of the Tiber, nor sight of the absurdly top-hatted statue in Piazza
Sonnino having been sufficient to derail my train of thought
from Giorgio's feet upward or from the imagination of a fully enacted scene in my bedchamber to some sort of future life above
and beyond feet—I glimpsed only with difficulty the sommelier
in question, and from behind. A tall figure, dressed in perfectly
correct black; big hands at the end of long arms cradling a mag-

num of first-growth Bordeaux while the large table of onlookers stared up at him as silent and motionless as though they were posing for a daguerreotype. Nothing so very surprising until one noticed that the wine in the bottle was white. It was a fish restaurant, of course, but Haut-Brion Blanc is so rare that it has never even risen to cult status. If this erudite professional was dealing in such arcana, and getting people to pay for it, he was indeed a maestro.

Then he turned around, and I found myself staring into the face of a teenager with what looked like an old man's stage beard. With hardly a pause to separate himself from his high-rolling clients, he recognized me from my telephone voice, called me *tu*, recollected that I lived in Chicago, and demanded, "You want to join the seminars? *Allora, che pensi dei* Bulls *questa stagione?*" If this was a test, I wasn't going to do well. I was trying to remember the difference between Michael Jordan and Michael Jackson when the learned man-boy in front of me let out a great laugh and handed me part of his share in the recondite white Bordeaux that was making the rounds of the table. In time, and very little time was needed, I understood that Sandro was about twenty-five, the uniform was borrowed, the beard was real, and most real of all was a spirit of extravagance and play.

The only problem with joining the tastings, it soon turned out, was *my* schedule. Fortunately, they did not conflict with the events at Clara's—no need to feel guilty, as Mauro did, of betrayal—but Sandro made it clear that his *lezioni* were a real commitment; attendance was mandatory. And my calendar was filling up. The Wednesday night group was already spinning into tree diagrams of association. Silvia had introduced me to a wine-selling ex–twelve-tone composer with his own Italo-Slavic band of sauvignon-swilling disciples; Vito and Marian were connected via someone's marriage to Antonio and Maria Rita, placid seventy-something ex-revolutionaries who now stitched exquisite leather purses in the shadow of Santa Maria sopra Minerva; through Ian, I had met an assortment of expatriate pediatrician–foie gras lovers; even Big and Little John, it turned out, had friends more sociable and talkative than they themselves. If Monday evenings became compulsory, would I be giving up too much?

Blame it on the Communists. While there wasn't much in my meeting with Sandro to give the upcoming events an ideological framework, except perhaps calling them *lessons* and insisting on perfect attendance, I simply had to be there when Marx met Margaux.

How shall I explain it? I was born in the middle of a war that I don't remember. But I remember the Cold War and Vietnam; I remember Selma and Dallas; I remember the Berlin Wall going up and the Berlin Wall coming down; I remember the Six Days' War and the Gulf War and the perfect cloudless sky over lower Manhattan on that Tuesday morning in September. But for all this remembering, what privilege, what merit should I be accorded, what authority do I deserve when I voice my politics? That question keeps me stumped and silent.

The thing is, my parents were Communists. Or at least I think so. The visible politics were innocently liberal—Stevenson was good, Kennedy less good, Nixon unspeakable—but there were a great deal of invisible politics. Secondhand evidence includes a whispered account from an unreliable narrator concerning my mother's unwavering support for Stalin when he made his pact with Hitler; a little altar of Henry Wallace paraphernalia, perhaps deliberately hidden; and, of course, heavy agony in the household during Army-McCarthy.

But it's the firsthand experience that remains most enigmatic and most haunting. It's my third birthday; my parents and I are celebrating at dinner. Presents in very small boxes have been loaded into a large bowl that sits between candlesticks. As the festivities near their end, it is somehow revealed that they have just sold the cottage where we spend summers. I become hysterical with grief; the party is over. I storm out to my bed, where my parents each take turns, fruitlessly, to console me. The cabin that was the subject of this trauma formed part of a Jewish Communist colony in Westchester. It remained a piece of family lore, narrated in cycles of legend that were alternately respectful and parodic, which I continued to absorb long after my third birthday. Everything about the place, it seems, was ideological, foreign, veiled in secrecy and suspicion: compulsory signs of poverty, such as a ban on indoor plumbing; a day camp that indoctrinated Soviet ideals; perpetual rumors that the Feds were about to march up Route 138; semiliterate immigrants quixotically acting out agricultural fantasies while engaged in disputes with self-taught intellectuals who would not make a move without consulting the works of Bakunin; group excursions to support victims of racism or red-baiting. I could hardly have understood, that teary night, why we had been there or why we were leaving, nor would I perhaps ever understand what act of separation I was bewailing. The truth is, I recall nothing about the colony myself; my memories begin on the night it departed from my life. Even so, the sharpest recollection from that occasion is not anguish at the loss, but the brand-new experience of how effective my sorrow could be. Indeed, I seem to remember the strategic act of exaggerating my grief. If so, the colony was teaching me my own system of subversion.

Second-earliest memory, some months later, another part of Westchester. I'm in the backseat of the family car, my grandmother next to me. We are in a very slow line of traffic. Then the cars stop altogether; there are people on the sidewalks

screaming; something about my father's silence frightens me
even more than it usually does. A lady of my grandmother's age
peers into the car; her eyes meet mine. She runs around to the
driver's side, gestures, but my father won't roll the window down.
She screams loudly, something like, "Go up that driveway. It'll
take you to the backstreets. They're throwing rocks up ahead.
Get the kid out of here." I remember that the driveway was very
steep, almost too much for our prewar car to manage. Then we
were lost in unfamiliar roads, but at least they were quiet, no
jeering crowds, no stone throwing.

Where we were coming from, where we were going: none of
this could I have been expected to understand. Certainly the
name of Paul Robeson would not have meant anything to me.
Had we been to hear him sing? Were we—mother, father, a
seventy-five-year-old lady, and a four-year-old boy—outside agi-
tators? Was it all an accident of misreading the map, as my
mother claimed? My own memories are of equal-opportunity
fear: the mob on the sidewalks, the relentless wedge of cars inch-
ing along, the lady who rescued us, the father who never spoke a
word. And then there's my infuriatingly apolitical clarity about
the most inconsequential things. At my birthday party, it's the
big, opalescent gift-bearing candy bowl whose sides flapped out
like a retriever's ears; on the road in Peekskill, it's the fawn-
colored tufted upholstery of the Studebaker and the matching
hue of my grandmother's absurdly out-of-date floor-length skirt.

I was going to Trastevere on a piece of unfinished business,
then. Not that the Italian Communists were staging wine tastings for my benefit; they had their own goals. Ever since the end
of Fascism, the cultural and intellectual life of Italy had been in
the hands of the political left, many of whom were as affluent
and ambitious, as showy and extravagant as the people we used
to call yuppies. But by the time I was ready to hand over a cou-

ple hundred thousand lire for my personal therapy, May 1968 was past, the radical terrorism of the late 1970s was past, and the Communist bloc of Eastern Europe was beginning to dissolve. Italy's leftist bourgeoisie was becoming disillusioned with grand ideological schemes and with all the puritanisms of monolithic political ideas. They were rediscovering local traditions, the history of daily life, and the work of women and family. They were discovering food and wine.

Communism in Italy was still a great social club, and the Party had spawned recreational organizations under the acronym ARCI, for Italian Recreational and Cultural Association but also meaning "arch," as in *archfiend*. Foremost among these was Arcigola, whose name added another joke, since *gola* can refer to either a gourmet or a glutton. Arcigola had had its defining moment—its Bastille, its Stonewall—when in 1986 McDonald's dared to open a fast-food outlet within sight of the Spanish Steps. Powerless to prevent this desecration, a band of leftist epicures brought into being a whole gastronomic ideology: localism, tradition, ecology, *la qualità della vita*—not fast food but, to give them the title that has spread through the world, Slow Food.

But if I expected the *lezioni* to untie the knot of my personal paradoxes, I was—happily—disappointed, wrong-footed by the simple hedonism of the occasions. Granted, the wine tastings had the trappings of pedagogy. Each session began with a lecture and slide show, sometimes overextended, about a French viticultural region. And we had to slog through an occasionally agonizing Q and A, as the members of the group, virtually all wine professionals, revealed their ignorance about a product that was made only a few hundred miles from their own vineyards and had stood for centuries as a benchmark of excellence.

For instance, an elderly wine merchant who has done much to popularize Friulian whites in Rome and who shows off his education by taking a great deal of time to express himself, demands contemptuously of Sandro how one could possibly appreciate the half-flowery, half-bitter flavors in an Alsatian Gewurztraminer.

"You must understand, *bel dottore mio*," Sandro replies, "not every region has the sun so perfectly poised between the mountains and the sea as in our own northeast. The Alsatians have cultivated these exotic aromas in response to what was lacking in their *terra*—and I think they have done it magnificently."

A sommelier from a restaurant famous for its deep cellar of Tuscan vintages sniffs a Chambertin, raises his hand instantly, and declares that the wine is defective because he smells volatile acidity, that slight sensation of evaporating alcohol which the greatest red Burgundies often emit.

"È *vero, è vero*," Sandro counters. "This wine would make a terrible Brunello. But Montalcino is one thing, Chambertin another. Smell it again, then taste it, and you'll see how that bit of tickle in the nose sends those fruit flavors into your head as though they were flying on angel wings."

The maker of a sweet wine in the Castelli Romani, long out of fashion, is intrigued by the complex apricot tones in his first-ever taste of Sauternes. But he is perplexed by Sandro's account of the much desired fungus—the noble rot, as we call it—that is responsible for producing them. "Even if I wanted that disease in my vineyard," he sputters, "I could only get it into the wine if I picked bunch by bunch, or even"—he could not contain his laughter—"grape by grape!"

"I have to tell you, *carissimo*," Sandro responds with a grimace of comic sorrow, "that there are many people in France who love their grapes so much that when they see them afflicted by *muffa nobile*, they declare a medical emergency and rush each and every victim, one by one, to the winepress. We could learn lessons from them."

In short, under Sandro's leadership, which he manages not like a commissar, but like an intimate best friend to each member of his constituency, everything is about the delightful harmonies of nature and nurture, about love of good wine conquering any boundaries imposed by the Alps, about the increase of knowledge begetting an intensification of pleasure. And it isn't just the talk, it's the wines. Sandro has a taste for the voluptuous, the immoderate, for wines that push the limits of their categories in just the way that is bound to startle, confuse, and educate his pupils. Whether it is the *vendange tardive* with the highest sugar weight ever recorded in France, which staggers the taste buds of a group already reeling from the surprise of Alsace, or the legendary super-concentrated Vega Sicilia—not French at all but from the deep interior of Castile—that Sandro plants with blithe irrelevance among the namby-pamby Loire whites, there is something about these weekly meetings that you might even call dialectical. Sandro was singing the Internationale in his own special way.

Then there were some guiltier pleasures of my own. My fellow seminarians needed these lessons because, like the rest of their countrymen, they knew nothing about French wines. For Italians, though they are far more cosmopolitan in many ways than we *anglosassoni*, globalism stops just short of the taste buds. Americans may not be the world's greatest polyglots or diplomats, but when it comes to food and drink, we're multinational sophisticates. I came, in short, from a gourmet culture where to know wine at all was to know foreign wine; and foreign wine meant French wine. As a consequence, on these Monday evenings I was Gulliver among vinous Lilliputians. And I was not above playing my long suit—at least so far as my Italian communicative skills permitted. The disturbing inaugural session on the wines of Alsace—the room ablaze with challenges that betrayed an inability to imagine any practices other than Italian

ones—was my chance to communicate. For all the improvements in my language ability over the preceding months, I had
never yet spoken Italian to a large public, so I knew I had to
choose my words carefully.

"*Forse sono l'unico straniero nel . . . ,*" I began, after Sandro
had recognized my cautiously raised arm. "Perhaps I am the only
foreigner in the . . ." But how exactly to say *room*? I was being de-
feated by the rapidity of my own learning curve, the mastery of
vocabulary without the corresponding mastery of usage. Clearly,
I still didn't have quite enough people to talk to, or listen to.
Camera sounded intimate, like a bedroom. *Sala* felt too grand,
like one of those frescoed spaces at the Villa Farnesina. *Stanza*
felt too domestic. *Aula* was a lecture hall. I looked around me,
with all these synonyms sharpening my vision. What sort of
room was it? A restaurant's banqueting space, once grand but
now slightly faded, a little small for the number of people and
glasses now crowding into it, a few peeling faux wall paintings,
unmatching chairs hastily arrayed, some at tables and others in
auditorium-style rows. I had no way of making the right lexical
choice, so I shifted from the place to the people.

"*Nel gruppo,*" I concluded my introduction. In the group.
"The gentleman over by the window says it is impossible for a
five-year-old white wine to be still drinkable. Perhaps that is
the experience you have all had. But I must tell you of other experiences. Only recently did I drink a stupendous Corton-
Charlemagne—that's a Burgundy—from 1966, and as for German
sweet Rieslings, even the 1959s remain lively." There was a
diminution in background chatter and quite a few looks of perplexity, whether at the language or the content I couldn't say.
But I wasn't finished.

"And the gentleman in the blue shirt—forgive me, I don't
know your name—is concerned that he is not familiar with a

single dish, *primo* or *secondo*, that could be accompanied by any of these wines. With that I am in complete agreement. But I must tell you that these might be perfect partners with other dishes. If I may say a word or two about Alsatian cuisine, you see, it is full of smoky and salty, sweet and savory, vinegar and sugar, fruit and meat. If you taste these wines again and think about those flavors rather than *pasta fagioli* or saltimbocca or fried *baccalà . . .*"

And here I trailed off, fearing that by cataloguing the clichés of Roman cuisine, I was in danger of sliding from welcome foreign informant to victim of community ritual sacrifice. I need not have worried. True, there were some strange glances in my direction during the succeeding weeks. But for the most part, with that little speech and a few similar ex cathedra pronouncements as the sessions continued, I landed somewhere between notorious and adulated, not just in that particular space (whichever word you want to use for it) but throughout the little world of professional wine appreciators in Rome.

I didn't specify what *kind* of foreigner I was, to begin with—not that I was trying to hide anything, it just wasn't part of my rhetorical gambit—and this led to a dizzying variety of speculations, both behind my back and to my face. At the end of the second meeting, a lady charged up to me and said, "*Signore*, I understood last time that you were from Alsace, but this week it seems you are Burgundian. How can that be?" Others worked their way through the particular polyglot identities that Italians are most familiar with: Was I Swiss, or perhaps from the German-speaking Alto Adige? Did I have some connection with the Vatican? Every one of these was politically suspect, and there was great relief when I answered all in the negative and could bask in acclaim that was unclouded by ideological suspicion.

Other kinds of positive attention were better informed, more valuable. Sandro did not work alone. Though he was affianced and seemed to lead a conventional enough private life, he also played pied piper to a band of attractive, clever, affectionate high bourgeois young men who were being seduced away from the earnest professions and toward a life of gastronomic pleasure. And I soon found myself seamlessly folded into the group as though a couple decades of age difference meant nothing.

At Clara's wine tastings I had met multiple Giovannis; here both official pourers were Marcos. One was heir to a family that operated a restaurant named for the gluttony circle of purgatory; I was immediately invited to partake of that least deadly of the seven deadly sins (according to Dante's very sensible reckoning, whereby lust is second least), and before long I enjoyed a parade of rabbits and ducks in various forms of galantine that were served in their chic underground establishment. The other Marco first introduced himself to me alongside his father, reportedly a famous scientist. They looked virtually identical, except that the older man was ramrod straight and rail lean, while the younger was bowed out in an immense curve of belly. No surprise, then, that he would make a gesture of excess: as soon as the father was out of sight, the son opened up a supersize briefcase of alternative wines—said to be Sandro's rejects for the current tasting—and conspiratorially offered a dozen samplings. I suppose this Marco really did belong in the circle from which the other's restaurant took its name.

If the two Marcos were foot soldiers in the Communist gourmet army, Paolo was more like a senior lieutenant. At one of the first sessions, I spotted him in a huddle with Sandro, both of them sporting expressions of extreme gravity when one bottle of Burgundy was raising suspicions that it was corked. But that wasn't the first time I had seen Paolo. On a memorably bleak and solitary Saturday night some weeks earlier, practicing my accustomed therapy of allowing Rome itself to keep me company, I had already concluded the chemical portion of the treatment by visiting a *salumeria* near St. Peter's, where the amazing fried cal-zone—available only between five and seven on Saturday after-noons and filled with leftovers from a week's production of every imaginable fatty pork product—could be purchased to go. It was my solution to the melancholy of the closing market that my poetess friend had chronicled. And now, my hands sufficiently degreased, I wandered into a used-book shop. Though such browsing had been a mainstay of life on my own as far back as I could toddle from my parents' house to New York's Fourth Av-enue, it was quite a different sort of venture in a country whose books were in a language I still found quite challenging.

It was a comforting place to be, nevertheless. Just to acknowl-edge the dust, the vagaries of the cataloguing system, the weird proliferation of titles on occult subjects: all this gave me a little sense of home away from home. I also enjoyed, as I had for decades, tuning in on the learned, quirky, obsessive conversa-tions that the clients of such stores engaged in with the staff. In this case it was an arrestingly intense young man with a beautiful face almost completely covered up in unkempt hair above and below, an ensemble somehow more comic than menacing. He spoke an Italian that was at once poetic, archaic, witty, and—biggest surprise—completely comprehensible to me. What he was looking for, it seemed, was everything that interested me: aesthetics, the philosophy of images, Renaissance painting, the scholarship of Warburg and Panofsky. The bookseller had noth-ing to offer. But what about me? As I stood there pretending to be engrossed in a section devoted to the history of mathematics, all I could think of was how easy it would be to pick up this young man, if only I opened my mouth. But I was frozen in place, still fingering a volume on the battle between Newton and Leib-niz over calculus, as he disappeared through the front door.

Now he was in front of me once again, and with the fate of a problematic Beaune-Bressandes '85 in the balance, I was being given a second chance. But before I could even begin to screw up my courage, he was talking to me as though we were old friends.

"*Senti*—" (Oh, that sexy second-person singular!) "You have probably tasted more Burgundies than anyone this side of Gevrey-Chambertin"—these were the fruits of my locally inflated reputation—"you figure this one out."

I am afflicted with a mysterious lifelong insensitivity to the proverbial cardboard taste of wines whose corks have gone bad, but I went through the motions of a long sip and spit, looked into the faces of Sandro and Paolo, the one a mask of anxiety, the other a mask of anxiety leavened with irony, and I declared, "Maybe yes, maybe no. Better skip it." The bottle was immediately put aside and a backup chosen. From that moment, Paolo and I managed to integrate words and images, philosophy and poetry, his work and mine, Burgundy and Barolo, gravity and irony. Of course, like all the rest of the *ragazzi di Sandro*, he had a girlfriend; still, he was usually free for dinner, he laughed at my jokes, and he wanted to translate me into Italian.

And so, courtesy of some forty-odd new colleagues, I was entering a new set of Roman communities whose gastronomic pleasures were spontaneous, passionate, multicultural. I became accustomed to telephone summonses for immediate appearances—because a 1971 Barolo was so magnificent that its tasters could not fully enjoy themselves unless I would cross town at midnight for a chance to put its pleasures into words; because a chef at a three-star restaurant had just re-created Renaissance peasant food and I was required to judge its authenticity before it got cold; because a Hungarian politico was in the midst of confessing half a century's officially sponsored neglect of Tokaji Essencia; because a bottle of Grands Echézeaux had inspired the tasters to make an immediate congratulatory phone call to its maker back in Vosne-Romanée and only my French was thought sufficient to the occasion.

If I felt myself poised somewhere between Roman *triumphator* and charlatan on the brink of fatal unmasking, that contradiction managed to play itself out at the climactic final session of the *lezioni*. Sandro staged a contest, the prizes being bottles of Alsatian eaux-de-vie. It took about twenty minutes to explain the rules, which were complicated because they involved dividing the fifty of us into separate groups, each of which had a leader. The groups were furthermore (and this only became clear to me later) divided by expertise, so that group one was the *più bravo*, and on down. What the leader of the group was supposed to do was never clear to me; what was clear to me was that I was the leader of group one. The whole thing was a nightmare, the more so because Sandro began by explaining that as leader of group one, I was the very first of the first. The question to our group was impossibly complicated, having something to do with giving a complete account of the climate and soil of Alsace and its effect on the wines. Fortunately, someone else, not the first of the first, answered Sandro's queston and was duly awarded a sampler of Poire, Kirsch, and Mirabelle.

After it was all over—and I was dreading this encounter from the start—Sandro appeared at my side, took me into the little prep room where I had given my unreliable opinion about the corkage of the Burgundy, and, waving his arms around, shouted, "*Come mi hai tradito!*" How you have betrayed me. Incongruously—but then, what wasn't incongruous in the Communist Gourmet Club?—all I could think of was Jesus and his disciples. Whereupon his face changed from tragic to comic mask, and he planted a full, moist kiss squarely on my lips. Those same disciples kept rearing their ugly heads. After all, the Italians had their contradictions, just as I had mine. As for the more immediate scene, however, nothing like this ever repeated itself. I was simply left to understand that I was now, warts and all, an initiate of some kind: archglutton, proud wearer of a Slow Food snail in my lapel, part Communist, part communitarian, eligible to play out my own dialectics wherever good food and good wine were being offered in Rome.

It would probably be too easy to say that the troubles with Giorgio coincided with my induction into the Communist Gourmet Club. For one thing, he had managed his own triumphant investiture there. A barrage of transgressive dicta, introduced with those signature formulas *secondo me* and *nella mia umilissima opinione*, made him just as much an object of curiosity as I, even if he was slow to disabuse his admirers of the fantasies they projected on him. This I learned one week when he was absent (another transgression!) and I was asked by a fellow seminarian whether my friend had returned Stateside to supervise his gourmet empire in Chicago, a city—indeed, a nation—where I knew that Giorgio the itinerant philosopher had never set foot. With or without these fabulations, Giorgio was proving a most desirable fellow traveler, a principle of exuberance less predictable than was the fashion at this party.

Then, too, we both undertook the pursuit of Sandro with the merriest of energies and with an unspoken sense that this would be a collective enterprise. Collective, but not precisely collaborative: to Giorgio's suggestion that we honor the occasion of the first Sandro dinner, at my house, by actually cooking *together*, I responded with the warier proposal that we cook *side by side*. It was an important distinction—*chacun à son plat*—but for a little extra insurance I designed everything on my side of the counter as hyper-French: immune, in other words, to his authority. The strategy was not entirely successful. I expressed nothing but reverence as Giorgio squeezed little sacs of squid ink into his pasta dough, but when it came time for me to insert strips of loin into the middle layer of a rabbit pâté, he was full of contrary opinions about the Cognac in which they had been marinated. No matter: for the next Sandro dinner, at Giorgio's house, I skirted such danger by providing a *bœuf en gelée*, which had to be braised, potted, and gelled to completion before it ever left my kitchen for his.

Indeed, it was something of a triumph and a sign of happy integration that there *was* a second dinner. Sandro was no easy man to plug into one's social calendar, what with his slightly neurasthenic fiancée, a six-nights-a-week job as sommelier, and a far-ranging gift of his own for convivial friendship. That he took time out for us, not only from his personal life but also from a demanding involvement in all the affairs of Arcigola, might speak to some subtly designed political praxis, but would Giorgio and I represent social climbing or proselytizing the unconverted masses? The evidence—Sandro's exquisitely well-tuned sense of what wines to put alongside our menus, like the profound yet remarkably soft-edged Vosne-Romanée Cros Parantoux that he paired with my *bœuf en gelée*—suggests that Sandro was there, as I was, for pure pleasure.

But then, how pure is pleasure, anyway? Things turned darker, or at least less gastronomic, on this second occasion, when Sandro revealed that he was quitting his sommelier position in order to work for his father at the family restaurant in an ugly provincial town halfway to Naples. In my life, such distancings have been more the rule than the exception; I take them for granted. Giorgio, however, had a sense of being at the center of the world—all roads lead to Rome, none away from it—and he became at once intensely emotional, as though a love affair were being nipped in the bud.

"But you mean that you are leaving us?" he asked.

"Well, not exactly . . . ," Sandro began to explain.

"We won't see you?" Giorgio continued in the lovelorn vein.

"Don't worry," Sandro responded, with just the beginnings of a perplexity in his voice. "Twice a week I'll be in the Campo de' Fiori."

"You will? But how come?" Giorgio asked eagerly.

To which Sandro responded with complete nonchalance, "To see my psychoanalyst."

Now, this exchange was not taking place on the Upper West Side of Manhattan, but inside a culture where such matters as, say, divorce, homosexuality, and countertransference were kept far from dinner-table conversation. Or so I had thought, particularly since Sandro appeared to come from the hardworking, traditional, and resolutely uncosmopolitan backbone of the Italian class system. Popping the cork of a recently disgorged Besserat de Bellefon, he went on blithely to clear up at least some of my puzzlement with a little too much information about the way in which it was, in fact, precisely these class origins—the conventional proletarian father turned rebellious jazz musician now turned back into reluctant family man—that led to his need for continuing therapeutic visits.

I was unsure what my options were. No one—not the timid fiancée, not the libertine Giorgio—was saying a word. And where was Sabina with her "Perhaps Leo was thinking . . ."? What *was* I thinking? Should I share news of my own favorite analytic breakthroughs? Ask what instrument Sandro's father played? (Drums.) But it was time to clear the antipasto plates and serve Giorgio's square spaghetti with oxtail sauce. I knew that he required no assistant for this, and I had reservations about playing such a role, but when Giorgio summoned me into the kitchen, I obeyed, marginally preferring whatever postmortem would take place over the stove as against further exploration of Sandro's personal history.

Without prelude, and in what I thought was too loud a voice, Giorgio said, "*È tremendo, tremendo.*" But what was terrible, terrible? The story of Sandro's life? The fact that he was seeing a shrink? The square spaghetti?

I began some all-purpose response, but I was quickly interrupted.

"The Campo de' Fiori!" Giorgio threw up his hands. "Every analyst who practices around the Campo de' Fiori is a charlatan." My zone of the city was being insulted. "You and I have to get Sandro a therapist from the right neighborhood."

It's just possible that Giorgio was making a joke. I couldn't tell from his face. But I allowed myself another of those out-of-proportion responses, like my refusal of a cream puff in place of dinner: "No, no, no. Giorgio, we are not going to interfere in Sandro's therapy or in his life." Maybe I had gone too far with *or in his life*. But for whatever reason—because Sandro was leaving Rome, or because he had revealed too much about himself, or because I wouldn't cooperate with the hunt for an analyst with a better address—Giorgio was from that moment uninterested in the three-way friendship. With Sandro and all his captivating *ragazzi*, I was now on my own, as, of course, I was with Giorgio.

Rome is a village. It is also a city of pedestrians. Put the two together, and you discover that once you have even a moderately voluminous address book of acquaintances there, you are bound to have chance meetings on the street. It's not a contrivance of storytelling, it's a fact of urban life. Mauro, Cecilia, and Dario had handed me the Communist Gourmet Club during one ten-minute stretch of encounters in Piazza Navona. At other times I might stumble on graduate students playing hooky from a research library or the proprietor of a wineshop checking up on the competition across town. When fortune especially smiled on me, I would be in the company of a friend visiting from the States when a drop-dead glamorous figure like the photographer with the tinted lenses or the urbanologist with the west-facing balconies would appear out of nowhere in mid-piazza to plant kisses on my cheeks.

A few days after the second dinner with Sandro I had an encounter that was different from these brief bits of happenchance, however. For one thing, it occurred when I was working. Not working, exactly, but doing what I do when work troubles me. That moment when my dinner and my note cards coalesced so favorably that the opening sentences of the book emerged full-blown from my forehead was only a moment, not a steady state. It wasn't that I started to have writer's block or to lose interest or to doubt the value of my subject. It was more that I fell into the state that Raphael had described: "On the one hand, this knowledge of so many excellent things has given me the greatest pleasure, on the other hand, the greatest grief."

Grief number one was that smart-ass at the Academy who had asked me how I could work on a bunch of art objects that were so ugly. Was my unearthed sculpture ugly? Of course, I could retreat into historical relativism: everything is beautiful in its own way; the moderns possess no special authority; every age sees with its own eyes. I needed more than that, however. I needed to love my statues. Winckelmann, who had inspired a couple centuries of aesthetes to make pilgrimages in their direction, was no help. I still can't see the *Apollo Belvedere* as art's highest ideal, the very essence of the Greek spirit, partly because I know that it is a copy after a copy after a copy, partly because I have the uncomfortable sensation that Winckelmann was more than a little turned on by shapely nude lads, and partly because for me this particular manly specimen registers more like a tranquillized runway model than as my dream date.

The business of the classical ideal was giving me other problems. The famous line about "noble simplicity and quiet grandeur" worked well enough for the *Apollo*, but what about all those statues in conditions of torsion and torture like the *Lao-coön*? What about the boy who is just pulling out a thorn, or the images of toothless old fisherwomen, or the episodes in bas-relief of rape and pillage and mayhem? If you look at Raphael's great painting of the School of Athens—order, harmony, companionship, and wisdom—and you try to write the story of how the bits of ancient rock that came up out of the ground at about the time he was composing it somehow inspired Renaissance classicism, you end up with dots that won't connect. How do you get from the twisted, bizarrely decorative, self-dramatizing earthbound fragments all the way to abstract perfections, the golden mean, and the harmony of the spheres? Not only that. In my research I was discovering that the reason why Renaissance Romans were digging up so many statues is that they were tearing down great ancient buildings: to build a neoclassical city, in other words, they reduced a real classical city to rubble.

This left me with the job of sifting through the bigger pieces of rubble, trying to write a book about stuff that was broken. If I had left behind the business of studying literature all by itself, it was because pictures are more beautiful than words. Words are just arbitrary marks on paper; their relation to things is so shaky that all you have to do is cross some political boundary line—between, say, Paris and London—and the words don't mean anything anymore. Somehow, that's what I had learned from my German friend on the train. Pictures, on the other hand, are the thing itself. Or better. Aristotle said we love looking at images of things we don't want to see in real life, like snakes and corpses. I agree. Pictures give pleasures that things don't always provide. And I was in it for the pleasure. Yet here I was spending my days in front of a hand, a shoe, a stump, a headless trunk. If these were pictures of something, they were pictures of handicap and mutilation.

If the comprehensive was hopeless, I needed to go into the

particular. Which brought about my day trip to Tuscany. That morning's reading contained, first, a scary admonition from no less a personage than Erwin Panofsky—"The subject of the appropriation of ancient art in the Renaissance is too large to lend itself to comprehensive treatment"—and, second, an anecdote about an ancient sarcophagus that Donatello praised so fervently that his friend Brunelleschi trekked all the way from Florence to Cortona barefoot just to look at it. So I followed Brunelleschi— it was easier with shoes and railroad—but when I finally looked at the object in Cortona for myself, all I saw was a gaudy, overdecorated mass with too many figures in a frenzy of too many histrionic gyrations. Perhaps it was out of embarrassment that I peered inside the box. Nothing much to be seen. Except that I couldn't take my eyes off some wadded clumps of dirt. They started to take on shape. This was, after all, a burial box. Dust to dust. I was staring at the biggest grief of all: my subject was death. These sculptures, whether inspiring or schlocky, were nothing more than coffins. And the big, monumental pieces so valued by the popes had been disinterred in much the same way as coffins had been; they were like thousand-year-old bodies dug from the ground. Ordinary people in the fifteenth century suspected humanists of being ghouls. Me, too: I was living with the Renaissance Undead.

More knowledge, more grief. Probably sorrow has no legitimate place in the scholar's reckoning. And why grieve, anyway? Perhaps I could tell an even better story, or maybe a sexier one, if the art I was chronicling could be shown to be bad, broken, overwrought, and marked with the grave. Still, I live for pleasure; failing that, at least the history of pleasure, and those same weeks that found me bonding at Clara's or frolicking with the Communist Gourmet Club were also the weeks when too much unpleasure was crossing my desk.

So I went looking for beauty elsewhere. Make of it what you will, but I have always been a collector of Narcissuses. Not the flower, but the boy who turned into a flower after he spurned the love of Echo and became the eponym of self-love. What other story is so perfectly classical and so perfectly modern? When Ovid's Narcissus looks in the mirror, he doesn't just fall into impossible, laughable love; he discovers himself—that is, he discovers he *has* a self. Two thousand years later, Lacan is still slogging upstream through the mysteries of identity formation with something he calls the mirror stage. In between, Shakespeare tries to define romantic love by uncoupling it from narcissism, and Milton imagines Eve's first instant of consciousness as the dangerously vain sight of herself reflected in a pool. Know thyself, love thyself, love thy neighbor as thyself: Who can untie these knots?

Most especially, I like to collect images of Narcissus, not just because I like mythological pictures but because, since they tell a story about seeing—actually about *seeing* and *seeming*—they are like the especially personal property of artists. This is why Alberti, back in 1435, said that Narcissus was the inventor of painting: "What else can you call painting but a similar embracing with art of what is presented on the surface of the water in the fountain?" And so my particular fascination with the meta-Narcissus, the way in which artists represent that picture inside the picture—the mirror image that Narcissus falls in love with, and that he *is*. Perhaps it's not surprising that artists don't often depict the reflection: maybe the competition of the mirror is too keen. Poussin gives us the dying boy, a few of his namesake flowers, and a decidedly nonreflecting puddle. Cellini sculpts nothing but Narcissus himself, except that the boy is holding his left arm around his beautifully coiffed head, so it looks as though the real body has become the reflection in an oval mirror. And, immortally, Roy Lichtenstein makes his break-through into comic-strip art with *Look, Mickey, I've Hooked a Big One*. We, and Mickey, can see that Donald's fishing hook is stuck in his own sailor suit, while he, staring at the reflection in the water, imagines a great catch of the day, not realizing that "the big one" is himself; but the artist does not permit us to see any-thing in the water.

This brings me to probably the greatest Narcissus of all, in which we *do* see the reflection, a painting usually attributed to Caravaggio. I had seen it in reproduction, and I had passed briefly by it once during my early visits to Rome. Now I really wanted to look at the surface of the picture; I wanted to engage in Alberti's painterly embrace. A slide could never reveal just how the artist fashioned the transition—indeed, the metamor-phosis—between the broad-beamed, sensuous, fleshy boy who is staring into the pool and his own perfect replication, identical but for a completely different painterly texture, and occupying exactly the other half of the canvas, the two joined by the arc of their widespread arms. No landscape, no Echo, no flower, just two different paintings that meet in a perfect circle.

As it turned out, however, neither Narcissus nor his reflec-tion was on current view. A couple of decades earlier, I had glimpsed the picture in a dark little museum on the Trastevere side of the river. Now it was fittingly in the process of being transferred to the brilliantly baroque confines of the Barberini Palace. Meanwhile—and meanwhile could last for years—noth-ing was open to the public, and I had to hit the streets, my intel-lectual occupation momentarily gone.

Then, ten steps outside the courtyard of the shuttered mu-seum, I saw Giorgio. He showed no surprise, merely quickened his already swift pace and declared, as though in the middle of a longer conversation, "Hurry up. Or else we'll be late for Gianfranco." I fought back the *Alice in Wonderland* sensation but could remember no Gianfranco in my Rolodex.

"*Scusami*, Giorgio. Gianfranco who?"

We were entering a botanical garden—I spotted a tree labeled WINGED WALNUT OF THE CAUCASUS—but almost immediately our stride was overtaken by a flotilla of little electric panel trucks that maneuvered among the succulents and began to unload cases of wine and wheels of cheese. It was evidently some sort of pastoral gastronomy fair.

"Gianfranco. *Non ti ricordi?* You can only see him by appointment," Giorgio clarified. And with that, we found ourselves on a sort of synthetic savanna that had been outfitted with tents against the brilliant sunlight, like some encampment for a biblical battle.

I didn't remember. All I could comprehend was that fate and my vain search for Narcissus had clearly caught Giorgio in the midst of some initiative from which I had been excluded. No matter: he graciously motioned me inside the tallest and most sheltering of the canvas enclosures. It was amazingly dark, then suddenly illuminated by photographers' strobes. A middle-aged man of strikingly careful coiffure and immaculately tailored in no small yardage of double-breasted pinstripe was in the spotlight but looking a little impatient with it. He dismissed the cameramen with a few abrupt gestures, and just as the lights were going dim again, I was able to identify the labels on the wine bottles arrayed in front of him.

CASE BASSE.

So this was Gianfranco Soldera, the author—no, *auteur*—of the great Brunello to which I owed my entrée into Italian society. Of course you needed an appointment. He was a notorious mix of recluse and publicity hound, part insurance salesman and part tortured genius, all smiles when he chose to be if you praised his wine, but capable of visiting mafioso-style vendettas on his critics.

Giorgio was taking the lead. "May I present a great American admirer of yours . . ."

So he was turning it into my show, as though I had been the very cause of this meeting rather than its accidental beneficiary. My mind was flexing through the linguistic skills I would need to express, interrogate, acclaim Signor Soldera's accomplishments. But fortunately, I was given more time as Giorgio pointed in my direction.

"*Questo signore,*" he continued—though it was obvious that Soldera was not used to being lectured at, and certainly not about someone else's excellences—"represents in America the great European tradition of culture, artistic and gastronomic. And I know that your magnificent 1982 Brunello has been for him the summit of what can be achieved with the grape."

Soldera smiled, now on more familiar territory.

"*Tutto ciò nonostante . . .*" All that notwithstanding? What reservations, what subjunctives would follow in Giorgio's loose-cannon oratory? A cloud seemed to pass over Soldera's broad features. "Despite his profound *formazione* in the great wines of Burgundy and Mosel, California and Piedmont, when I offered him a taste of your 1985 Rosso di Montalcino"—he was taking the liberty of pouring himself this very wine from an open bottle on the table—"do you know what opinion he brought forth?"

A brief wine lesson. Every producer in Montalcino makes two wines: Brunello comes from the most privileged vineyard sites and is matured in cask at least four years prior to bottling, while Rosso is made from younger vines and aged only twelve to eighteen months. It's a pleasant necessity of the market that a winemaker be able to release an expensive five-year-old and a reasonably priced two-year-old wine at the same time, but for all their family resemblances, the two wines must be conceived quite differently, lest the profundity of the Brunello or the charm of the Rosso be compromised. One had only to look at Soldera to realize that he might not have a head for charm. *Tutto ciò nonostante*, in the court of public opinion, the tidal wave of enthusiasm that had greeted his '82 Brunello had engulfed, or at least trickled down, to its lesser '85 sibling. But when Giorgio brought the wine to one of our more contentious dinners, I had not shared that positive opinion. Clearly he had taken my criticism personally. This was payback time.

"He maintained that it was completely out of balance. He said that the unripe fruit couldn't support the high alcohol, that the acidity was buried in harsh tannins, that no amount of time would *smorzare* the watery middle and the bitter finish." It was me, more or less verbatim. Except for *smorzare*, which hadn't ever entered my vocabulary. Giorgio handed me the glass of Rosso out of which he had already sipped. "What do you think? Has it balanced out yet?" *Smorzare* that, his face seemed to say.

What sort of performance must this duet have seemed to Soldera? Half Wizard of Oz, half Citizen Kane, in a single motion he uttered some proverb about "so many persons, so many opinions"—the first words I had clearly heard him speak during the entire encounter—and waved us out of his tent. The appointment was over.

But if the two of us were waging a war of triangulation whose battles were fought over—or at least in the company of—third parties, why was it that Giorgio was at his most passionate, most intuitive, most available, when we socialized with friends of mine visiting from America? At one dinner in the Piazza dei Satiri, Giorgio plunked himself down on a bench next to my old friend Peter, turned abruptly to face him, and declared that he had beautiful eyes. Peter, who in middle age was taking his first tentative steps into declaring himself homosexual, needed no translation as he blushingly replied that Giorgio's voice was so powerful as to shake the seat they were sharing.

At other times translation was necessary, even part of the pleasure itself. There was my pixie librarian friend Irwin, who speaks virtually every European language, probably including Basque and Ural, *except* Italian. Pursuant to a widely diffused belief, he decided that all he had to do was speak Spanish forcefully and it would be understood as Italian. Refusing to limit his conversation to the requisite polite interchanges, he declaimed at top voice, while extending his petite frame to hidalgo proportions, a disquisition, filled with Castilian trills and lisps, on the Jews of Scandinavia, as though he were some sort of Don Quixote whose demented knight errantry had led him to comb the Baltic for the Lost Tribes of Israel. Giorgio was enchanted with all this, and enchanting.

To say nothing of dinner with Gregg and Annette, making their first-ever trip outside the States. Earlier in the day, things had been rocky. True, the three of us lunched at my favorite trattoria, and we all took it as a divine sign that this was the very noon on which the spring crop of fresh porcini mushrooms hit the stalls. But to this pleasure-loving couple, gastronomic delights were one thing, high culture another, as I discovered during an ill-advised tour of Santa Maria del Popolo. The church has much to recommend it, but I steered them past Caravaggio and Bernini to impose their rapt attention on Pinturicchio's *Adoration*. Why I forced my two jet-lagged, truculently nonacademic, and resolutely Jewish friends to absorb the baby Jesus dancing on his back, with the Holy Spirit as a hovercraft high above and the soulful glances of ox and ass in front of the manger, I can't say. Worse was to come: when they escaped me and discovered in the very next chapel a grand expanse of parti-color marble, with columns and pergolas and gilding, I foolishly pronounced that the work they were admiring—to my eyes a mess of rococo schlock that looked like it came from a high-end subdivision in Teaneck—was forbidden to give them pleasure. For this I was punished with an afternoon of not always good-natured mockery.

But the dinner at Giorgio and Sabina's apartment that followed was nothing less than a cosmic realignment on the subject of pleasure. I can't explain what it was that instantly put these four individuals on the same wavelength, perhaps a tone inaudible except to swarthy-faced, sexy, confident heterosexuals. What few things they had in common—Gregg was a psychotherapist; Giorgio knew someone who knew someone who knew Anna Freud; Sabina made jewelry; Annette had worn jewelry in the seventies—had little to do with it, though everyone loved food and wine and we all listened with rapt attention to Giorgio's sententious discourse on how you must never buy any oil whose olives are not handpicked. Rapt attention but, presumably, little comprehension. And I suppose it was all this intuition beyond the authority of words that managed to erase the art-historical debacle of the afternoon.

It was actually the olives that got us going. "Tell Giorgio that I've known a few extra-virgins in my time," says Gregg. Annette snorts. Sabina darts a look at her. "I mean, in my therapeutic practice."

I attempt something, though I am out of my depth in vocabulary. Giorgio begins to rephrase my efforts into better Italian for Sabina's sake, but what comes out is: "He deflowers virgins in his spare time." Unsure whether the mistranslation is his doing or mine, error or repartee, I waver between laughter and pique. Annette, either oblivious or else capitalizing on all this floating signification, understands *flower* and says, "Tell Giorgio we're sorry we didn't bring flowers. We couldn't find a place to buy them."

I decide to introduce some deliberate error into the system: "They want you to know that they would have bought flowers, but they were too stingy."

By this time multiple discourses are afloat. Giorgio is giving a speech to Annette on the theme that great food never makes you fat, while in another corner of the room Sabina is carefully pouring Gregg a glass of the 1963 Dow that I had brought back from England. Annette, giving up on understanding him, is feeding Giorgio a slab of Stilton, while Gregg is ripping through his phrase book to work out what I actually said about the flowers. I am called upon to translate the verb *grouse* from my own conversation and the expression *spin the bottle* from another. Thus, through a multitude of pathways, we arrive at a moment when my Chicago friends insist that I recite in Italian my favorite narrative of gourmet life in England.

This is a shaggy-dog story that involves a peer of the realm, the head of an Oxford college, the date being August 12, when the shooting season begins in Scotland and it is annually permitted to eat grouse (the bird, not the verb). A solemn feast is celebrated at high table, during which we underlings are constrained, before tucking into our own leathery, buckshot-ridden serving and before the ritual decanter is passed around by way of antidote, to await with ever increasing suspense the verdict from the head of the table. Really, the whole point of the story is the pregnant pause after everyone is served and our noble leader, barely visible from my end of the table through all the distance and dim candlelight, considers the food in front of him, seizes a morsel, chews it contemplatively, looks down at the long row of eager, hungry faces, and exclaims, "FROITFUL!"

Imagine the many difficulties of my task here. It wasn't just that my lexicon of fowl fell short; how could I capture the hierarchies of an Oxford senior common room or convey the special flavor of that cockney diphthong, which, for the cognoscenti, was the true climax of the story? It didn't help when Gregg insisted that I include the notion that the grouse was *well hung*; nor was it fortunate that I had gone for the generic term *uccello* in the face of my inability to render the precise species we were consuming. In the end, I fear I left the Italians with the picture of a member of the House of Lords conducting the yearly ritual of chewing on his own sexual organs and finding them "*SPAVENTEEHHVOLE!*" No matter: uproarious and authentic laughter from all nationalities, atop which Giorgio started crooning, "*Fiducia! Fiducia!*"—trust, faithfulness, confidence—as a blessing on the whole human and linguistic enterprise. Whatever is the opposite of the expression *lost in translation*, this was it.

Giorgio's predictable postmortem phone call arrived as I came through the door. No retrospective on the evening's events, however, no *ti voglio bene*; just an invitation to join him and his daughter, Giulia, on Saturday afternoon at the beach. The Communist beach, he was careful to specify, where artists and politicos, dope smokers and toddlers cavort peacefully together.

"Is it already beach season?" I hazarded to ask.

"*Meglio ancora.*" Exactly what Don Giovanni says when the possibility arises that he has been fooling with Leporello's wife.

Perhaps it is Giorgio's odd silence—and Giulia's—during the drive that extracts from me a strangely articulate monologue; indeed, as I speak, I am almost as conscious of my own fluency as I am of the things I'm saying. I narrate the backstory of my ill-advised lecture to Gregg and Annette in front of Pinturicchio, and from that blunder I free-associate into a whole autobiography of embarrassments. Some are of recent, Roman date, like

hunting for sex at the railroad station or telling a poetess more
than she ever wanted to know about Corton-Charlemagne. Others range broadly through the decades of my life, though I do notice as I go along that they array themselves in two categories:
Talking Too Much and Looking for Love in the Wrong Places. I
like to tell stories against myself. Perhaps that doesn't charm
everyone as much as I think it should. Perhaps that explains
what happened at the beach.

We are more or less alone on this stretch of shore, but Giulia
amuses herself with impressive independence at the game of almost going into the water. It is a complete departure from my
usual scene with Giorgio: not his house, not my house, no food,
no wine. A little at a loss for subject matter, I watch Giulia and
comment on her charm and intelligence and self-reliance.

"You don't understand the first thing about what it means to
have a child," Giorgio says. This is a strange enough insult in
translation, I suppose, but even more enigmatic because he is
saying *voi* rather than *tu*. You-all. And *voi* becomes the operative
pronoun for the whole chain of his discourse.

"*Voi* live for yourselves, taking off across the ocean whenever
you want . . ."

"*Voi*—how much time do you really spend teaching students?"

"*Voi*, coming here to the provinces from the center of the
empire . . ."

It is easy enough to dismiss the politically fashionable cliché
about America being the new Roman Empire and Italy one of
the outer provinces: call it Giorgio's *hommage* to the Gramscian
shades of the beach where we found ourselves. But the glimpses
of his life and mine in some sort of fun-house mirror are more
disturbing. How have he-and-I turned into you-and-them? I
think about the ways in which my life during these months—

comfortable, defined, even self-assured, but also lonely, frustrated, needful—has been displaying itself before Giorgio. I also think about the parade of my friends whom he has so charmingly cohosted. Did they constitute the plural of me? Are we collectively the lazy, childless, imperialist objects of Giorgio's anger?

In particular, I think of another visiting friend, a brilliantly successful scholar with an air of unflappable and infectious self-confidence, apparently comfortable in his gayness, his attractiveness, his triumphant intellectual success. Gordon remained decidedly—and doubtless visibly—unsmitten with Giorgio. If Giorgio saw in him a version of me with no stories to tell against himself, and if that version of me didn't really care for Giorgio at all, perhaps . . . But it all remains guesswork. Still, I must say something, and I choose to bypass all the details of accusation against me-plural. Instead, I circumvent my life and leap to some conclusions about his.

"*Carissimo,*" I begin. "One of the things I love about you—*per cui ti voglio bene*—is that you succeed in deriving so much satisfaction in your life even if, *magari*, you haven't realized all your professional hopes . . ."

What can I say about this blunder? That maybe it sounds a little less dreadful in Italian? Certainly, I gave careful thought to *love*, *succeed*, and *satisfaction*. I also am preparing to say that his contentment is deliciously contagious for me, that it has taught me how to appreciate who I am even when I'm cut off from the security of being a professor and from the assurance of my own language. But the look on his face silences me. Of course, he can talk all he wants about how little he cares for his job; he can engage without restraint in eloquent chimerical schemes concerning international academic exchanges, making the whole world learn Italian as a *second* foreign language, bringing European civilization back to formerly Italian colonies in Africa. *Tutto ciò nonostante*—it is not for me to put these pieces of his frustration into a package, and certainly not to turn them into something weirdly, patronizingly positive.

"Leo, Leo, Leo." Giorgio speaks my name in a tone part ironic and part operatic, then gets up and walks away. Giulia is at about ankle level in the surf, and he yanks her back onto dry sand. "I didn't tell you this before," he says when he has returned to his seat beside me, "but you remember last week when you served us that big plate of *pappardelle?*"

"Yes, I remember." Where is this headed?

"Those meatballs were so tough you couldn't chew them. Too much bread, too much egg, too much pepper. Sabina thought she had food poisoning. I nearly had to take her to the hospital."

"*Dio mio!* Is she all right?" I hope I am doing a good job of pretending I believe him. The slide from gastronomic dissatisfaction to toxicity seems highly suspicious.

"*Non capisci un cazzo,*" he says with real anger. Roughly: You don't understand a fucking thing. My mind races between Giorgio's denunciation—were we breaking up? could I even use that term?—and the recollection of those *pappardelle.* The recipe was made famous by a fancy restaurant in Bologna that had been trashed by rioting students in '77. The American empire, the Communist beach—was that somehow where all this was coming from, or going?

He unleashes a tirade on his old theme of *lasciarsi andare.* Now, courtesy of my reminiscences in the car, he is fueled with even juicier anecdotes of my inability to let myself go. All my accomplishments are just a screen, and they don't prevent me from being *un cretino* about love, *un coglione* about sex, *un deficiente* about companionship, *un fesso* about loneliness.

Inspired by the lexicon, I fight back. "*Se mi manca qualcosa*"—if I'm missing something—"what harm is it doing *you?"* And I unload a few months' worth of resentments, detailing my reactions to everything from his story about sex with a nineteen-year-old girl to his Rosso di Montalcino performance in front of Gianfranco Soldera. Along the way I find my own lexicon: *mascalzone, disgraziato, figlio di puttana, testa di cazzo.*

I think of one of the standard family jokes: A mother, angry that her child is still playing outside when it's dinnertime, shouts out the window, "You dirty rotten *&%£$¢#*@!* get back in here!!!!" The kid replies, "*You're* a dirty rotten *&%£$¢#*@!!!*" The mother, to herself: My God, where does he hear such language?

Giorgio's thinking is clearly on the same track: "How the hell have you learned to be so vicious in Italian?"

It is true, I have learned this. *Don Giovanni* served me well, finally, and Giorgio, too. Now I hear how his wife, his child, his job, his prospects for advancement in the world of philosophy, are suffering because he is spending time with me. I've had this conversation before, in other countries, in other languages. If I have learned anything, it is not to fight back on the ground that the married man has chosen. This is the moment, then, to turn the other cheek. To tell him that this isn't about language lessons in viciousness, but the opposite. I want to say that he has taught me I could be lovable, could be loved, in Italian. But all I manage is, "Let's not finish it like this. My time with you has been the best part of my year in Italy."

"*È stato, è stato!*" he repeats. "You're right. The time is over. *Tagliamo la corda.*" Let's cut the cord.

How did we get from *not* finishing it to finishing it? And what, exactly, is finished? True, the afternoon at the beach is over; we are coaxing Giulia out of the surf and wordlessly packing the car. But have I just declared that my year in Rome is over, or is it my relationship with Giorgio whose cord has been cut?

The perils of the verb. I meant to say *has been*; what I was forced to say was "*è stato*." In English, what *has been* may still be going on; in Italian, if something *è stato*, it is completely finished. In fact, I had just been learning how many pasts the two languages have and how irreconcilable they are. When you get to be quite an advanced student of Italian, you may start wielding a tense called the *passato rimoto*, which includes strange, unexpected forms like *fu* and *ebbe*. Or, you may find it in the earliest lines of *The Divine Comedy*, precisely in that meeting between Dante and Virgil that was always for me the most mysterious and most inspiring model for encountering history. It's Virgil who says, "*Omo già fui, poeta fui.*" I *was* a man, I *was* a poet. Except not like *was* in English: what he is really saying, I was, *and finished being*, a man; I was, and *finished being*, a poet. It's over, *tagliamo la corda*. Just as Don Giovanni loves women, according to Leporello.

So this perfect tense, as they call it because it refers to things that have been *perfected*, was teaching me about all sorts of pasts. When Dante has Virgil say *fui*, it's because he wants to make it perfectly clear that Virgil, man and poet, is completely enclosed in the past. But it was my scholarly business to dis-enclose the past. Dante, looking at the colossus of ancient literature, or Raphael looking at the Arch of Constantine, may have had a stake in separating themselves at the same time as they were embracing their predecessors. But I was stuck with a broader band of possibilities for past and present, and possessed of later, looser, more hybrid languages to shape my thinking about it: *was, has been, used to be*; *era, è stato, fu*.

The afternoon on the beach, with its linguistic crisis, was only half of what sent me down this path of reflections. On a warm May Sunday, when Rome felt even more shuttered than usual, Giorgio chose to reconnect with me by making repeated appearances at my door. About which I knew nothing, because I was in fact engaging elsewhere in my own kind of aftermath and process that day. It was the moment for an art pilgrimage, and this time Narcissus would not suffice. I had patterns for such activity, particularly on Sundays, when it became a challenge to rebel against the city's nearly universal closure by seeking out its few open venues. This time I enjoyed the astonishingly serene arithmetic of Borromini's Sant'Ivo during its infinitesimal window of accessibility, and I followed that up with the somewhat more practical project of carrying *Mein Führer*—not a dictator but a fanatically painstaking German guidebook to antiquities— through a couple of rooms at the Capitoline Museum, where I could make my way through the several fine-print pages of erudition devoted to every single shard on display. The therapy was insufficient. By the end of the day, with Sunday past, I remained in need. On Monday morning I required something more passionate than Borromini and less demanding than a hall of remnants viewed through the sharply focused lens of Teutonic scholarship.

It was probably no accident that it had taken me so long to return to the Sistine Chapel. In the days of my annual vacations in Rome, it was so inevitable a stopping place that I had my own patented technique for encountering it without crowds: 8:30 a.m. at the door to the Vatican; the elevator rather than the stairs; learn the shortest route through the labyrinth of approved pathways; speed past phalanxes of sightseers distracted by Bramante, the Etruscans, and several miles of monotonously displayed papal tchotchkes; make the painful decision to bypass the Raphael rooms; deliver oneself down the narrow stairway into Michelangelo's sanctuary a good quarter of an hour before it was occupied by the carnival of world tourism.

If over the year I had been repaying my debt to all the Vatican treasures I had previously circumvented, paying regular visits to everything from the post office to the *Laocoön* but drawing a circle around Michelangelo, it was probably because the ruckus over the cleaning had kept me away. These were the violent glory days of the battle over whether the frescoes were being ruined or saved by their fifteen years of restoration—in retrospect, it appears like high culture's chance to satisfy the perpetual need of the media for manufactured sensation—and voting with my feet had been my way of remaining in less controversialized realms of art. Still, on this particular Monday morning, with the sense of an ending that Giorgio had imposed on my consciousness, time seemed to be running out on my chance to stand on the battlefield where sixteenth-century pigment met twentieth-century prophylaxis. Perhaps that was the logic which led me to take my familiar walk across the river and repeat my crowd-busting itinerary inside the papal palace.

No luck, it appeared at first, with my strategy. But it wasn't tourists who crowded me in the Sistine Chapel; it was an army of workers and their tools. Coming through the little door into the big space, before I saw any art at all, I was confronted with masses of plywood, bright lights, and contrivances of scaffolding that resembled some hydraulic reconception of the structures that made painting the ceiling possible in the first place. Drawn by the remarkable colors on the ceiling at the far end, I passed through the two-thirds of the space where the work was not yet done, or currently being done, as though it were so much static.

My gaze landed first on a bald, bearded man with a book, wearing flaming pastels. I had never before seen Zacharias cast a shadow, since in the old days everything was shadow. He had all the weight and presence of an animate being, and yet there was a darkness in his face—what before was all *scuro* was now *chiaroscuro*—that made him appear immobile, like an icon. Not so the two putti behind him, now revealed as a blond and a brunet, whose shadings of rose and ivory made them seem more like flesh and blood. Framing all three were pairs of sculpted putti—not really sculpted, of course, but painted to look like sculpture—whose distinctness in hue and texture located them in yet another order of nature, or art. Fresco paint was everywhere being turned into architecture, sculpture, bodies—no veil of uniformity, but separate categories of being. Michelangelo seemed to assert the irrevocable boundaries of life and death but also to place the human body on an infinitely shaded continuum between those extremes.

My eye fell on the *ignudi*, those naked, hunky supernumerary figures who have no theological meaning but only hold up a series of biblical medallions: suddenly they stood out from the whole architectonic construction as living persons. Michelangelo had even designed a plumped-up cushion under one of them, as though his naked rump might get too chilly from the painted marble on which he was destined to sit forever. I had a long professional interest in these characters because their form owed the most to the artist's love for ancient statues. Now I could see that they were also the most alive of any figures in the room. The entire space had become a phantasmagoria on the difference, and the not-difference, of art and life.

It was that cushioned nude—for the first time I realized that he looked a bit feminine, a bit mixed-race, say, Moorish—who formed the boundary line between the cleaned fresco and the work in progress. The room was perfectly trisected on that Monday morning: first a kaleidoscope of fresh color; then, in the middle, the superstructure of contraptions behind which nothing was visible; and lastly the uncleaned frescoes as we had known them all our lives. It took only the briefest glance at the restored images for me to shed any anxiety about the project; clearly, this

would be the Sistine Chapel as Michelangelo had painted it, and
it was even greater than we could have known. My fellow
tourists, now swarming in, bunched themselves so disproportion-
ately at the gleaming end of the room that if the chapel had really been Noah's Ark instead of a metaphor for Noah's Ark, we
might have been on a sinking ship. If only to avoid the crowd, I
felt myself finally drawn from the far end to the center.

The unseen center: as I stood under it, restorers were at work
on the Creation of Eve. The Expulsion from the Garden, its
cleansing already completed, was partly obscured; the Creation
of Adam, also half covered, was not yet begun. I was at the exact
midpoint of space in the room and time of its renovation. Above
my head, the most famous scenes were shrouded. To one side of
me, the reborn clarity of the Noah scenes, which generally receive so little attention; to the other side, the as yet untouched
panels depicting the first days of creation, whose unrepre-
sentability was fittingly served by the gray cloud inside which the
old, dirty Sistine ceiling seemed uniformly encompassed. As I
planted myself in the blank epicenter and turned my torso, like
one of those athletic medallion wielders, first toward the light,
then toward the darkness in which God said "Let there be light,"
and then back again, I started to feel the layers of the past as
though inside my own body.

Was, has been, is. The days of creation, the years of frescoing
the Sistine ceiling, the centuries of its afterlife. No mechanical
reproduction here: the real thing, Michelangelo in the flesh.
Michelangelo made paint into flesh; flesh decays; art decays.
What is the real thing? These are sixteenth-century visions, but
I cannot see them through sixteenth-century eyes. They are
beautiful outside of all time and history, but they show the effects
of time, and they have a history. At this moment, one-third of
the ceiling is newly made as if original—"repristinated," the Ital-

ians say; one-third is in the form that several centuries have known and loved it; one-third is under subjection to a surgical process that only our present times dared undertake. Not one of these thirds can be frozen in time; every one of them has a present and a past. What *was*, still *is* but is different, even when it is put back as it *was*.

I would like to say that I had a complete revelation about my work as I stood on that liminal site, but the truth is that it was the ritual twenty-minute walk back to Satyr Square, past the madhouse and the bullet-shaped penthouse windows and the oversize bathtubs, during which things fell into place. Somewhere between the outer circle of Pompey's Theater and the hundred and three steps, my questions started to have answers.

I reflected on the calumnies against my unearthed sculptures, and on my own accusations, mostly—that they were bad or broken or kitschy, that they formed a map of death or were merely remnants of heedless demolition. In the Sistine Chapel I felt as though I were at ground zero of unstoppable flux, on the factory floor of history's work. On the one hand, time; on the other hand, everything else. The one hand was God's, the other hand Adam's. By the dawning of the Renaissance, my statues had had a thousand years to grime up, to become faceless, to go out of style; by my time, Michelangelo had had five hundred years to do the same. You can love the grime or clean it off; you can restore what is broken or be inspired to make something new. You can look at the past across an unfathomable distance of incomprehension; you can deny the distance; you can salute the past as a long-lost friend.

If the *Apollo Belvedere* failed to turn me on, if Heemskerck's shoe was too scanty to build on, if *Laocoön* seemed to be overacting, if the Cortona carvings had a touch of the middlebrow—

they all were what gave me my own historical work to do. I wasn't repristinating, like the workers on the scaffolding, but maybe doing something more humane, more faithful—like Giorgio crooning *"Fiducia!"* when we all lost and found ourselves in translation. I was mapping the distance between moments in the past without erasing them, mapping the way Michelangelo did his own mapping of his own past. God knows, I wasn't painting the Sistine ceiling or cleaning it, but maybe I wasn't enrolling in the Academy of the Superfluous either.

When I got upstairs, I went straight for my dining-work table and jotted notes. Some of them, years later, turned into a couple of sentences from the book that had progressed out of my projected *Art from the Ground Up* and *Archaeology by Accident*:

> The modern culture which appropriates the classical past in part seeks to make something out of nothing. That "nothing" may in the end be less about artistic quality than about historic distance and all the inevitable erasures that come with fragmentation, loss of context, and illegibility.

Something and nothing: particular stories of making new things out of old things had been vexing me. Renaissance artists loved those ancient sarcophagi that were covered in mythological carvings, but they never put Venus and Adonis or Diana and Endymion or the processions of Dionysus on their modern coffins. That would have been un-Christian. What they did do—and it was almost as surprising—was to build wedding chests, trousseau holders, in almost exactly the shape of the sarcophagi and cover them in paintings of scandalous pagan myths. Now it all made sense. The ancients had wanted to think of death as an embrace of carnal, heavenly joys. Christianity had a different story about death and enforced it pitilessly. But that universe of pleasure, where intoxication and triumph meet with sexual desire, was in the end irrepressible. *Liebestod.* Where death was, there marriage shall be.

My note-taking was interrupted by the doorbell. "I'm giving you a second chance," Giorgio shouted up from the street as I dropped the key in his general direction. Purveyor of his own special logic, he had concluded from my absence the previous day, as I later learned, that I was refusing reconciliation. In the course of the next few days, there was one phone call that was friendly but cautious and another in a tone of appeasement, with references to how painful—though necessary—our separation had been, how much he had missed me, how he now felt completely delivered from the problems that had started it. Between the two calls he made yet more appearances on my doorstep, with tokens including a bunch of flowers (what century were we living in?) and a bottle of 1978 Barolo that was extremely strenuous to consume at 11:00 a.m., the more so because it was accompanied by postmortems aimed partly at resolution and partly at reawakening hostilities. We had dinner the next evening at a restaurant of my choosing, distinguished by its spaghetti with shellfish and its clientele of breathtaking long-haired soccer stars; here, in contrast to the previous morning's conversation, nothing but small talk was spoken.

Finally, we met again at a supernumerary tasting in Clara's shop. Not only was it outside the regular series, but it threatened to be the last of the season—possibly the last ever—since Jeffrey, our *magister ludi*, was rumored to be discontented with his employment there. Was it his malaise that explained the preposterous premise of "Pinot Noirs from Lombardy and Santa Barbara"? That evening everyone, and not just the grape, seemed to be outside their comfort zone, *fuori zona.* Jeffrey, generally so strong-willed, was passive, garrulous Ian tight-lipped. Little John strutted wine expertise no one had heard before; Silvia withheld her accustomed charms from the suntanned California boy who was presenting his lamentable products; Long John's discourse, usually terse and blunt, was abstruse and ironic; Giorgio and I were almost completely silent.

When the evening was over, we found ourselves huddled just outside the doorway of the shop.

"*Senti,*" he began. "Sabina and I want to take you with us to the sulfur baths in Saturnia. We'll soak ourselves in mud. We'll wash away all the bad humors together. *Così ci salutiamo.*"

You say goodbye, I say hello. *Ci salutiamo* can mean anything from a casual greeting to an eternal farewell. It was difficult to know which to expect from Giorgio in Saturnia. It's true that the sense of an ending had already started to close in on me. Not a sad ending, not a happy ending—no simple dramatic genre suffices—but more like a period at the conclusion of a sentence. Better to think of my life as grammar than as theater.

Clearly, though, Giorgio preferred theater. Now that I was faced with the promise of a big finish in the Etruscan slime of Saturnia, I realized what had most upset me since the afternoon on the beach. Between not knowing whether our relationship was over—was that a subspecies of not knowing whether it *was* a relationship?—and not knowing whether I wanted it to be over, and feeling like a fool for investing so much in it, and worrying that Italy was going to go down the drain if Giorgio did, I realized it was this last quandary that left me most battered.

Had Giorgio become Italy? I had told him he was the best part of my year in Rome. But even if that was true, was he all of it? As I followed one of my familiar homeward routes from Clara's shop—no crowded Corso this time, or the Jews' racetrack, but the Tomb of Augustus and the melancholy lowlands that had regularly been inundated by Tiber floods until the end of the nineteenth century—I thought about the evening's cast of characters. I thought about the furniture in Giovannone's apartment, about Long John carrying me up the Arch of Constantine; I thought about Vito and Marian's leather people and the music of Silvia's atonal composer and Ian's Christmastime tasting of duck versus goose foie gras. Clara's group had opened up into the Communist Gourmet Club, and that had led me to Sandro. Sandro had led to the Marcos and to Paolo. Paolo had led to Vincenzo, radiologist and collaborator with his girlfriend in the making of fresh hams and in-house smoked salmon, farmer of rabbits and wine grapes at the end of the subway line.

I thought of people I couldn't even remember how I had met. How exactly had I ended up crammed into a sports car with a young doctor and his two—yes, *two*—girlfriends as they spontaneously decided that we would head for the beach at 3:00 a.m., only to be sidetracked by a repeated high-speed circuit of the hallucinatory, hidden-in-plain-sight Piazza Mincio, an early-twentieth-century complex of buildings in a style, to put it mildly, eclectic, that mixed Pre-Raphaelite with Pharaonic with Mayan; or was the place quite normal and just our consciousnesses that had become eclecticized? And what was I doing wearing headphones in the mountains of the Veneto as a new friend, scion of a Prosecco-making family, appointed me chief sound mixer on a recording project to be entitled *La musica del vino*? Or, closer to home, in Frascati, how did I get my hands in molten curds of warm milk, attempting to form mozzarella balls under the encouragement of a beaming tenor-voiced lady winemaker who was my guide on a gastronomic odyssey that culminated in a home-cooked meal etched in the memory by, among other things, a pasta sauce of cherry tomatoes deep-fried until they turned mahogany?

Sometimes your life can pass before your eyes even when you're not drowning. As I approached Satyr Square that night, reconstructing my life in Rome, now something like three-quarters elapsed, I thought, Buy a camera. Then I thought of Isherwood, half a century earlier in Berlin, saying he *was* a camera, and then I thought of Liza Minnelli in front of the camera, and then I thought, No. I spend too much of my time with other people's pictures, other people dead for hundreds or thousands of years, to be satisfied with shooting my own. Still, there is something special about images, the way they capture the frozen moment and keep it still through time. I thought about Giorgio and how for six months I had felt as though I were on some wayward arc of a journey with him, some parabola speeding in directions I couldn't predict or control. Maybe that was why I took refuge in Caravaggio or Michelangelo when the going got tough. A picture could stop time, could stop motion, could silence fearful questions about present and future. Italians are said to live for the moment: Was that why they painted such beautiful pictures? If I wanted to take back my time in Italy for myself, wrest it from Giorgio's exclusive dominion, I had to record its moments, its images. Which is exactly what I determined to do from that moment onward. *Ekphrasis*. Snapshots, if you like.

Ekphrasis—words that describe a picture—was, after all, my perpetual subject. And these days, with Bukowski long since relegated to his original position on the living-room shelves, my bedside book was a little bilingual version of the founding texts in the history of *ekphrasis*, written by Philostratus in the third century A.D. Perfect nightly reading, since the *Eikones*, or Pictures, consist of chapters so brief that I might even assay the Greek before too much fatigue set in. The fiction is that the author is walking through a museum and lecturing to his pupil on exactly what to see, chapter by chapter, in each painting. In reality, it seems, the pictures were invented, painted first in Philo-stratus' mind and then turned into florid exercises of rhetoric. He, too, was making something out of nothing. I loved these texts because in a space of two or three pages you could move from Phaëthon to Ariadne, from Pasiphaë to Perseus, just as though you were in the perfect picture gallery of the mind. It was like crossbreeding my favorite lists with my favorite modes of snacking.

But it wasn't only the shape of the *Eikones* that delighted me. I loved what Philostratus saw in pictures because he used so much more than his eyes. When he looked at painted Cupids, he could smell the apples they were gathering. He could hear Pan's pipes and Amphion's lyre and the din of Bacchic revelry; he could relay whole paragraphs of speech from an image of the god Apollo. He could read the emotions off the grimace of the slave who is about to flay Marsyas. He could tell that the Heliades were about to turn into amber trees and Cadmus and Harmonia about to become serpents. In the world of sensible reason, no one can literally see such things in pictures, of course, but I loved Philostratus most of all because Renaissance artists read his de-scriptions and engaged in the blissful illusion that they could communicate all these impossibilities in pigment and stone if they played their genius right.

Philostratus, to be sure, would never have painted himself into any of these pictures. But I take the liberty of making that modification.

The scene is a sun-dappled, terraced hillside; cypress and poplar suggest Tuscany. From our vantage point it is possible to see old brick stables now converted into some vernacular form of Bauhaus modern, as well as a baroque palace with turrets and belfries through whose windows bits of fading pastel frescoes in the manner of Tiepolo are to be glimpsed, and, between them, a sparsely tended topiary garden whose fantasy animals are only occasionally identifiable. Though these are only the first days of spring, it is already the perfect median temperature, not too cold to sit outside in shirtsleeves or too warm to sit in front of a baronial hearth where lazy-burning olive logs give off a perfumed warmth. The *padrone di casa*—slight, smiling, myopic; architect, professor, winemaker; his dress a little tweedy, his speech a little poetic—is jubilant with the pleasure of offering an afternoon's hospitality to some twenty wine lovers. He occupies these noble surroundings not through ancient inheritance, as might appear, but because his father bought them cut-rate after the nobleman who belonged there lost his fortune in a disastrous postwar building scheme.

The *padrone* can be seen in many places at once. Here, like an Age of Enlightenment lord of the manor, he is demonstrating how an oven of his own design constructed expressly out of chestnut wood is roasting an *ocio*, or gander, that has been specially fatted up for lunch. There, like an eager sophomore, he is confiding in one of his visitors the information that he has put the technical direction of his wine production into the hands of a certain Dr. Science (apparently a vineyard consultant really named Scienza), and he pulls out an invoice of French grape varietals whose seedlings he has just ordered from Montpellier, having recently discovered how good French wine can be. The visitor looks at the list and responds with a paean to the rare and costly Viognier, while his interlocutor faithfully writes down a series of attributes ("guava, crème fraîche, primroses") of this grape in the margin of the invoice. In a third place, he appears more as a moderator, perhaps the secretary-general of some U.N. of hedonism, as he orchestrates a partly spontaneous and partly patterned set of public exchanges among the visitors, wherein speeches about archaeology and tractors, about the culture of roses and the influence of psychoanalysis on art, are interwoven, amid laughter, with quips in multiple languages that remain just shy of hurtful, the Viognier-touting visitor contentedly at the polyglot center of it all.

In a separate scene, later, when most have gone back to the city, a circle of specially privileged guests roast sausages in the fire, receive tastes of experimental concoctions—grappa, Vin Santo, the first Gamay this side of the Alps—and when they retire to a myriad of bedrooms that have been prepared with freshly pressed linens and newly cut flowers, one guest says to another as they go their separate and solitary ways, "There are some times that are so perfect that they make you sad, because you know that your future life will never return to this level of perfection."

No, it's not *Israelites Adoring the Golden Calf*, it's one Israelite in search of a statue he has longed to see in the flesh. We find ourselves at a series of receding vistas among the Vatican antiquities. Laocoön and the Belvedere Hermes are at the limits of our peripheral vision as we greedily focus on the next chamber, whose menagerie of kitsch—a Panther Sinking Its Fangs into a Goat, a Bear Fighting with a Bull, an oversize beast whose label reads, in Italian, MOUSE (RAT)—hardly satisfies the ravenous eyes of our two viewers. On one side, it is the urbanologist, who has done herself up *alla giapponese*, with long yardage of an intricately folded silk kerchief that is supposed to retain the traces of all its crinkles even when made to stretch, as now, from neck to ankle. But no genius of Asian textile could have anticipated what flaccidity would result from the wild convertible ride that has brought these two, on her imperious caprice, from a lunch party occupying two of her apartment's three terraces, where she flirted consecutively with an American antiquity restorer, two graduate-student wine pourers, and several unidentified citizens of non-European nations.

Her face appears flushed with whatever passion it was that propelled her so liberally through the susceptibilities of her guests, then out of her house with the feast still in full swing, her trademark smoked salmon nowhere near exhausted, then in a dizzy, *carabinieri*-defying sequence of Tiber bridge crossings while she embarrassed her fellow traveler—who felt neither deserving nor appreciative of the favor of her company—by shouting obscenities at all drivers who got in her way. His face, too, reflects high stimulus, but it is neither the wind-borne pollutants that have lodged in his eyes nor the prospect of an ambiguous tête-à-tête; rather, he has caught sight, just beyond the marble zoo display, of an open archway where previously a barrier had always stopped him.

The object of his desire is a larger, older, and even more exotically clad female. The prospect of seeing her reclining figure in all its burnished marble lassitude, her chastely crossed legs balanced by an almost lurid pileup of draperies at her midsection, the complete self-absorption of her somnolent countenance confuted by an enveloping, beckoning gesture of forearms that seems to insist on a viewer's entry into her secret space—all of this propels him to leave his traveling companion some meters behind and only dimly recollected. When, finally, he stands in the long-desired statue's presence, he realizes that so accidental was this encounter that, accompanied by the merest little touristic guidebook, he has none of the extensive scholarly materials he needs to enter the centuries-old contest to name her, to decide whether she is Cleopatra or Ariadne or a Sleeping Nymph from the shores of the Danube. He must return properly equipped.

To which end, he wonders whether there is some algorithm in the rota of the Vatican Museums whereby he can be assured that this room will be accessible during a certain predictable moment in the week, or month, or year. Nothing so straightforward, he learns from a conversation with one of the uniformed employees. "Not to worry, *signore*, you can call each morning to find out what is open or closed on that day." Wherewith the burly guard surprises him by seizing the Baedeker out of his hand and writing the phone number on its back page with a broad-tipped indelible pen. His companion glimpses the transaction from afar and, once she has herself arrived in front of the statue, says in a tone of petulant competitiveness, "Were you making a date with that man?" It was she, after all, who many months earlier had left on his notepad the invitation to spend a sunset on one of her terraces.

Allowing for some centuries of difference, you could say that the scene looks a little like the "Who, me?" of Caravaggio's Saint Matthew. A little crowd of diversely dressed patrons, younger and older, sit sipping intently around a table in a space dramatically lit by a setting sun that reflects golden through the wide opening of the shop as radiated off the peach-colored palazzo opposite. It's no marble-appointed, high-vaulted wine bar like others we have seen. Is it just a neighborhood dive where the artisans from a small radius of workshops pile in daily to swig a cheap glass of rotgut? Not exactly: if we look closely at the shelves—and you have to look closely, since both bottles and persons are jammed tightly in the space—you can make out ordered hierarchies of the finest wines. On one set of shelves, labeled PIEMONTE, the eye moves upward from Dolcetto to Barbera to Nebbiolo to Barbaresco to lordly reclining magnums inscribed with legendary *crus* of Barolo. In a deeper sanctum of the space, wines from across the Alps, under the notably recherché heading ALSAZIA, are once again displayed on a vertical continuum, beginning at the bottom with mere grape varieties and reaching an apex with labels sporting the magic words RANGEN DE THANN, which sounds foreign in every language.

Perhaps the populace makes some sense of this paradox between squalid interior and exotic treasure room of the vine. All the faces but one are certainly *romanissimi*, even if the dress code and the professions that go along with it vary radically. A handsome young fellow, his fine features going a bit puffy, is suited in a plaid that tries to be both old money and slick; he probably sells high-end automobiles. An elderly gentleman with an aristocratic shock of thick white hair is incongruously dressed in a workman's smock, and he grasps a wineglass that reflects the dancing golden light on his fingertips, which are far from clean: perhaps he fixes cars, perhaps he sculpts masterpieces. No mistaking the actress, however. Her hair, her face, her long, form-hugging suit, all shimmer with impressionist highlights designed to dazzle but also to deflect from any too rigorous inquiry about age.

Only those denied admission to this paradise of friends would be so mean about them. They are certainly not mean to one another, nor does any of them seem to be denied admission. *Anzi,* the lone foreigner seems to be the special object of affection, the mascot, the favorite son, the *passepartout.*

This scene isn't about him or them, however. The wine bar's owner, half pixie-philosopher and half entrepreneur-promoter of the remarkable collection of souls whose party he hosts every evening, is giving a performance such as no one has seen from him before. He has taken a large sheet of paper from the art student who moonlights as his stock boy, and he is busy doing some preliminary folds while quietly demanding widespread attention.

"So," he says, "Mary has just told Joseph that she's expecting *un bambino.*" The paper is taking on a less rectangular shape. "Right away her husband starts worrying. 'Where will we put him? I'm sure there's no room' "—he executes one more fold so as to produce the suggestion of a chimney—" 'at the INN!' "

The audience begins to pay more attention. He turns the paper ninety degrees and executes a few more swift alterations on either edge, so that it has become a little open box, like a feeding trough. " 'And we certainly can't let him grow up in a MANGER!' " Much sleight of hand; the next changes are too rapid to follow, but all at once it emerges as a six-pointed star. " 'And the TEMPLE? Well, it's too full of money changers.' " Laughter all around, almost. " 'Then, what'll we do if he brings all his friends home to SUPPER?' " Wherewith the paper, now much smaller and returning to three dimensions, turns into a long table, suitable for thirteen. " 'But I'm such a poor old carpenter, I can't manage all that work. So what *can* I build to house our child?' " He pauses, takes the paper out of view, but as he returns it, he is still manipulating, so that the tabletop narrows and the legs rotate and widen. " 'I got it. Here's where the baby is going to live. *Ecco!*' " In the sharp rays of late afternoon light, he holds up a perfect origami cross. Amid the laughter and applause, he tosses his artwork to the one foreigner, about whom it is rumored that he is soon to return home. "Take it as a souvenir," he says.

Call this one a *moving* picture. It begins with a fava bean. In the shadow of Giordano Bruno, a young man of the market is showing off the freshness of his produce. His customer, who has become well practiced among these displays, has learned to admire not only this stall's merchandise but also the deep complexion, high cheekbones, and curiously elegant speech of the salesperson. Now, to demonstrate that these are the very first favas of the season, the young merchant motions for his customer to hold out his hands, and he rewards him, in what is almost a gesture of communion, with a little pyramid of beans. As a few glints of moisture on them catch the morning light, the shopper has his first taste of raw fava. He orders half a kilo, the pods tumble into a sheet of paper that is expertly folded, and then, after an extra moment of eye contact, the young man reaches into a bin behind him and deposits something else, a little clandestinely, into the bag. The whole movement is almost too swift to be seen.

Next, on the top level of a tower, we see the same shopper unwrapping his packages in the company of a sturdy lady who shows only mild interest in the culinary contents while she focuses on folding laundry. It has been less than a year, but our shopper has learned to trust her in all matters domestic: Had she not, after all, taught him how to improve on his risotto, how to fold and stack freshly washed shirts so that they did not need ironing, and how to thwart the imperialist designs of the landlady, whose attempt to gentrify by raising the apartment's roof while he was still occupying it was threatening the viability of his beloved loft bedroom? Now, as he disentangles the folds of the almost gift-wrapped fava beans, a fat bunch of lacy greens pops out of the package first. He knows it is nothing that he bought, and surmises that it was the little lagniappe offered by the market lad, whose face and bearing had always reminded him of the way Florentine painters imagined the most exotic of the journeying Magi.

What are these gauzy fronds, exactly? Dill, or perhaps the salad green that Italians call "monks' beards"? And why were they spontaneously included with the fava beans, like a foregone conclusion, in the way that a Roman greengrocer would automatically toss in a bunch of basil when regular customers bought tomatoes? And yes, there had been a sprig of wild oregano from the same young man many months earlier. A quick taste reveals the inimitable flavor of anise, but exceptionally sweet and gentle. At just this point the lady concludes her linen work, glances over, declares, "Wild fennel!" Both pairs of eyes move from fava to finocchio and back. Something disquiets him about their interconnection, especially given her saintly company, but she surprises him by joyously crying out, "It's the season of *frittedda*!"

Is *frittedda* her word for summer? he wonders, being used to her habit of doubling consonants. But the location shifts. Together, they are at another market, different from the first, said to be built atop the mountain of pottery fragments left by the ancients. He gazes in perplexity as she slides a well-trained fingernail through mounds of peapods, rejecting with contempt anything more than half the size of a cherrystone. Then she pushes him through a rapid triage of artichokes. They had all looked pretty much the same to him before, but as she labels them with derision, he begins to notice difference. *"Mammole! . . . Romanesco! . . . Violetta!"*: apparently none of them is what she is looking for. Suddenly she says, *"Cerda!"* and places in his hand the spiniest little cactus of an artichoke he has ever seen. Gently, so he won't be lacerated, she retracts the vegetable, pulls out a pocketknife, and feeds him a raw slice. Miracle: the outside was murderous, but the interior is soft, chokeless, and luscious to the taste.

Fava beans, wild fennel, peas, artichokes. Now he understands that they are ingredients in a special dish whose window of possibility, since everything in it must have just barely sprung from the ground, is a scant ten days in May. "The fried thing," they call it in its native Sicilian. She is leading him onward, toward a remote part of town. What more can they need?

"*Cipolle!*" she exclaims. His face registers doubt. Traversing all five bends in the Tiber just to find the right onion? She is implacable, and the shopping is complete only when she has found the perfect little red sphere, of a sweetness legendary since Phoenician times, at a market on the site where, Christians say, Constantine saw a cross in the sky and was told, "Under this sign shall you conquer." Holding the magical vegetable out to him, she says, "Now we will begin."

Once its constituents had been appropriately trimmed, sautéed, braised, finished with surprising touches of vinegar and nutmeg, and allowed to rest the requisite twenty-four hours, the *frittedda* might have served as a centerpiece for the next picture. But in truth it would hardly have been visible on a table groaning with *timballi* and *fondute*, *arrosti* and *tielle*, and the real truth is that, glorious as they may be, all these dishes are little more than a blur in a panorama of festivity whose real highlights are the persons and the conversations. We are looking at a festivity designed to lament and celebrate the end of one man's year in Rome.

The site, with its marble bar, cracked mirror, and fading walnut cabinetry full of wine bottles, is by now familiar. So, too, the guest of honor, momentarily visible in a back room, where he appears to be exchanging sharp words with another figure we've seen before as they act out opposing intentions with the knife poised over a *torta di ricotta*. As for the crowded and indistinct canvas of other celebrants, we shall have to identify them by their attributes, like the saints lined up on a medieval altarpiece. On the edges of the action, out on the street, a dignified older gentleman is struggling to maneuver his luxury vehicle into a compact space while, nearby, a strapping younger man, who has easily parked his mini, is struggling to extricate his own body from it. Closer to the action, a glamorous photographer manages to snap candid shots even though she has not removed her own tinted glasses. Elsewhere, a lady of a certain age, wearing something like a lace dressing gown and a confused expression, sits alongside a sprightly young man who is entertaining her with clever descriptions of himself as reflected in his passport picture. Meanwhile, other contingents of the young eschew such frivolity: one group argues over the day's newspaper; another commiserates about the imminent summer closure of the archives; a third worries whether the evening's wines are cloudy.

Then there are the gift givers. The sorceress of *frittedda*, its brief season already past, produces a covered dish containing pasta with sardines. Another lady—a country cousin with the look of rustic aristocracy—unveils a brace of still warm mozzarellas that she has transported directly from the Castelli Romani, while a much younger man shows off the capocolla that he and his girlfriend have produced an hour's ride away on the A line of the Metropolitana. A whimsical young fellow in the background is spinning a disc of his own making into the stereo system, which includes tracks with names like "Pomerol" and "Song of the Grape." Brightest spot of all in the picture is a beautiful billfold, each pocket of which forms a rainbow of gorgeously polychrome leathers; it is being presented to the guest of honor by a smiling older couple who are dressed in a timeless elegance that suggests well-to-do bohemians from a more civilized past. Less visible is the gift of a sheaf of papers from a wildly unkempt young man: if we could get close enough to read the words as well as the guest of honor can, we would see that it consists of an Italian translation of his own first chapter, the original itself only barely completed: "*L'*Apollo Belvedere *rientrò nel mondo intorno al 1490.*"

But now a game is in progress, a little joke at the expense of the foreigner who is the occasion for these revels. The shapely young woman who looks too young and pretty to be mistress of this whole domain calls the company to attention and at some length introduces her associate, who, she says, will give a proper speech. Her slightly awkward and ill-attired colleague commences, in exquisitely formed but ear-cripplingly pronounced Italian, what sounds like an oration until it suddenly compresses itself into a mere introduction of yet another speaker. The new speaker—either an old man inside a young man's body or the reverse—declares that he, finally, will rise to this solemn occasion, only to derail into a witty introduction of the young lady who began the whole circuit. Whereupon she, now that the game seems to be over, announces that it is she who has been granted the privilege of making the speech. After a few introductory formulas, however, all she does is to ask the guest of honor to rise, and once he is indisputably the center of attention, she announces that he will give the evening's speech on the theme of everything that has happened in his life since he first entered this space. Unprepared, and looking at all these faces in their varieties of anticipatory enthusiasm, he feels as though he has been turned around and around in some dizzying game of blindman's buff, or like someone who has knocked on his own door and found himself a different person on the other side.

The farewell party at Clara's wineshop—where I know there were at least forty-two people, since that was the number of micro-portions Giorgio and I managed to eke out of two cheesecakes—did not really take place at the end of my stay. Fearing a mass summer exodus, we scheduled the event almost a month before my actual departure. Joyous and triumphant as it was, with the participation of even long-lost and problematical persons such as Gabriele of the painting, or my landlady, who had been so generous with *fodera* but later became connivingly secret about construction work on the building, which produced floods far graver than the one that greeted my earliest days there, I felt by the end of the evening that I was poised on a sort of lame-duck period when I would be back in solitude while my friends left the metropolis for their various exurban family seats.

I need not have worried. The pace let up a little, to be sure, but what events there were took on grand valedictory significance. The *last* rump roast with the jeweler, the *last* sunset on the urbanologist's terrace, the *last* discussion of French varietals with the architect, the *last* sighting of the poetess in the street market, the *last* necropolis excursion with the antiquity restorer: what had been casual was now an occasion.

On the other hand, some events insisted on being momentous, like Giorgio's long-heralded road trip to the famous Tuscan sulfur baths. When, exactly, did Satan take charge of this journey to Saturnia? It would probably be a mistake to see his malign hand in the planning stages. Better to blame Giorgio for making, canceling, and misremembering the appointment several times. And better blame myself for the farce of waiting with my newly purchased swimsuit in front of the wrong Trastevere landmark, thus producing a delay that got, somewhat illogically, blamed—*ne parleremo dopo*—for Sabina's absence from the excursion, which deprived me of that voice which was always ready to tell me what I was thinking.

The shades start closing in a little later, when Giorgio and I drive by eerie Etruscan ruins whose bulky, bristly shapes seem like mystic love children of Celts and Aztecs, and when we travel through a village that advertises itself as Little Jerusalem, with tourist signs pointing to a synagogue and matzo factory, but—according to the guidebook—not a single remaining Jew. The name of the Archenemy himself is at last invoked a few kilometers from our destination. As we stop to look at the magnificent arch of the Roman Gate to the village of Saturnia, a toothless, self-appointed local guide urges us to follow him into the valley below, where a land and rock formation commemorates some prehistoric good-and-evil escapade of legend, from which, he tells us half coherently, it takes the name Hoof of the Devil.

We decline his offer, then come upon a spectacular panorama of rocky strand crowded with bathers frolicking in roiling waters, which could have served as the title sequence for a California surfing movie if the Pacific happened to have turned boiling hot. Or it might have been something Gustave Doré designed to illustrate an upper circle of Dante's hell, where the damned labor under the illusion that they are enjoying themselves.

Were we heading for another Communist beach? On the contrary: with the briefest of dismissals, Giorgio speeds past these lower-class diversions to a Grand Hotel, where it is said that with a little sleight of hand we might pass for residents and be entitled to a choicer experience of the waters. As though to confirm, or qualify for, this preferential status, we are required upon arrival at the private spa to make our way, shoes and socks in hand, down a sodden trough in a tufa-lined hallway, so that we are cleansed for the baths themselves. Giorgio soon jumps a few spaces ahead in the queue and becomes invisible. The pace of forward motion is regulated not only by the very old and very young who trudge single file ahead of us but also by the extensive signage screwed to the walls.

Here again the netherworld seems to reach out. The first text, carved in pseudoclassical lapidary mode, recounts the ancient legend of these hot springs. The melancholy god Saturn, it seems, became wrathful with human beings because they were forever at war with each other. Wishing to penetrate the bowels of the earth, on this very spot he hurled down a thunderbolt that simultaneously created the boiling waters and calmed mankind's bellicosity. I have plenty of time to ponder the tale's paradoxy. Was this act of violence a good deed or a bad deed? Or was Saturn the first in a long line of leaders who claimed to make peace by making war? The next plaque, made to look like a rough-hewn boulder and engraved in a faux-Carolingian font, recounts that in the Middle Ages it was believed that this was the spot where the devil exited from the underworld whenever he wished to tempt mortals into damnation; hence it was said to be the place of black masses, witches' sabbaths, and the like. A perfect historiography: as time marched on, pagan gods became Christian demons; what was for the ancients man's multiple nature became for the medievals a war between God and Satan.

A few more sludgy steps and the writing on the wall changes to stark modernity. The print is reminiscent of newspaper columns, and the text is simply a catalogue of diseases that these waters are reputed to cure. I can never resist a list. As I think longingly of those proletarians who enjoy taking the waters amid sun and surf, I have leisure and solitude to work on translations. Gastritis, obesity, duodenal ulcer . . . Asthma, bronchitis, emphysema . . . Sterility, uterine inflammation, vaginitis . . . The illnesses seem to be organized in groups. Herpes simplex, psoriasis, seborrheic dermatitis. It all makes sense: we've given up hell but gained the germ theory of disease. I think about the hot mud at my feet and ponder whether it is miraculous or fraudulent or, more likely—given the long line of customers who have come to partake of it—fulminantly contagious.

Then, finally, when we see the light at the end of the tunnel, the last and briefest of informative placards, announcing simply that the temperature of the waters where they issue from the earth is, and has always been, precisely 37 degrees. At last I am impressed: whatever else Saturnia's waters may be, they share the temperature of the human body. The devil be damned. Submerged here, I should feel exactly in my element.

How wrong I am! Unaccustomed to the bright sun after our trek through the earth, I am almost blinded by the sight of the baths themselves. The celebrants seem to be taking the cure by treading water in a basin of unlimited acreage: to join them, I have to revisit my childhood and jump into the deep end of a pool. Alternatively, I can choose the confinement of a little cave, which is the actual site where the jets exit from the split earth. But in this space the roar is deafening and the bathers, cheek by jowl, appear to be the most in need of cure, many of them seizing clumps of muddy algae and rubbing it on parts of their bodies—gums, buttocks—I would rather not notice. In addition to which, large signs inform the clientele that it is dangerous to remain in this confined space for more than five minutes. Common to both sites is the cloud of sulfur—surely it is the devil who is in his element here—whose stench outrages the nose and whose density blinds the eye. Yet somehow there is one thing I see with perfect clarity. As I waver between pool and cave, I come upon Giorgio, by now well ensconced in a kingly central space in the open pool. He is wearing the barest suggestion of a Speedo.

The next couple of hours are blurry. Giorgio ridicules me for my reticence. I take periodic refuge in the cave, paying scrupulous attention to the five-minute warning that goes unheeded by the rest of those who congregate there. Periodically, I join Giorgio, who meets me halfway in some shallower part of the big tub. Everywhere the haze, the roar, the reek. Giorgio's bulge.

My visits to the pool develop an intermittent continuity.

Giorgio talks to me as though he were delivering a single monologue insensible to the five-minute hiatuses—sometimes shouted and sometimes whispered, always in desperate competition with the sound of the waters.

"Ouagadougou . . ."

He notices the perplexity on my face. "When you go to New York, I go to Africa . . ."

". . . We had to fit Giulia for a pair of glasses today. She's six years old, and I cried because it's the first time I realized that she's mortal . . ."

". . . It's not true that the lightness of being is unbearable. You bear it with taste and style. Harmony is the opposite of euphoria . . ."

". . . We'll meet one day in some city or other in the world without recognizing each other, but the hot traces of recollection will outlive us. For example, the fact that Giulia, following your suggestion, is learning to play the cello, there's the sign . . ."

". . . In the green hills of Africa, I'll shoot buffalo and lions and send you trophies to hang on the walls of your house. I'll travel to the mines of King Solomon. I'll read the adventures of Aladdin on my way to Zanzibar . . ."

". . . That San Francisco earthquake? Do you think it happened because there are so many gays there? . . ."

". . . Do you remember that first Christmastime, when we were alone together?" I don't. "You were carrying Raymond Carver, and me, outrageous and impudent, holding that phallic packet of mullet roe? You serious, you joyous, you enraged like the Furies, and you sweet and carefree, while I sink deeply into that maternal sofa in the Piazza dei Satiri . . ."

". . . If Vito *ti piace*, why don't you go after him? Or Sandro. Or Paolo. Or"—a big laugh—"Long John? . . ."

". . . A proposal: write a novel . . ."

". . . More and more I have been preferring the perversions of speech to the perversions of sight . . ."

". . . Last night I dreamed about Achilles and his furious lament over the death of Patroclus . . . I thank Dionysus, who brought us together . . . One of the most beautiful meetings of my life . . . I've changed. Like Bogart in *Casablanca* . . . You'll see. You're leaving, and the gods are abandoning Rome . . ."

". . . When you and I had that furious fight on the beach, all those words like stones, maybe we were just making violent love to each other. That was the erotic perversion of speaking . . ."

". . . Why Africa? Because I like black women . . ."

". . . Between Apollo and Dionysus, isn't there some *tertium quid?* . . ."

". . . It wasn't true: Sabina didn't really get sick from those *polpettine* . . . Remember that time at the Domus Aurea when I told you about the nineteen-year-old girl? I invented that . . . Sometimes, I have to confess, I talk Italian fast on purpose so you won't understand me . . ."

Maybe it is because he says this or because he starts to talk faster after he says it, but his speech is becoming harder and harder for me to comprehend. God knows, there are enough distractions. I hear him say something like *"Vivan le femmine, viva il buon vino, sostegno e gloria d'umanità!"* No, it can't be. That isn't Giorgio. His line, that first night we met, was *buon vino, buona cucina, buona letteratura, buon sesso.* Still, everything is starting to sound like *Don Giovanni.*

Scellerato. Malandrino. Sciagurato . . . If the scene begins too sweetly, into bitterness soon it may turn . . . *Se fosse costei stata mia moglie?* . . . Provided she wears a skirt . . . *Sposo. Amico* . . . But in the Congo, *son già mille e tre.*

The vapors are so thick, the mud so dense, Giorgio so near to naked, and the stench so unremitting. I think of Dickens's London canceled by its shroud of fog, of Kafka's K., who botches his big chance to reach the Castle because he is too sleepy to listen to the instructions. I think, Cryptic, uncanny, deracinated. I think of Michelangelo's shades in the Sistine Chapel, some of them lightened, some still dark, some in perpetual hell. *La perversione erotica del dire.* The real work of the devil is the loss of sensation, the obliteration of memory. Putting the devil in hell. The sulfur fumes of hell, the last cry of the Don as he plunges under the stage . . . *È l'ultimo momento* . . . *Du mußt dein Leben ändern.*

Pace Mozart. *Pace* Rilke. You can't change your life. Even if you do, you can't change anybody else's life. Drained and dried but still fragrant, we pile into Giorgio's car, now unbearably confining, on our way to a restaurant that promises regional cuisine. Though I say nothing about it, I worry that we will stink up the place. Speeding along in the dusk, we barely escape collision with a wild boar who chooses that moment to cross the highway. Was it the devil lying in wait for us? The highlight of the trattoria menu is a local specialty, which Giorgio and I spend the rest of the evening almost wordlessly enjoying: wild boar, though presumably not the same one. Maybe it is the sauce, exceptionally pungent with onions and vinegar, or maybe just the passage of time, but after a while I realize that everyone in Saturnia smells of sulfur, that it is their element, now our element, and that we are all getting used to it.

Sulfur on the nose, once more, on an ordinary evening that turns out to be an occasion. I am seated in another *enoteca*. None of my now vast circle of wine acquaintances in Rome has ever mentioned Il Goccetto. I came upon it by mere chance and stayed only briefly the first time, feeling a little intimidated by the closed circle of its regulars. But a few unaccustomed acts of social bravery later—probably owing to the threats of summer loneliness—and I began to be inside that circle.

These are not the posh surroundings of Jeffrey's tastings or the slightly faded grandeur that surrounds Sandro's, but something a little more raffish, in a neighborhood where captains of industry and leatherworkers are shoulder to shoulder. In place of Clara, in place of Jeffrey, in place of Sandro, there is Sergetto—gentle, frisky, direct, occasionally fantastical. No formal tastings here, no professorial master of the revels who has come from across the sea to instruct us, just an ongoing seminar about Sangiovese and Nebbiolo, pecorino and mozzarella, as well as the dreadful inhumanity of those who support the Lazio soccer team against Roma.

Then, too, changes are afoot chez Clara. She herself is edging toward a sequence of romance, marriage, and motherhood that will resituate her in the conventional life to which she was born. By whatever parallel course of destiny, Jeffrey is distancing himself from her enterprises, replaced by a new man—Italian, from a wealthy family, humorless—whose first efforts as dean of tasting struck me as unpromising.

In a matter of mere days, it is almost a quotidian ritual that I am sipping something on the third seat at Sergetto's bar. As elsewhere, I tend to arrive too early, and I have to mark time with some little Dolcetto or Soave until the crowd shows up. But there is one other habitual early bird. Despite the uncharacteristic punctuality, he is certainly Italian, though I know little else about him, since we have not yet spoken—he's shy for an Italian, too—except that he is plump, bespectacled, awkward, and, as is evident from his ill-sorted dress, quite without vanity.

None of this prepares me for his entrance this evening, when he fixes me in his sights from across the street, strides to the bar, and says, "*Bravo* for last night."

Apparently he is also ungifted with conversational gambits.

"Uh . . . what did I do last night?"

"Daniele," he responds, holding out his hand. But then he is immediately elsewhere in the shop, scrutinizing the well-stocked shelves and focusing only on the upper registers. He works with intense concentration, seizing bottles, perusing them carefully, then changing his mind and returning them.

"At the tasting at Clara's—"

"*Mi scusi.* I didn't see you there."

"Let's call each other *tu*. I wasn't there, but everyone is talking about that *deficiente* Carlo, who's taken over from Jeffrey." He is clutching a couple of wines against his opulent midsection, their labels hidden. "You humiliated him."

The term is too strong. True, there had been no end to Carlo's blunders. We were supposed to compare identical wines as between single bottles and magnums, but he chose only recent vintages, evidently not knowing that it takes years for these differences to manifest. There were too many people and the pours were too small. Worst of all, he browbeat the tasters when they disagreed with him, notably about a beautiful recently issued Barolo that he lacked the subtlety to appreciate.

"I hope not. I just pointed out that everyone's opinion changed after he issued his ex cathedra pronouncements." Daniele laughs and completes his selection from a far wall of the shop. "And maybe I suggested he should shut his mouth until we were all finished tasting."

Sergetto seems to know the drill. He takes three bottles from Daniele, mixes their order, and lines them up facing the wall.

"I suppose you know that Carlo *è laziale.*" Worst opprobrium of all: he roots for Lazio. "*È praticamente fascista.*"

Three glasses are placed in front of each of us. Sergetto pours ominously small quantities in each, then hands out napkins on which we are to identify the wines in secret. I hate guessing games, and I'm not very good at them. "Do I get to know what we're tasting?"

"*Ma certo, professore.*" How did Daniele know what I did for a living? "The Barolo Granbussia, whose defense you master-minded last night. Vigna Rionda, from the same vintage—in my humble opinion its nearest competitor"—it sounds as though he might actually believe that his opinion is humble—"and . . . *cazzo!* . . . I don't remember which was the third one I chose." Clearly, Daniele can't produce a dramatic climax even if he tries. Sergetto sidles up to the bottles, shields them from our view, and announces, "Brunello Case Basse."

Sometimes the shades lift. Sometimes the angelic messenger is waiting for you, the one that lives in the volatile air of the wineglass. I put my nose in front of the three samples. There is a whiff of sulfur in number one—nothing like Saturnia, but just the reminder that certain devices of preservation have not yet precipitated out of this wine. I recall no sulfur from the other wines. I've never had Vigna Rionda; this could be it. As for sniffs two and three, what can I say but that one's life is one's memory? And if you love wine, I guess you can say that your nose is your life. That's where the angels find you. Granbussia is a vivid recol-lection of barely twenty-four hours earlier. Case Basse is—I have to paraphrase Socrates—written on my soul. By some mixture of recollection, inspiration, and the process of elimination, I write down the three names in that order—Rionda, Granbussia, Case Basse—without ever touching the glasses to my lips.

Daniele smiles broadly at the unveiling of the labels, wonder-fully unfazed when he discovers that he himself has mixed up the two Barolos. Suddenly he is pulling wads of newspaper out of his overstuffed jacket pockets. Looking at him, I think, My God, I'm meeting myself.

"You know that we have started to produce a food and wine

magazine. It began with Arcigola." He hands me some lively-looking sheets that are somewhere between samizdat and psychedelic. "We've been publishing it once a month in *Il Manifesto*." This is the ultra-Communist newspaper, not the mere mainstream leftist *Unità*. I am bemused by a mental picture of Stalin, Mao, and Gianfranco Soldera lined up like the three bottles against the wall. "But we're going off on our own. *Il Manifesto* is a little too . . . *communista*." He smiles. The irony of the politics is not lost on him. *"Ti va di raggiungerci?"* Would you like to join us?

"Join you?" I've been here before, but not exactly here. In another bar, on another day, a lifetime earlier. "Unfortunately, I can't. I'm just about to return home. My year's sabbatical is over."

"Meglio ancora!" That, too, sounds familiar. "We could use a man in New York. That way you'd take a little Rome back with you, and you'd bring us some America." Coming from him, the word *America* sounds full of music and promise. It sounds Italian.